CONVERSATIONS WITH TODD McFARLANE

Conversations with Comic Artists M. Thomas Inge, General Editor

Conversations with Todd McFarlane

Edited by Jake Zawlacki

University Press of Mississippi / Jackson

The University Press of Mississippi is the scholarly publishing agency of
the Mississippi Institutions of Higher Learning: Alcorn State University,
Delta State University, Jackson State University, Mississippi State University,
Mississippi University for Women, Mississippi Valley State University,
University of Mississippi, and University of Southern Mississippi.

www.upress.state.ms.us

The University Press of Mississippi is a member
of the Association of University Presses.

Library of Congress Cataloging-in-Publication Data

Names: Zawlacki, Jake, editor.
Title: Conversations with Todd McFarlane / Jake Zawlacki.
Other titles: Conversations with comic artists.
Description: Jackson : University Press of Mississippi, 2024. |
        Series: Conversations with comic artists series |
        Includes bibliographical references and index.
Identifiers: LCCN 2024017518 (print) | LCCN 2024017519 (ebook) |
        ISBN 9781496853509 (hardback) | ISBN 9781496853516 (trade paperback) |
        ISBN 9781496853530 (epub) | ISBN 9781496853547 (epub) |
        ISBN 9781496853554 (pdf) | ISBN 9781496853523 (pdf)
Subjects: LCSH: McFarlane, Todd—Interviews. |
        Cartoonists—Canada—Interviews.
Classification: LCC PN6733.M34 Z46 2024 (print) | LCC PN6733.M34 (ebook) |
        DDC 741.5/973—dc23/eng/20240627
LC record available at https://lccn.loc.gov/2024017518
LC ebook record available at https://lccn.loc.gov/2024017519

British Library Cataloging-in-Publication Data available

Major Works by Todd McFarlane

AS ARTIST

Coyote #11–14 (1985)

Infinity, Inc. #14–37; Annual #1–2 (among other artists) (1985–1987)

Incredible Hulk #330–34, 336–46 (1987–1988)

Detective Comics #576–78 ("Batman: Year Two") (1987)

Batman #423 (cover only) (1988)

Amazing Spider-Man #298–323, 325, 328 (1988–1990)

Marvel Tales #223–39 (covers only) (1989–1990)

Spider-Man #1–14, 16 (1990–1991)

Spawn #1–15, 21–24 (full art); #26–34, 50 (along with Greg Capullo); #195 (along with Whilce Portacio); #196 (along with Rob Liefeld); #245–46 (along with Szymon Kudranski), #258–66 (along with Erik Larsen), #300–301 (among other artists); 302–3, 305 (along with Jason Shawn Alexander) (1992–2019)

Spawn/Batman #1 (1994)

Image United #1–3 (among other artists) (2009–2010)

AS WRITER/PLOTTER/EDITOR

Spider-Man #1–14, 16 (1990–1991)

Spawn #1–7, 12–15, 21–150, 185–275, (wrote #201–19 under pseudonym Will Carlton), 278–323, 327–42 (2018–present) (sometimes as cowriter, coplotter, script, additional plot, additional script, additional edits)

Sam and Twitch #20–26 (2001–2004)

Savior #1–8 (2015)

Spawn Kills Everyone #1 (2016)

Spawn Kills Everyone Too #1–4 (2018–2019)

Gunslinger Spawn #1–28 (2021–present)

King Spawn #1–24, (as additional dialogue, additional script, additional edits, back-up stories) #25–30 (2021–present)

The Scorched #1–26 (2022–present) (as additional dialogue, additional script, additional edits)

AS INKER

New Mutants #85–89, 93 (covers only) (1990)

Guardians of the Galaxy #5 (cover only) (1990)

Spawn #35–37, 39, 41, 43, 45, 47, 51–73, 100, 185–200, 240–42, 267–75, 306–8 (1995–2020)

Haunt #1–18 (2009–2011)

Gunslinger Spawn #4 (2022)

Batman/Spawn #1 (2022)

CONTENTS

INTRODUCTION

Todd McFarlane is one of the most polarizing figures in comics culture whose personality sometimes garners more attention than his creations. With his dramatic monologues prefacing the *Spawn* HBO animated series, appearances on MTV, high-profile purchases of million-dollar baseballs, and his total rejection of the comics establishment, it's unsurprising that he's garnered the reception he has. Embodying the antiauthoritarian brashness that defined the youth culture of the 1990s, McFarlane spoke his truth everywhere he could. For many, that brashness was distilled in his now infamous 1992 interview with Gary Groth of the *Comics Journal* when he made many statements readers perceived as crass such as, "I didn't let some little thing like not being able to write stop *me*."[1]

For some, that may encapsulate everything there is to know about Todd McFarlane: arrogant, egotistical, and willfully ignorant. The readers of *Wizard Magazine*, however, might remember McFarlane's vaunted status as a new paragon in the field. "Your style of drawing is revolutionary. You practically rewrote the rules of drawing comics and have since become one of the biggest names of the field."[2] In reading the interviews for this volume, readers will find an artist, writer, and entrepreneur more nuanced than the flattened images represented in the pages of the *Comics Journal* and *Wizard*, and the image McFarlane himself has often presented. Instead, readers might find those criticisms rooted in the very reasons for his success.

The mythology of Todd McFarlane begins with over seven hundred rejections from Marvel and DC, a number that grows as the story ages. This often-told origin story underscores the tenacity and relentlessness with which McFarlane pursued his comics career. After receiving his first paid gig on Marvel/Epic's *Coyote* in 1985 and DC's *Infinity, Inc.* shortly after, McFarlane began testing his style through formal experimentation with paneling and page layout, incorporating design elements that blurred the fixed lines of panels by incorporating unexpected shapes into his compositions. Taking inspiration from comic artists such as Michael Golden and Jack Kirby, McFarlane was drawn to compositions that imbued a sense of action and energy.

Coyote #11, p. 27, March 1985. Marvel/Epic, Credit Marvel Comics. Even in his earliest work, McFarlane's formal experimentation with nontraditional panel borders and design elements draw the reader's eye to the shrinking panels.

It was this experimentation and willingness to break with tradition that emboldened McFarlane's later work. From 1987 to 1988, with Peter David as writer—the same Peter David who McFarlane would memorably debate at ComicsFest in 1993—McFarlane's aesthetics helped breathe life into an aging *Incredible Hulk* series through his busy linework and dramatic action poses. Paired with David's strong writing and narrative risk-taking, the two gained public attention—and more importantly, attention within Marvel—ultimately landing McFarlane artistic duties on *The Amazing Spider-Man*. To say he was an overnight sensation may be bit of an exaggeration, but within only three years, McFarlane had moved from small titles to the main stage at Marvel. There, he found even more success as the cocreator of the popular antihero Venom, and left his mark on the character of Spider-Man forever.

McFarlane introduced the most drastic aesthetic turn in the history of Spider-Man, blurring the line between man and arachnid, with *Wizard* even placing McFarlane's rendering, alongside Steve Ditko and John Romita Sr.'s, as one of the three most pivotal in the web-slinger's evolution. The famed wall-crawler's body became more and more opposable, making manneristic poses so twisted and contorted as to be physically impossible. Stories often took place at night, incorporating a neo-noir aesthetic rarely used in Marvel comics at the time. Despite some criticisms of his anatomically impossible positions, the "McFarlane style" was incredibly popular with readers. After a mere twenty-seven issues on *The Amazing Spider-Man*, Marvel handed McFarlane the reins to a fourth monthly ongoing title, the "adjective-less" *Spider-Man*.

It was on *Spider-Man* that McFarlane took on all responsibilities of writing, drawing, and inking, responsibilities he admits a bit of uncertainty about. When asked by Len Wong of *Amazing Heroes* about the new *Spider-Man* comic, McFarlane said, "To tell you the truth, it's not even that I want to be a writer; it's more that I wanted to have control of the artwork."[3] While the writing of *Spider-Man* would be criticized, McFarlane's control of the artwork pushed his style to its most extreme expression up to that point. Spider-Man's mask eyes grew even larger on his suit, poses became even more arachnoid, and layout experimentation challenged the limits of the sequential medium. His take on the beloved character proved incredibly popular, with the first issue selling a record-breaking two million copies. McFarlane's *Spider-Man* also marks a pivotal point in comics history: one that helped spark the speculation bubble of the early nineties, with foil variant covers that would help lead to a catastrophic crash for the comics industry. When confronted about his role in Marvel creating multiple cover variants for the speculator market,

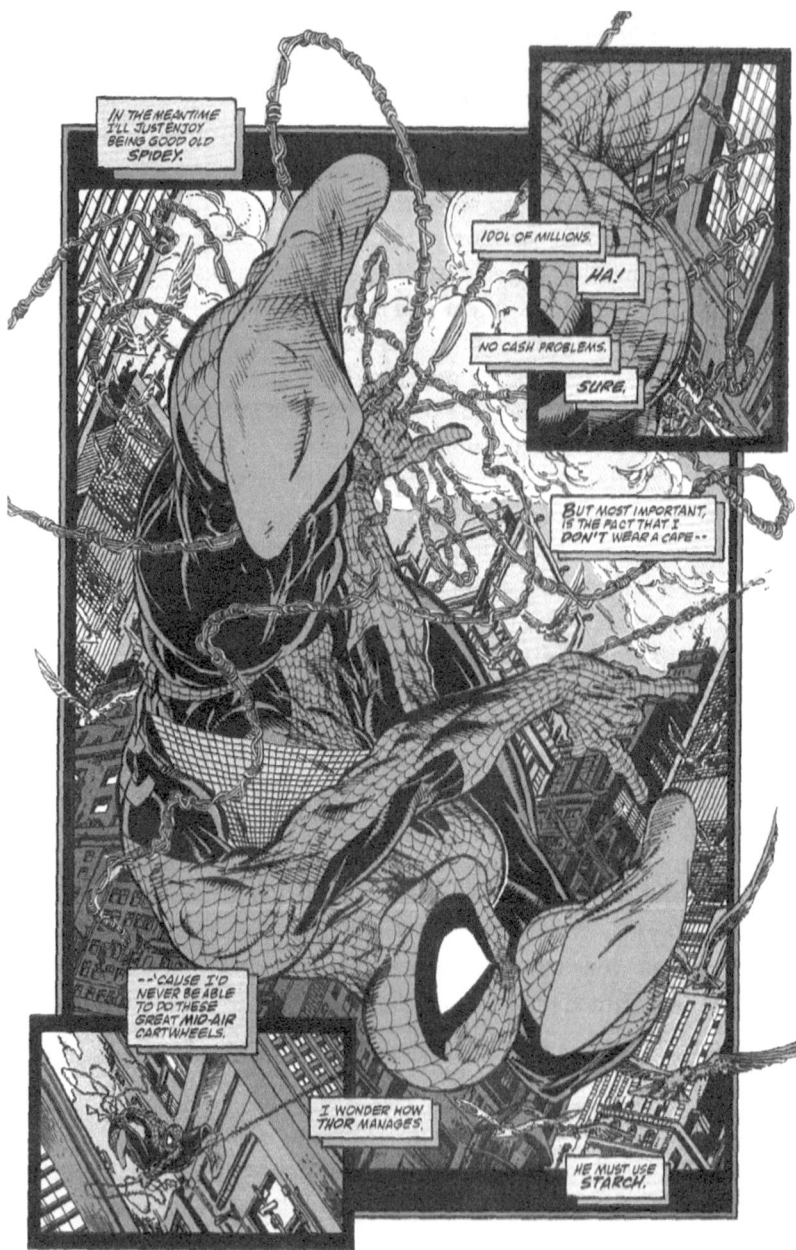

Spider-Man #1, p. 25, August 1990, Marvel Comics, Credit Marvel Comics. In *Spider-Man*, McFarlane often pushed the limits of the sequential medium to a degree that challenged the linear reading of the comic book page.

McFarlane said, "Everybody is either to blame or to be patted on the back for that, I guess it depends on your view of it."[4] The ensuing crash would not only change the comic market forever, but would also end an era of manic fandom where popular comic creators, like McFarlane and his fellow Image Comics cofounders, were treated as rockstars with fans lining up around the block to wait for a thirty-second autograph.

McFarlane's run on *Spider-Man* also marked a pivotal moment for the Comics Code,[5] putting McFarlane face-to-face with the aging restrictions, ultimately causing him to sidestep it altogether. Because of his work's incredible success, Marvel allowed McFarlane unprecedented artistic freedom. However, that autonomy was challenged by the Marvel editorial board over a violent panel depicting the blinding of the villain Juggernaut. These artistic constraints, along with McFarlane's frustrations with the work-for-hire system and his desire to earn appropriately according to his value (despite being the highest paid comics artist at the time), led him to consider a career beyond Marvel.

In perhaps the second most important event in the mythology of McFarlane, he, along with popular *X-Men* penciler Jim Lee and Rob Liefeld of *X-Force* and *New Mutants* fame, met with Terry Stewart, the president of Marvel, and editor Tom DeFalco to announce their departure from the company. That same day, as the story goes, the three of them went to DC Comics, a company that had recently developed more creator-friendly contracts, to tell them just because they were leaving Marvel didn't mean they'd be headed to DC. Instead, Lee, Liefeld, and McFarlane joined ranks with Marc Silvestri, Erik Larsen, Whilce Portacio, and Jim Valentino to found Image Comics.

With seven extremely popular artists at its core, the announcement of Image Comics in 1992 was a national news sensation unlike any other independent comic publisher before. Marvel's stock price dropped upon its announcement, and young readers across the country waited to see what Image and its founders had in store. Within its founding year, Image Comics surpassed DC as the second highest-selling comic book publisher. Titles from the creators broke multiple sales records, and McFarlane's *Spawn* #1 sold 1.7 million comics, holding the record for the highest sales of an independent comic book to this day. *Spawn* was instantly the "tentpole" series of Image Comics, a status it has maintained for thirty years.

With the success of *Spawn* emboldening McFarlane and his brand, he decided to step back as the primary penciller and writer after just twenty issues, thus freeing him to venture into other entertainment. McFarlane founded his own toy company in 1994, Todd Toys, which would later become McFarlane Toys in 1995, and immediately distinguished his products from chief competitors

Spider-Man #16, p. 18, November 1991, Marvel Comics, Credit Marvel Comics. McFarlane's rendering of the blinding of the supervillain Juggernaut led to a confrontation with the editors at Marvel over what was and wasn't allowed under the Comics Code. It also added to his many frustrations and would cause him to leave Marvel altogether.

Hasbro and Mattel by producing toys with an unprecedented level of detail and style. His unrelenting pursuit of high-quality toys not only bridged toys with the statue and figurine markets, including partnerships with artists such as H. R. Giger and Clive Barker, but eventually commanded the attention of his former competitor DC Comics, which granted him permission to produce DC characters under the McFarlane Toys line.

That same ingenuity expanded into animation and then film in the late 1990s. In May 1997, McFarlane executive produced an animated adaptation of *Spawn* for HBO. Lauded as one of television's greatest animated series, it won a Primetime Emmy Award for Outstanding Animation Program and ushered in a new wave of mature animation for television. While the live-action film didn't enjoy the same critical success as the animated series, it holds an important place in film representation: Michael Jai White was one of the first African American actors to portray a major superhero character.

McFarlane began a directing career with Pearl Jam's animated "Do the Evolution," for which he was nominated for a Grammy for Best Music Video, Short Form. Shortly after in early 1999, he directed the animated portion of Korn's "Freak On a Leash," earning him a Grammy for Best Music Video,

Short Form. Within a decade, McFarlane had gone from famed *Spider-Man* artist to founder of Image Comics, creator of *Spawn*, Emmy Award–winning producer, and Grammy Award–winning music video director.

The early 2000s weren't nearly as expansive as the late 1990s for McFarlane. Rather, they represented a period in which McFarlane was embroiled in lawsuits regarding the very reasons Image Comics was founded: character ownership and creator rights. After settling legal disputes with Neil Gaiman over character ownership from *Spawn* #9 and a lawsuit with NHL player Tony Twist over the use of his name within the comics and HBO animated series, McFarlane returned to *Spawn* as a writer.

While he is still primarily known for his artwork, McFarlane has produced significantly more writing in the comics medium than drawing. Since his return to *Spawn* with Issue #185 in 2008, McFarlane has written or plotted over one hundred issues of the series using the "Marvel Style" of operating from page layouts instead of a finished script. While his writing still holds a similar tone to his early Marvel work, this significant aspect of his career as a comics artist has received little critical attention. Though *Spawn's* sales numbers and popularity have declined since their record-breaking peak in the 1990s, a recent resurgence in popularity has occurred as a result of the expansion of the *Spawn* universe.

2022 marked the thirtieth anniversary of Image Comics and *Spawn* at a time when three new *Spawn*-related titles were released: *King Spawn*, *Gunslinger Spawn*, and *The Scorched*. Surprising the industry and even McFarlane himself, *King Spawn* #1 sold just shy of half a million copies, more copies than any number one issue released by Marvel, DC, or Image in the last twenty-five years. With McFarlane writing the scripts for *Gunslinger Spawn* and drawing variant covers for the different series, he's just as involved in comics now as he's ever been.

In a career path wholly unique for a comic artist, his aesthetics have shaped traditional comic characters in Spider-Man and Batman, invented new ones in Spawn, defined a successful toy company, enlivened mature animation, touched the music industry, and continue to impact comic books today. He is a rare example of an artist whose ambitions have exploded beyond the bounds of his initial medium. That explosion also propelled itself from an underlying frustration with the status quo that seemed to follow him along throughout his career. As Greg Hyland notes in the introduction to his included *Hero Illustrated* interview, "I learned that to truly understand the horror that Todd endured being paid millions to draw for Marvel, you have to be Todd."[6]

Being Todd McFarlane is a horror unknown to anyone else, but it's a horror (and perhaps, a pleasure) that we might be able to glimpse through the many personas presented in this volume. At times McFarlane is an enemy of the interviewer, at times a friend, at times a god, and in those rarest of moments, a human. Placing these various Todd McFarlanes in conversation with one another is the main benefit of collecting these interviews for the first time. Not only do we see the outspoken and bombastic McFarlane of full Image Comics fame, but we also get a glimpse of his humbler beginnings outlining his early work on Marvel and DC titles before discussing the upcoming and as-yet-unreleased *Spider-Man*.

We also get a rare insight into the softer-spoken McFarlane in an interview with Cliff Biggers of *Previews* where he relates how *Spawn* is a personal book. In this interview, McFarlane does not yet have the burden of needing to defend the series's writing or his choice to bring on guest contributors as he did in the *Comics Journal* when Gary Groth asked, "Did it ever occur to you that a lot of these artists might not know how to write?"[7] The *Previews* interview offers a moment where McFarlane voices uncertainty, an uncertainty that all but vanishes after the massive commercial success of *Spawn* and Image. That overconfidence couldn't be better described than in Gary St. Lawrence's transcript of the included debate between McFarlane and former collaborator Peter David at ComicsFest in 1993. He writes, "*Throughout the introduction, McFarlane is visibly undressing behind his podium and donning yellow boxer shorts and a bathrobe, slinging a towel so that it completely covers his head and shoulders.*"[8] All of McFarlane's confidence, however, wouldn't be enough to topple the intellectual in David. While McFarlane didn't land as many rhetorical punches as he might have liked to, admitting to Hyland, "Peter David gave Todd McFarlane and Image Comics a kick in the butt," he did it his way.[9]

These interviews also span the genres of McFarlane's career in rock 'n' roll, film, animation, and toy collecting, showing the different ways he's viewed through different mediums. Some readers may be surprised by the lack of any interviews with *Wizard Magazine*, perhaps the most vocally pro-McFarlane publisher in the early 1990s. In one speculative article guessing what the comic book world would look like ten years in the future, the headline proclaims, "McFarlane Buys Marvel" and describes McFarlane as a "comic mogul."[10] These praise-heavy promotional interviews have been exchanged for less popular magazines such as *Combo* and *Hero Illustrated*, where McFarlane gives similar responses, but where the interviewers can reach a bit further into his mind. After all, the versions of Todd McFarlane who appeared in the pages of *Wizard* and the *Comics Journal* were perhaps the best-known versions of him in the first decade of his career: McFarlane the comic convention god, and McFarlane the cussing antagonist.

For instance, in response to Groth calling McFarlane a "maverick," McFarlane stated, "I was very talented, I was a trailblazer and I was a fuckface and an asshole. To me they're all the same thing, I wear all those names with a badge of honor. It's a lot better than being afraid, or being content. To me, the guys who change the world are not the guys who follow, they're the guys who lead, because if everybody keeps doing the same thing there is no change in the world."[11]

Without exaggeration or embellishment, Todd McFarlane's career has impacted the comics world in a profound way. This collection of interviews illustrates an artist pushing beyond the status quo at every turn. Not only can McFarlane's career help us understand the linkages between comics, toys, film, and games in an interconnected media landscape, but it can also show the advantages that come with refusing to play by the rules.

A few months after the infamous *Comics Journal* interview, McFarlane was asked by Jim Salicrup, friend and former editor on *Spider-Man* in the included *Comics Interview*, "So Todd, why *did* you do that interview with Gary Groth?" "I knew," McFarlane said, "that every one of my peers was going to be reading it. So, all the guys who *hate* me, I gave them a *reason* to hate me."[12] That contrarian logic might not be perfectly clear by the end of this introduction, but the interviews within offer a glimpse into the sometimes frustrating, thoughtful, ambitious, reserved, arrogant and, in the rarest of moments, humble character of Todd McFarlane.

JZ

Notes

1. Emphasis in original.
2. Gareb Shamus, "Spawning a New Image," *Wizard*, no. 11 (1993): 11.
3. Len Wong, "Spider-Man Artist: Todd McFarlane," *Amazing Heroes* 1, no. 179 (1990): 25.
4. Gary Groth, "'That's the Spice of Life, Bud': The Todd McFarlane Interview," *Comics Journal*, no. 152 (1992): 54.
5. The Comics Code Authority of the Comics Magazine Association of America is the independent body that regulates content in comics.
6. Greg Hyland, "The Last Todd McFarlane Interview," *Hero Illustrated* 1, no. 21 (1995): 57.
7. Groth, "The Todd McFarlane Interview," 46.
8. Gary St. Lawrence, "The Peter David-Todd McFarlane Debate," *Comics Buyer's Guide* 1, no. 1044 (1993): 92.

9. Hyland, "The Last Todd McFarlane Interview," 63.

10. Rob Samsel, William A. Christensen, and Mark Seifert, "A Comic Odyssey," *Wizard*, no. 29 (1994): 136.

11. Groth, "The Todd McFarlane Interview," 49.

12. Jim Salicrup, "Todd McFarlane," *Comics Interview*, no. 119 (1993): 7. Emphasis in original.

CHRONOLOGY

1961   McFarlane is born on March 16 in Calgary, Alberta, Canada, to Bob and Sherlee McFarlane. He is the second of three sons.

1977   At the age of sixteen, McFarlane develops the prototype for the character Spawn in a sketchbook.

1979   McFarlane meets Wanda Kolomyjec, his high school sweetheart. He tries out for the Gonzaga University baseball team but could not afford to attend. Instead, he plays baseball at Spokane Falls Community College for one year.

1981   McFarlane attends Eastern Washington University on a baseball scholarship, studying in a self-directed program in graphics and art. He also works as a janitor on campus, part of the requirement of an on-campus job, and works weekends at Comic Rack, a local comics shop.

1983   McFarlane suffers a serious ankle injury during a game against Washington State University, limiting his prospects of playing professionally.

1984   McFarlane tries out for the Toronto Blue Jays' farm team in Medicine Hat, Alberta, but ends up being ranked just shy of the roster, ending his professional prospects. McFarlane graduates with a bachelor's degree and pencils his first backup story in Marvel/Epic's *Coyote* #11 with Steve Engelhart.

1985   McFarlane begins his career in earnest, drawing for DC's *Infinity, Inc.* over the next two years, and Marvel/Epic's *Coyote* from issue #11 until its cancellation in issue #14. Despite being drawn months apart, McFarlane's first art on *Infinity, Inc.* and *Coyote* appear on the shelf on the same day. He also guest-pencils DC's *All-Star Squadron* with Mike Clark for issue #47.

1987   McFarlane pencils the last three issues of DC's *Batman: Year Two* storyline (*Detective Comics* #576–78), *Daredevil* #241, *G.I. Joe: A Real American Hero* #60, and *Spitfire and the Troubleshooters* #4, where he's recognized by Marvel editors as being able to draw bulky characters. He then begins work on Marvel's *The Incredible Hulk* with writer Peter David.

1988   McFarlane joins David Michelinie on Marvel's *The Amazing Spider-Man*, beginning on issue #298 and gains industry-wide fame for his unique style. He also illustrates the now-classic cover of *Batman* #423.

1989   McFarlane pencils the first two issues of DC's *Invasion!* miniseries. He also begins drawing cover art for the Spider-Man reprint series *Marvel Tales*.

1990   After a twenty-eight-issue run on *The Amazing Spider-Man*, McFarlane tells Marvel editor Jim Salicrup he wants to write his own stories and would leave the book on issue #328. McFarlane is granted his wish and pencils, inks, and writes the new "adjective-less" *Spider-Man*. *Spider-Man* #1 sells 2.5 million copies; Marvel sells six variant covers of the comic, thus kicking off the comics speculator boom of the 1990s. He also pencils a Prowler story in *Spectacular Spider-Man* Annual #10, and inks *New Mutants* covers penciled by Rob Liefeld for issues #85–89 and #93.

1991   After writing and illustrating fifteen of the first sixteen issues of *Spider-Man*, McFarlane takes a break after the birth of his first child, Cyan.

1992   McFarlane, along with fellow Marvel artists Rob Liefeld, Jim Lee, Marc Silvestri, Jim Valentino, Erik Larsen, and Whilce Portacio, founds Image Comics. The company places creator control at the forefront, meaning each artist retains all rights and control of the characters they create. Upon the announcement, Marvel's stock drops. In May, McFarlane releases *Spawn*, the second Image Comics-published title, which sells over 1.7 million comics, making it the highest selling independent comic to this day. McFarlane wins an Inkpot Award and the Award for Best Comic Book by the National Cartoonists Society.

1993   Responding to criticism about the writing of *Spawn*, McFarlane hires Alan Moore, Frank Miller, Neil Gaiman, and Dave Sim to guest write issues. At the Philadelphia ComicFest, McFarlane debates Peter David, former colleague on *The Incredible Hulk*, on whether Image Comics is treated fairly by the media. He also inks the cover to *Satan's Six* #1, drawn by Jack Kirby and part of the Topps Comics line.

1994   After negotiating with Mattel about how to produce action figures for the *Spawn* characters and signing over licensing rights, McFarlane reclaims the rights and founds Todd Toys. In December, he introduces the first line of action figures titled "Spawn I." McFarlane teams up with Frank Miller to write *Spawn/Batman*, the first major crossover of Image Comics and DC Comics. He also inks Jack Kirby's cover to *Phantom Force* #3, a copublished book between Image Comics and Genesis West. McFarlane hands over the art responsibilities on *Spawn* to Greg Capullo in *Spawn* #26.

1995   Mattel pressures McFarlane to change the name of his toy company as to not be confused with Barbie's younger brother, Todd. McFarlane then changes the name of the company to McFarlane Toys. Acclaim Entertainment and Sony Electronic Publishing release *Todd McFarlane's Spawn: The Video Game* for the Super Nintendo Entertainment System console.

1996   McFarlane illustrates the album cover for the American heavy metal band Iced Earth titled *The Dark Saga*, based on McFarlane's *Spawn*. He also founds Todd McFarlane Entertainment, a film and animation studio.

1997   *Todd McFarlane's Spawn*, an animated series based on the comic, airs on HBO. In August, *Spawn*, a live action film, is released and is a moderate commercial success despite being critically panned. It is one of the first superhero films to feature a Black leading character with Michael Jai White playing the titular Spawn. Sony Computer Entertainment releases *Spawn: The Eternal* for the PlayStation console.

1998   McFarlane codirects Pearl Jam's "Do the Evolution," which is nominated for the Grammy Award in the Best Music Video, Short Form category. McFarlane also completes the album artwork alongside Greg Capullo and Brian Holguin for Korn's album *Follow the Leader*. An avid baseball fan, McFarlane pays $2.6 million USD at auction for a baseball that St. Louis Cardinals first baseman Mark McGwire hit for his then record-breaking seventieth home run, and pays $175,000 for Sammy Sosa's sixty-sixth home run ball.

1999   McFarlane directs the animated segment of Korn's "Freak on a Leash" music video. The video would win the Grammy Award in the Best Music Video, Short Form category. The music video also wins the 1999 Metal Edge Readers' Choice Award for Music Video of the Year and was nominated for a 1999 MTV Video Music Award. Konami publishes *Spawn* for the Game Boy Color console. *Todd McFarlane's Spawn* also wins an Emmy Award for Outstanding Animation Program (Longer Than One Hour).

2000   *Spawn* crosses the one-hundred-issue milestone. Capcom publishes *Spawn: In the Demon's Hand* for arcade and the Sega Dreamcast console.

2001   Then a part-time owner through the Edmonton Investors Group, McFarlane designs the Edmonton Oilers' third jersey. It remains part of the lineup until 2007. McFarlane begins writing *Sam & Twitch* with issue #20, taking over the *Spawn* spin-off from Brian Michael Bendis, and continues on until the series ends at issue #26. McFarlane Toys releases the *Clive Barker's Tortured Souls* toy line, a series of six action figures designed by the horror genre master Clive Barker, each including a chapter of a novelette.

2002   Neil Gaiman, former collaborator on *Spawn* #9, sues McFarlane regarding royalties of characters he cocreated: Angela, Cogliostro, and Medieval Spawn. McFarlane produces the animated sequences in the film *The Dangerous Lives of Altar Boys* by Peter Care. He also directs the live-action music video "Breathe" for Canadian hip-hop group Swollen Members featuring Nelly Furtado, which wins the 2003 "MuchVibe Best Rap Video" award (the Canadian equivalent of a Grammy), as well as the "Western Canadian Music Awards Outstanding Video" award. McFarlane creates the character Necrid for the cross-platform video game *Soul Caliber II*. Spawn is a platform-exclusive playable character in the Xbox release.

2003   McFarlane illustrates the domestic and international album covers for Swollen Members' *Heavy*.

2004   Hockey player Tony Twist files a lawsuit against McFarlane because a mobster character was named after him in *Spawn*. The lawsuit was settled out of court for $5 million. Konami releases *McFarlane's Evil Prophecy* to the PlayStation 2 console. McFarlane Productions publishes a new Spawn story in *Image Comics Summer Special* #1, part of Image Comics Free Comic Book Day offerings. McFarlane Toys produces *Li II*, a sculpture based on the Swiss Surrealist HR Giger's painting of the same name.

2005   McFarlane wins the National Football League's 2005 Artist of the Year Award for his work on program covers for the Baltimore Ravens. He also creates the artwork for the heavy metal band Disturbed's album *Ten Thousand Fists*.

2006   McFarlane directs Disturbed's music video for their cover of Genesis's "Land of Confusion." He also joins Boston Red Sox pitcher Curt Schilling in his venture to create 38 Studios and serves as Creative Director for all games in development, including *Kingdoms of Amalur: Reckoning*. The company would file for bankruptcy in 2011.

2007   McFarlane designs two wireless Xbox 360 controllers with custom artwork from *Halo 3*.

2008   McFarlane takes on coplotting duties on *Spawn*, beginning on *Spawn* #185.

2009   *Haunt*, a series whose title character was cocreated by McFarlane and Robert Kirkman of *Walking Dead* fame, is released with Kirkman writing, Greg Capullo drawing, and McFarlane inking. He also draws his portions of the Image Comics founders collaborative comic *Image United* in issues #1–3.

2010   McFarlane draws the cover to Disney Press's *Prince of Persia: Before the Sandstorm*, an anthology published prior to the film release of Disney's *Prince of Persia*.

2011   McFarlane is inducted to the Canadian Comic Book Creator Hall of Fame on June 18. He also begins writing *Spawn* under the pseudonym "Will Carlton" and continues to do so until issue 219. McFarlane serves as creative director for the Stan Lee and Yoshiki-created comic *Blood Red Dragon*.

2012   *Spawn* celebrates Image's twentieth anniversary with *Spawn* #220 and a series of homage covers. McFarlane sues former employee Al Simmons, from whom the name of Spawn's former identity was derived. According to a lawsuit lodged in Arizona federal court, Al Simmons published a book called *The Art of Being Spawn*, in which Simmons purportedly suggests that his own life was the inspiration for the Spawn character. McFarlane's position was that Simmons violated the terms of his employment pact and breached his duty of loyalty. The lawsuit was settled in December 2012 when McFarlane came to an agreement with Simmons. The terms of any settlement were not made public.

2013   McFarlane delivers the keynote speech at one of two graduation ceremonies at his alma mater, Eastern Washington University.

2015   McFarlane cowrites *Savior*, an eight-issue series, with former collaborator Brian Holguin.

2016   McFarlane writes the Image Comics one-shot *Spawn Kills Everyone*. He also draws a variant cover for *Reborn* #1.

2018   McFarlane begins writing *Spawn* at issue #283 and continues for the next three years. He also writes the four-issue miniseries *Spawn Kills Everyone Too*.

2019   *Spawn* breaks the record for longest running independent title at #301, surpassing Dave Sim's record on *Cerebus*. McFarlane draws his first interior artwork in over twenty years.

2021   McFarlane expands the Spawn universe by introducing three new ongoing titles in *King Spawn*, *Gunslinger Spawn*, and *The Scorched*. He also takes on scripting duties for the newly launched *Gunslinger Spawn* series.

2022   McFarlane works with long-time collaborator Greg Capullo on the DC Comics and Image Comics crossover of *Batman/Spawn*, the characters' first meeting since 1994. McFarlane also codirects the music video for Ozzy Osbourne's "Patient Number 9" with M. Wartella.

CONVERSATIONS WITH TODD McFARLANE

Todd McFarlane

JIM SALICRUP AND DWIGHT JON ZIMMERMAN / 1990

From *Comics Interview* 1, no. 81 (1990): 7–21. Reprinted by permission of Jennifer Bush-Kraft, administrator, estate of David Anthony Kraft.[1]

That Todd McFarlane loves drawing the adventures of Spider-Man is a matter of record. What he said, in fact, was that he would stay on the book for as long as Marvel would let him. So it was quite a shock when late in 1989 he announced that he would be leaving *The Amazing Spider-Man* to go on to another project. Of course, what we did not know then—those sneaky Marvel folks waited a few more weeks to make the big announcement—was that the new McFarlane project was a new series starring our favorite web-slinger. What's coming up? We asked Spider-Editor Jim Salicrup, and he delivered this exclusive . . .

Jim Salicrup: Why don't you tell me about your trip to the Philippines?

Todd McFarlane: The trip to the Philippines? I went to Singapore and I did a convention with Mike Grell—in Singapore they're pretty big on Marvel and DC superhero comic books. And at the end of this convention, it was late at night, a couple of reporters from Malaysia came over and wanted to do an interview with Mike Grell and myself. It was getting pretty late, so Mike took them to his room and was going to do a short interview with them, and then they'd come over to my room and do a deal with me, and we'd be done with them. It was about eleven o'clock at night when Mike took them away.

Then all of a sudden it was two o'clock in the morning and they still hadn't come over, and I was getting groggy and drowsy and stuff. So I phoned Mike and said, "Mike, where are the reporters?" They were still at Mike's room doing *his* interview, and he said they would be along in five minutes. Another

3

Amazing Spider-Man #299, p. 2, April 1987, Marvel Comics, Credit Marvel Comics. The second issue of McFarlane's run on *Amazing Spider-Man* shows his novel reimagining of Spider-Man with larger eyes and an arachnoid posing that breaks traditional anatomy.

hour went by and they still didn't come, so I get in bed and phone up Mike a second time to say, "Forget it, I'm not doing the interview. It's too late, you guys aren't being very kind." Then I heard a knocking at the door, and the two reporters came in. So I said, "You guys got five minutes and then I have to kick you out 'cause I got to get some sleep, you know."

So they want me to get dressed to take a picture! It's three o'clock in the morning and I'm not in a terrific mood, so I go, "Wrong. This is what we're going to do: I'm going to sit up in bed and I'll give you a smile, and you can take a close-up and crop it and slap it on your article." So they took their picture and they went their merry way after asking a few questions. And about two months later, I started getting deluged with mail from Malaysia. My wife started opening it up, right. There's pictures of women and marriage proposals, statistics of how much they weigh. [*Laughter*]

You name it, it was there. We were getting bundles every single day, mostly from Malaysia. And we found out, finally—one of the letters was from a guy and he sent me this article—what they had done was they took that picture of me in bed but they never cropped anything. I was in bed, sleeping in the buff, and I had the blanket down to my waist, and because I had propped myself up I'm flexing kind of, bare chested. [*Laughter*] And anybody who's seen me playing sports and stuff, I'm not a bad looking guy, I'm still in pretty good shape. So they put this picture in there, and they put my home address in the article, and a bogus seven-figure salary that I was pulling down. [*Laughter*] In US dollars, no less. So we got close to two hundred letters from both the women *and* the men, and it was pretty funny.

Salicrup: We'll do that in *Comics Interview*, run that same picture with your home address.

McFarlane: Let's make it an eight-figure salary. [*Laughter*] Todd "Donald Trump" McFarlane. [*Laughter*]

Salicrup: Let's go right into *Spider-Man*, how did that work out?

McFarlane: How did it work out—it's still working out. It's been doing okay. I came into the *Spider-Man* office, kind of told you some of the changes I wanted to make—although it was probably a four- or five-month gap by the time I started. I think a few of the changes that I brought up were maybe forgotten by the time that they saw print. I think I gave you guys a bit of a heart attack on some of the things.

Salicrup: What were the changes?

McFarlane: *Cosmetic* changes, nothing that big. The ones that you can see now, the bigger eyes, more black in the costume, more webbing in the costume—the spaghetti webbing as Tom DeFalco dubbed it. Just trying to make him a little more funky, you know. It was my way of kind of going back to the first, maybe, three or four issues of what Steve Ditko did but without actually *doing* Steve Ditko. It was my *perception* of doing Steve Ditko, and what my memory of Steve Ditko's Spider-Man was, without actually looking at the artwork. I'm just kind of putting it in there with my style for the 1990s, kind of *updating* it.

Salicrup: What made you come up with that crazy webbing?

McFarlane: That crazy webbing? I actually can't take credit for that. The webbing idea came from an old black-and-white piece. Years ago you guys used to put out these black-and-white portfolios, around 1980 or something like that, and there was one piece that was the *Defenders* by Mike Golden, and for whatever reason he had Spider-Man in it. He did this great Spider-Man with this funky webbing, and I *kept* that piece out of all the pieces. And I go, "If I ever turn into a comic book pro, and if I ever work for Marvel Comics, and if I *ever* get to do Spider-Man, I'm going to do webbing like that!"

And this was in 1980, so I was just a baby collecting comic books. [*Laughter*] Nineteen years of age and it just kind of *hit* me like a bolt, so when I finally got my chance I go, "Yeah, it's time to dig out that drawing that Mike Golden did and do the spaghetti webbing!" He had to do it *straight*, it was my idea to make it kind of like a cowboy guy; but the ultimate origin of the spaghetti webbing, the honors go to Mike Golden.

Salicrup: What about the big eyes?

McFarlane: The big eyes, I'll have to give credit on *that* to Steve Ditko. Looking *back* on the stuff, he didn't actually make them as big as I thought he did. And *that's* where a lot of the stuff that I did with Spider-Man . . . I *thought* that Ditko did it, you know. When I look at it I see he didn't really, but my mind was telling me that he did these things—the eyes were real big and the costume was real black and that there was ten times as much webbing and stuff like that. If you ask me to go back and *dissect* it, from a professional point of view, he didn't do a lot of that stuff. So it actually turned out better that I didn't actually look at the stuff, that I just kind of pulled from my memory what I *thought* was in it.

Salicrup: You also beefed him up.

McFarlane: What?

Salicrup: You beefed him up.

McFarlane: I beat up Spider-Man?

Salicrup: You beefed him up, added more weight.

McFarlane: Oh, *beefed* him up—ah! I beat him up. *No!* [*Laughter*] Yeah, I guess I did beef him up a bit, although I still like the scrawny-looking

Spider-Man. Sometimes I go for *that* look, the odd time. I was actually *trying* to make a leaner guy, you know, but it didn't work out that way. I guess because I have a tendency to put another ripple in the arms and stuff like that. But he isn't big and chunky like the Hulk. And the kids today, I find, don't really *like* the scrawny superhero, they like their guy to look like he's solid.

Salicrup: You haven't mentioned John Romita.

McFarlane: John Romita, when I first went into doing Spider-Man, in *my* mind John Romita did the definitive Spider-Man. I mean, Ditko created the character and refined him, but the Spider-Man that I remember and that I think most everybody else remembers, from cartoons and from all the merchandising and stuff, *comes* from John Romita, you know. When I took over the book it wasn't that I didn't *like* John Romita's Spider-Man, it was quite the opposite. I was in such awe of his stuff, and thought that he did such a perfect job, that I would have been a *fool* to try to emulate what he had done.

I could either do a bad John Romita imitation or I could kind of pull some of the things I liked from John and some of the things that I liked from Steve Ditko, and some of the stuff that I was doing at that point, and kind of meld it and throw it onto the page with a nineties look and hope that it was different. My attitude was never that my way was better than anybody else's way, it was just that it was different. That is *always* my attitude when I do *anything*, from the inking to the writing, hopefully. I might fail sometimes, and I might succeed other times, but I'm going to try to do something different and hopefully keep you off base.

Right now I'm at this cocky point in my life, and that was all it was. It was *more* of a tribute to John *not* to draw like him, although it seems the opposite. I would have been a fool to do a bad John Romita style. I guess I should have made that more clear when I went off in my direction—I don't think my stuff is any better or any worse than anybody else's.

Salicrup: What about the critics who don't have kind things to say about your anatomy?

McFarlane: [*Laughter*] The critics? I'm not one for saying bad things about people, so. . . . The easiest answer would be: If you don't like it, don't buy it. It's simple, you know. It's over. The nightmare is over, just stop buying it and you don't have to have any problems with it. Really, I don't *worry* about the critics all that much, because at this point they can't really take anything away from me—as a matter of fact, *any* lip service I can get at this point in my career, I'll take it. I actually—being the naïve young child that I am—take it as a compliment. If somebody's got something bad to say, then it's like I know that I'm one of the top guys in the business at that point.

When I was doing *Infinity* and even my first year at Marvel, nobody gave a shit about me. I could have dropped my drawers in the middle of the Bullpen and nobody would have even cared, you know. But *now*. . . . If you *look* a different way, then it's news to people, so whatever. Like I said, I'm not really that concerned about what they say. What I'm concerned about is whether the kids who are *buying* it *like* it, you know. If the sales go down then that tells me they don't like it, and the sales go up then that means they do. And the sales have gone up a little bit since I've been on the book, so I take it as the people who buy it *like* it. If you're buying it and you *hate* it, that doesn't make any sense to me. Go buy a book that you like.

Salicrup: How did you like working with David Michelinie?

McFarlane: He was, he was, he was . . . I'm kind of like a weird artist. I worked for Roy Thomas a few years and I had *some* contact with him because he was my editor, but I worked for like a year and a half with Peter David, then two years with Dave Michelinie, and you can almost count on one hand the amount of times I have talked to the writer. I kind of take a stance that I don't talk to the writers, tell them anything about their writing, and they don't have the right to talk to me about my artwork.

I've found that the writers that I've worked for, especially David, actually *wanted* feedback from me. He wanted me to give him story ideas, he wanted me to have more input into it—but I kind of took that stance. And by the time that I felt that I *had* some ideas for the book, I felt it wouldn't be fair to him to, like, change the rules of the game. The book was doing okay with him doing the story and me doing the artwork, we weren't really suffering or anything like that. Maybe I frustrate the writers that I work for because I don't ever talk to them, but it's worked out for me. Everybody does their own thing.

Salicrup: What made you decide to write your own Spider-Man book?

McFarlane: [*Does an Eddie Murphy laugh*]

Salicrup: The question everybody wants to know.

McFarlane: You're pushing me. You want me to come up with something, like, gooey and greasy, right?

Salicrup: Just the facts. [*Laughter*]

McFarlane: Just the facts, there we go. The facts, if you know me, I'm kind of a cocky young kid. When I was pencilling, the reason I broke in being a penciller was that I thought that most people would send in their samples because they think that they can do it better than the guys that *are* doing it, or *most* of the guys that are doing it. And the same thing happened with the inking, you know. I wasn't satisfied with the inking and I thought I could do something a little bit different and be a little more true to what I wanted on the page.

And then once I became a little bit more adept at inking, it's like, "Well, let's go to the next thing." And right now the next thing is writing. After doing two years on the book, a lot of ideas that I have are stores in the back of my mind and there's only one way to get them on paper, that's to write them myself. It wouldn't be fair to David to all of a sudden graft my ideas to his. Maybe not, maybe that would have been the way to go, but I'm at the ballsy stage.

A lot of the guys that I collected, the Millers and the Chaykins and the Byrnes and the Pérezes and the Ordways, all turned out to be pretty decent writers and still continued to do their artwork. So I guess I was kind of molded in *that* venue. Those were the people in the last five years that I've admired, and they went on to do their own gigs. So I'm just seeing if I can do my own gig.

Salicrup: So, what's coming up in the new Spider-Man book?

McFarlane: What do you mean, you're the editor, you know! [*Laughter*]

Salicrup: But they want to hear it from you.

McFarlane: Oh, okay. We're planning it—because in your inimitable wisdom you have deemed it that I *don't* have to tie this book in with the other Spider-Man books, which I think is a good move because of my lack of writing ability . . . it would be another burden on me that I probably wouldn't be able to get over. So, if I remember right, you told me you wanted the new book to kind of play it like "miniseries within a series" where the stories have their own beginnings and own ends, whether it takes one issue or takes four or five issues to tell the story, and then we just pick up another story and not have to carry stuff from the other Spider-Man books.

So, going on that premise, it's been working out rather well. The point is all I've got to do is come up with three ideas and stretch them out and I've got a year and half's worth of books. [*Laughter*] I don't have to come up with that many ideas, actually. But in the *first* five issues because I found out through you and your Spidey office that some of the villains were already taken by the other Spidey books—we'll have to do a villain draft next year—[*Laughter*] But I decided to do a five-part story and bring in a female villainess, because there's not really *that* many *bad* female villains. I'm going to see whether I can make a bad female villain. The character, in my mind, I tried to come up with something bad to equal the bad of Dr. Doom in a female character.

So, the first five issues of the new book will be . . . basically the first issue will be a setup issue, and then the next four issues will take place in the span of maybe two to four hours—it takes us four months to get those four hours. [*Laughter*] It's just going to be one long night, a bad night for Spider-Man, and at the end of this *bad* night . . . it's going to look for these first few issues like a Spidey and Lizard story, but by the end of issue #2 or in issue #3 there's going to be a little bit of a U-turn and you're going to see that it's not what it seems—it'll turn in a different direction.

Salicrup: And we're calling this book *Legends of the Arachknight*.

McFarlane: Yeah, and we're going to do a protective cover! [*Laughter*] And we're going to give our reason why—because it sells more copies! [*Laughter*]

Salicrup: And there'll be sixty-four different editions.

McFarlane: We could possibly top the thirty million-mark on this book! [*Laughter*] We'll suck everybody into buying sixty-four copies each, you know. It would work, even if they did have to stop buying every other book for the month.

Salicrup: The people reading this will think you're the most crass and cynical guy in the world. You have to bare your artistic soul for them, Todd.

McFarlane: Oh, no no no no. I just have to give the critics a couple more things to take jabs at me for. [*Laughter*] Then I get more lip service, more advertising. If there's one criticism that a person wants to give, it's that I probably won't ever give you the "formula" comic book. If I have control over it, you're not going to get a "formula" comic book. If you *want* a "formula" comic book, if you want a "formula" type of drawing and some other things, I'm not the man to give it to you.

Salicrup: Anything else you want to say to the boys and girls out there?

McFarlane: To the boys and girls out there, as Jim will testify, I'll listen to the readers more than I'll listen to my editors. [*Laughter*] That's part of the cockiness that goes along with the package right now, of dealing with me. But, in looking back on it, Jim Salicrup, the man of the hour, has been either one of the nicest guys or one of the dumbest guys in the business to put up with a lot of the stuff that I've done. At this point it's a risk to even give me a big-name character like Spider-Man, to *write* a book when I don't have any writing experience, to kind of let me go off in my direction and see if I can't do something a little bit off center and let the audience decide whether it's better or worse or anything.

So, don't always believe all of the stories you hear from people about different people. Jim Salicrup and Roy Thomas have been two of the nicest guys I've ever worked for, but other people would tell you different. I've been happy with my career so far, and maybe in a couple of years somebody else can come in there and take over the book and do a good job and I can kind of fade into oblivion. [*Laughter*]

You probably aren't very interested in hearing about problems such as the ones which plagued this interview. Suffice it to say that Jim and Todd spoke at length, and as much as could be was salvaged from the tape. Now let's join Dwight and Todd to fill in some gaps . . .

Dwight Jon Zimmerman: So, the Spider-Man comic that you're doing, how is that going to be different from the other Spider-Man comics?

McFarlane: We answered this question, Jim and I went into it *thoroughly!* What's the next question? No, I'm just kidding you, I can't even remember what we talked about.

Zimmerman: Well, what I have from the transcript is that it's going to be outside of continuity.

McFarlane: Yep.

Zimmerman: How about other heroes and villains? Are you going to be having many guest stars?

McFarlane: That will depend totally upon my mood. If I get moody and I just want to do Spider-Man and a bad guy or something, then I'll stick to that. If I decide I want to throw Captain America in there, if I want to draw Captain America, then hopefully I can work him in for some kind of storyline and make some kind of sense. I don't really have anything *concrete* right now because we *are* doing it out of continuity and we're trying to make most of the stories between three and five issues, you know. I don't want to start thinking about *too* many things and they won't come out until four or five years down the line. I don't want people to be waiting that long.

Zimmerman: What do you really like about Spider-Man? What is there about Spider-Man that really grabs you?

McFarlane: *Ooo-huhuhu!* Hey, good question! That's a deep one! You know, to tell you the truth, I guess I'm kind of like a simple kid when it comes down to it. I haven't really sat down—I guess I should, being the writer of the book—and *dissected* the guy. I've been drawing him for a while and I just know how to draw him. He's a young kid and he might have a few common things with me in my life, something like that, but . . . you know, I really haven't gotten that deep into the guy. I've been doing him for two years and he seems like he would be the easiest guy to do right now, because everybody else I'd have to be starting from scratch and figuring out how to draw them, how to write them.

I think the *biggest* disappointment for people, really, is I don't really have anything deep to say about it. I just kind of do it because it's kind of something fun for me to do. I get a kick out of this: It's kind of cool. That's about as deep as I get on this stuff, you know? I'm not the kind of guy that can ramble about inside Peter Parker's head for two hours. I'd rather talk hockey.

Zimmerman: Hockey? Okay, which one, Gretzky?

McFarlane: We'll talk all of 'em! [*Laughter*] I'm sorting the cards as we talk, I just picked up a case of nine thousand cards.

Zimmerman: So, when you're not drawing you're either working out with your baseball bat or collecting hockey cards?

McFarlane: Yeah, yeah. Actually, I am the co-owner of a cards and comics shop right now.

Zimmerman: You are?

McFarlane: Yes. So besides it being a hobby and stuff, we also do a little bit of business with those old cards and stuff, and sell the comic books. Between the drawing and that and trying to spend some time with my wife, I'm usually pretty busy.

Zimmerman: Well, as a retailer, how do you view the wacky business?

McFarlane: As a retailer—[*Laughter*]. You never try to guess why somebody—and this is Todd and not the words of wisdom for everybody out there—I stopped trying to figure out *why* a lot of people want this stuff and really see my duty more or less to supply what the demand is. Some guys feel that they have to go out there and kind of educate the readers. "Don't read *that* garbage," and whatever else. But . . . I mean, I guess to a small extent, but I'm not there to do that. I'm assuming the kid's reading the book because he likes it. And yeah, I'm going to point out the books that I might think are of a little bit higher grade or quality or something like that—

Zimmerman: Like yours?

McFarlane: No no no no no. I mean, I'll ram mine down their throats if they want it, but I don't make a judgment on my stuff. I never have. I like to let everybody else make the judgment. And I'm talking mostly, like, from the artistic point of view, or from the content. Plus, you have to look at it—I think a lot of guys get caught up in the book and they don't look at the age of the reader. Yeah, there are certain books that are kind of nice and they're pretty deep and whatever else, but that's not what an eight-year-old kid wants. I think a lot of people get caught into a groove and it's either got to be all or nothing. But, you know, a ten-year-old kid is going to be more inclined to follow a certain kind of book, a fifteen-year-old another kind of book, and at twenty-five and above there's going to be more inclination towards these other things. To try to sell *everybody* the same books is ridiculous. And I love superhero comic books, I can guarantee I'm going to be selling them for a long time.

Zimmerman: But will you be trying to give a little bit of your story to everybody, trying to reach as broad an audience with your—

McFarlane: Yeah, yeah. Personally, I think that *probably* the toughest thing to do as a creator is to keep a wide audience. I could write something, or could draw something, that would be real nice and clean and simple, and I would hit a decent audience on that. Or I could go for something that is a little bit deeper or something, and *again* I'd hit an audience. But either way, doing one extreme or the other, you limit yourself. What I'm hoping for is to kind of be somewhere in between where the storytelling is clear and the story has got enough action and stuff like that that the kids are going to like it, but there's enough nice art stuff and enough reading between the lines and having to think your way through the storyline that the guys that are a little bit older, and even a lot older and still want Spider-Man, will be able to pick it up and say they haven't seen it a thousand times before. That's about as much as I can hope to accomplish.

Zimmerman: Do you think that your success has given you more freedom or less freedom than before?

McFarlane: [*Does an Eddie Murphy laugh*] I'd have to say, on a creative point of view, *more* freedom. I'm probably getting away with things, and *could* get away with things if I wanted to, than other people who aren't quite as successful as I am at this point in my career. They wouldn't be able to get away with some of these things. I'm not talking about style or things like that, but . . . just becoming a writer, number one. I wouldn't have gotten away with that if I could only draw stick men, I guess. I pretty much used my artwork as the crowbar to get into writing, and it worked out where I was able to get a gig where I could write *and* draw. It might be the worst move that I've made, or the worst move that Marvel Comics has ever made . . . I don't know.

I flounder around with stuff like that. The creative part of it is . . . Jim Salicrup, who is the editor, and other people at Marvel have been . . . they've been easy with me, you know. I haven't had no complaints. I keep waiting for them to, like, drop the axe every now and then. I guess at this point they're kind of letting me have my head, and if I make a wrong turn I'm sure they'll be the first to let me know. So for now things have been successful, the sales haven't gone down or anything, and hopefully this new book will be fairly successful. I guess if it's a commercial success they'll probably keep letting me do what I do.

Zimmerman: Have you ever looked at whether . . . scratch that question, I'm floundering now.

McFarlane: You sorting hockey cards too? [*Laughter*]

Zimmerman: Let's get back to your retail store. When did you start that?

McFarlane: The store opened the ninth of December of 1989.

Zimmerman: So this is a new thing.

McFarlane: Yah.

Zimmerman: Is it in Vancouver or where?

McFarlane: It's just outside of Tacoma, Washington, in a town called Puyallop. My brother-in-law runs it.

Zimmerman: What gave you the bug to go in on a store?

McFarlane: I had a *huge* comic book collection, I gotta tell ya. I think the final count was around 25,000 items, heavy multiples of everything. It didn't go back that far, maybe twenty years. I'd been holding onto them and it just got to the point where I had to make a decision, and I decided I'd put them into the store. And plus, I had a lot of baseball cards too. We'd always collected cards. The only two things I really am an expert about are comic books and cards—I don't really know much of anything else. I couldn't talk politics or religion, but I can talk cards and comic books, so I thought, "Why not put that knowledge to use!" And I'll tell you, I know more about sports cards than I know about comic books—and I know a lot about comic books.

Zimmerman: So, what's the hot sports card?

McFarlane: The hot sports card—hey hey, you want my inside investment tips here? For basketball, Michael Jordan is gold. For football right now, Joe Montana seems to be the hot man. For baseball, Nolan Ryan is gold. And for hockey, Wayne Gretzky and Mario Lemieux, *gold!* Any kid buys those cards, they're not going to lose.

Zimmerman: Have you ever gone to games and stood in line to get autographs?

McFarlane: Get a player's autograph?

Zimmerman: Yeah.

McFarlane: Yeah, when I was a kid, sure. Everybody did that. You stand there and you're kind of shy and you go, "Mr.—Mr.—Mr.—." You didn't even care who it was. I mean, yes, you knew who the big guys were, and you always had one or two favorite guys, but you were happy as long as you got *an* autograph, and I think the kids are the same way today.

Zimmerman: Who's influenced your art most?

McFarlane: Who's *influenced* my art the most? Uh . . . to tell you the truth, no one guy. I could tell you who I think is the greatest, just visually I'd say Mike Golden is *stunning!* I've never seen a bad Mike Golden job, I love his stuff.

But I'm kind of like a sponge—I think most people are pretty much the same. You end up being like a sponge and pulling a couple of things that you like from this guy, a couple things from this guy, from that guy, and after hodge-podging it all together and playing with it for a couple of years, you end up coming up with your own style. I've had some people come up to me and say my stuff looks like some guy and, like, I've never even cracked one of his books open. It's all in the eye of the beholder. I think most guys will tell you that.

And the reason why most guys become, like, their own style, is that once you get to a certain point and you're turning out so much work, you don't really have time to look at other guys' stuff. You've got to crank out your pages and you don't have time to analyze another guy's work. You've got deadlines; as a matter of fact, that's probably the best thing, because it forces you to become you.

Zimmerman: Do you try to read other comic books, or do you find your schedule is just too full?

McFarlane: Yeah, yeah, my schedule is pretty full. I stay on top of a few things. That probably is going to disappoint people. I think—I don't know whether it's egotistical or whatever—but I think that the *less* stuff that I actually look at that's comparable to the type of work that I'm doing, the better it is because then I don't have any preconceived notions about it. Especially on the writing end of it. The sponge, I do the same thing with the writing. I'll look at things that wouldn't directly tie into a superhero comic book, or a Spider-Man-type comic book.

My *biggest* thing that I want to accomplish on the book is to make it a little bit different. I think if I read too many superhero comic books then I'm going to get caught up in kind of a certain way of presenting something. If I'm staring at a blank wall all day then I've just got to flounder my way through it; and hopefully within a year I will have dropped the bad habits and kept with the good habits and we'll have a nice product.

Zimmerman: What does Todd McFarlane enjoy drawing most, Spider-Man in those wacky poses, the action scenes, or the women? [*Laughter*]

McFarlane: You know, to tell you the truth, I don't really think that I'm that good of an artist of females. I've had lots of people tell me they like the women, but I can rattle off twenty guys that can draw women a lot prettier and they've got the bodies down a lot better than I do, and they've got the body *language* down. It seems like it comes off more natural, you know?

Zimmerman: For instance?

McFarlane: I've seen Marc Silvestri draw some dynamite women. Mike Golden. George Pérez. There's a lot of guys, actually, that's what their forte is.

As for Spider-Man, it's not so much that I get off drawing Spider-Man per se. I would say, if I *have* to nail down one thing that I like to draw, I like to draw big and exciting things. Maybe that sounds dumb. I can remember . . .

Infinity, Inc. #36, p. 19, March 1987, DC Comics, Fair Use. McFarlane's love of capes is clear from his early work on *Infinity, Inc.*, where the cape not only covered the body and added a sense of visual drama, but was also incorporated into the design of the page.

I didn't start collecting comic books until I was seventeen, so I'm one of the late bloomer guys. I guess the reason my attitude is the way that it is that I wasn't one of those guys who'd been reading comic books since he was five. I kind of got in it as an afterthought. I was going to school and playing ball and I was going to be a baseball player—that was my *life*—and I kind of tripped into comic books.

So for me, mentally, I just do what I like to do. I just like to draw big visual stuff. As an artist, up until recently, I had no control over the storyline, really. I didn't know who was going to be in it, why they were going to be in it, what kind of motivations they had—I had no control of that. The only thing I had was that I was in control of the visuals, so I had to make it as visually exciting as possible. So, I love drawing big stuff. There's a lot of guys, Pérez and Adams and Silvestri, who can draw a million tiny little guys, and I *envy* them. I can't draw them—I like the big stuff.

And that *probably*, in a roundabout way . . . Kirby, as much of a Kirby influence that you can see in me, my stuff is patterned after this perception of Kirby. Kirby seems to always hit you over the head with big visuals, and that's all I do. If you're going to buy *Spider-Man*, I'm going to give you big visuals, a big Spider-Man. If I were to draw *Iron Man*, then I would draw a big Iron Man. If I were to draw *Wolverine*, I guarantee you I'd give you some big Wolverines. I assume that there's a reason why you're buying that book, and visually I'll hit you over the head with this stuff.

Zimmerman: Did Spider-Man give you more of an opportunity to play around with those visuals than other superheroes would? Spider-Man being Spider-Man, did what he is, and his environment, give you more of an opportunity to play around and get into extremes of posture and angles and anything like that, as compared, for instance, with Iron Man?

McFarlane: Yeah. Because of the characters I'd say that's true. Going in. I don't think it really . . . maybe it did, who knows? But I don't think it really expanded me or contracted me as an artist. What I find is when I get on a book and I'm totally floundering—if I was to jump onto a new character I would be floundering on that book for the first four to six months—by doing repetition—and I like the books that have single characters, too—after four or five issues I start to get a feel for what I'm drawing. For the first couple of months—this is why I try to stay away from fill-in issues—it's, "Okay, his belt's like this, the boots go here." You go through the paces and gradually you start to know what you're doing.

This is why I'm sticking with Spider-Man, is that I can now dive into the new *Spider Man* book with the whole repertory behind me. If I went over to *Iron*

Man, for instance, I would look at him totally different. I would say, "Okay, what can I do that's different?" I think Bob Layton's done the definitive Iron Man, but I would say, "How can I make him glide through the air in a way that's never been done before? What kind of high-tech stuff can I add that's never been done before? What hasn't been done before that I could do?" Doing a shot of Iron Man here and there doesn't allow me to think about it for eight hours a day.

But I'm drawing Spider-Man eight hours a day and I have to, like, problem-solve the guy, because otherwise you're just going to see the same picture over and over. What was I . . . oh, yeah, about Spider-Man being any different being Spider-Man. I don't think so because on any other character I would have done the exact same process and gone into the directions of that character.

Zimmerman: Is there a character that you haven't drawn that you'd like to take a crack at?

McFarlane: You know . . . again, I hate to buck the notion that I have all these things that I'm just cracking to do. I've got a lot of energy, I gotta tell you that—and I'm sure my wife and Jim can verify that. I just don't do it because I have to do it, but I go to each job first as a professional—this is the book I'm doing. I'm going to do the best job possible.

If you push me into a corner, other than Spider-Man right now, I wouldn't mind taking a crack at Batman. Not because I have any great fondness for Batman, but he's *probably* one of the easiest guys to *draw!* You just put that cape around his body and you never have to draw anatomy. [*Laughter*] The odd hand and the odd foot, the head, and this cape all over the place, and you're done! You don't have to worry about whether his biceps are in the right place. That's why I like capes, 'cause capes cover up a lot of the anatomy.

Zimmerman: Will we get to see Spider-Man with a cape?

McFarlane: No, no. The reason that I do the *webbing* the way that I do is because it's in lieu of a cape. I've always loved capes because I think they give a great sense of depth and a great sense of motion. I could have Batman standing there in a majestic pose just picking his nose. Literally! Doing nothing but picking his nose. It would look like there's a lot happening because there would be this majestic stance, and the cape would be billowing in eight directions in the wind, you know. He'd look like a god figure.

And Spider-Man never had that. Everybody's perched him up on top of buildings and whatever else, and I needed to add something *more*. So I go, "He doesn't have a cape but he's got *webs!* Wouldn't it be cool if it looked like the webs were all over the place, like blowing in the wind!" That's why I do the webs the way that I do.

Zimmerman: Is there anything special that you'd like to add?

McFarlane: Oh, something *deep* you mean? You've come to the wrong well.

Zimmerman: Not necessarily deep but something Todd.

McFarlane: Ah, Jesus, now you've put the pressure on. I would like to say that because I've been on the book that I've been on—I happened to be at the right place at the right time, really—I know in my mind that I've got no place to go but downwards. And I know that as I'm going down in the eyes of the audience, which is okay because everything's in cycles, that I'll be turning out better work. If people think they've seen the best that I've got, I've got plenty more years that I hope to be in the business and hopefully it's going to get better. I've just begun to get geared up.

Note

1. Throughout all interviews, emphases are in original.

Spider-Man Artist: Todd McFarlane

LEN WONG / 1990

From *Amazing Heroes* 1, no. 179 (May 1990): 24–40. Reprinted by permission.

Amazing Heroes: I suppose the most obvious place for us to begin would be with your new *Spider-Man* title. I was wondering how it came about.

Todd McFarlane: It came about after being on the *Amazing Spider-Man* book a couple of years. I just got a little bit antsy to broaden my horizons, I guess, and since I already do the penciling and inking on the book, the next obvious step was to get into the writing. To tell you the truth, it's not even that I want to be a writer; it's more that I wanted to have control of the artwork.

AH: So there were no hard feelings over you leaving *Amazing Spider-Man*? Your departure there was sort of abrupt, wasn't it? I mean, they had announced plans that you were going to do a Spider-Man/Wolverine/Punisher team-up and—

TM: Yeah, yeah, yeah. That's true. To tell you the truth, in comic books, there's never a good time to leave a book. Never ever ever. If you phone up the editor and say you're quitting the book, not too often they'll say, "Uh, yeah, okay. Next issue—that seems good." Yeah, I guess it was abrupt, because in some respects I kind of built my career on the book.

If there was any scandal to anything, then for sure I wouldn't be working on Spider-Man, with the new Spidey book, and for sure I wouldn't be working with the same editor. As a matter of fact, I think that that might throw a few people for a loop, because usually when you quit, you're supposed to go, "Aw, fuck you," and run to the *Comics Journal* and blow your horn, and—but no. It was just a decision that I made. I basically was just going to try to blackmail people into giving me writing with my artwork. And they fell for it.

AH: It's just interesting that you'd leave a Spider-Man book to do—

TM: —a Spider-Man book! I know! Well, like I said, when I was going to do the writing, I thought that I would have to start at a low book and learn the trade. I'm pretty cocky—uncoachable—because, for the most part, when I've done things that I've wanted to do, they've worked out. So I'm not really that lenient to listen to other people's thoughts on some of the things. I'm good at listening to people after they've shown me that it doesn't work, but it drives me nuts when they try to stop you before they even give you the chance to attempt it another way.

But anyway, because I quit the Spider-Man book when things were going good and they still wanted me to do some Spider-Man stuff, they came up with a new Spidey book and, not being foolish, I knew that Spider-Man was a hot commodity. It wouldn't have been my choice to bring in a fourth Spider-Man book, but I wasn't fool enough to say no to it.

AH: Besides the fact that you're doing everything, what's going to make your book different from the other three?

TM: What, that's not enough? [*Laughs*]

AH: No, I mean, is it going to be a "Spider-Man of the Week" thing or—

TM: Well, that will be the underlying theme of the whole book—trying to justify a fourth Spider-Man book out there. Fifth, I guess if you count the reprint book. But my main concern is to try and make it as different as possible from the other three or four books, not because the other books aren't good or anything, but if I'm just going to do the same thing that's happening in *Amazing* or *Web*, then there is no rationale for having another book. It would almost be like taking one of the other books and going biweekly.

So what I'm trying to do is come up with a different slant on presenting Spider-Man. Obviously, some situations are going to call for the standard way that Spider-Man acts, but I'm just trying to show people that I think there is more than one way, two ways, three ways to present Spider-Man.

AH: Are you just talking in terms of the artwork?

TM: I'm talking in terms of the artwork, in terms of storytelling, in terms of the way the writing is. It's not going to be—I don't want to use the phrase "formula-type book," but I guess that's as close a phrase as I can come to. I'm trying to stay away from a formula as much as possible, literally to the point where I'd rather do something stupid and wrong than do it the way that it's been done before.

For me to repeat the same thing doesn't make any sense to me. I mean, why would I want to do it? You've seen it, I've seen it.

AH: According to the Marvel press release, your book's going to basically be standing on its own, not part of the continuity with the other books. So, for example, they're not going to have this "Spider-Man gets superpowers" thing going through your book—

TM: Well, you know, if it's something major like that, I'll probably make some kind of comment on it, but no, I don't have to do that. That's going to be up to the editor and up to myself.

Right now the plan, as suggested by Jim Salicrup, is to save ourselves all a lot of headache, and not tie into anything, and make it kind of a miniseries within a series. So I'm going to do my five-part "Lizard Saga," and then the next one will be my six-part whatever saga, and it's just going to be little finite stories.

It's good for me because all I've got to do is come up with one idea and it carries me for five months, so I don't have to be brainy and come up with five stories. I don't think I could do a regular-type comic book that has pacing and all the characters moving through it in twenty-two pages. I don't have that knowledge right now.

What I need to do is take one story, drag it out for a hundred pages, get everything in that I need, and make it a nice finite little story.

AH: So they're just putting you off in your own little corner, to play with their stuff.

TM: Yeah. If there's major ramifications in the other books, or if he gets a certain haircut, I have to keep things the same. But I think it allows me a lot of freedom. If I don't want to put him in New York, then I can just say he happened to go to the desert for that week.

AH: Are there any plotlines you'd like to reveal to our readers right now?

TM: Oh yeah. I phoned up and got all the plots on *The Avengers* and *X-Men*, so I'll blow those. [*Laughs*] No, the first five parts are going to be a Spidey, Lizard, and somebody else story. I've got a mystery villain in there who hopefully won't be the obvious choice. This character was suggested to me by Glenn Hardling, who was assistant editor on *Spider-Man* until recently.

The Goblin and a lot of the other guys I wanted to use had been spoken for, so my choices were kind of limited. The Lizard was hanging around, and then I decided to throw in somebody who has been shooting around the Marvel Universe, but—

AH: You don't want to reveal who it is?

TM: Well, no. They don't have to buy the book then. I'm a rookie writer—I need to get people sucked into this.

Hopefully, there'll be a few twists and turns on it, but that's not really my main goal on the storyline right now. I want it to kind of look like a Lizard story, and then go left with it and show you it's not really a Lizard story.

I really like the Lizard. I think he's a great visual character. And I'm trying to present him in a fashion that I don't think he's ever been presented before.

Because my story takes place in the span of two days, I think I can get away with saying he just acts like this for two days. Somebody else—the next writer who picks him up—can worry about why he did do this. So in the five issues that you see him, you don't ever see Doc Connors. There's very little mention that he's even the Lizard. The dialogue refers to him as "the creature" or "the monster," which is exactly what I play him as. He doesn't speak, that's the other thing.

AH: Lots of growling?

TM: No growls. I'm not big on sound effects. But he won't talk because it drives me nuts.

I've given him bigger fangs than the last time, and his clothes are torn more, and he's 80 percent more in the shadows, and the story takes place at night, so visually, I think he's a good character to use. But it kills me that you've got this guy that looks like he's going to rip your throat apart, and he comes out from the corners, and he goes, "I'm gonna kill you, Sssssspider-Man! And you're going to die a sssssslow death!" And he comes out talking with this lisp. They do that to all the lizard and reptile guys. They always put ninety "s"s on everything, and to me, it's corny. I'm doing this book so I don't have to give this character a voice; it's as simple as that.

And so, with the Lizard, I'm playing him like the creatures in the *Aliens* movie, where the good guys come around the corner and the big guys were there. Especially at the end—the big mother was sitting there and she just opens up her jaws about fourteen feet and then about two pounds of saliva hits the ground. You don't have to say, "I'm going to kill you. You better watch out, Sigourney—I'm a bad one." I mean, it was there. It was evident in the picture.

When the Lizard comes jumping down at you and he's got his teeth bared, I've got to assume that the average intelligent reader is going to assume that he's going to inflict some kind of pain. I don't have to put "Sssssstand ssssstill while I sssssslay you," you know? Jesus, we'll worry about that when I do Daffy Duck. [*Laughs*]

AH: Do you have any previous writing or plotting—

TM: [*Laughs*] Credits? No. Zippo. Nada.

AH: So they're just throwing you right into the water?

TM: Yeah! Actually, I don't look at it as if they're throwing me—I'm throwing them! They're giving a number one Spidey that's going to sell because the character's their big guy. I guess a lot of kids like Wolverine, but to the average person walking the street, the biggest guy that they know in Marvel is Spider-Man. I think they're taking a bigger chance than I am.

Probably the best thing for that will be to wait until the book comes out and to listen to some of the critics—constructive criticism, not that it's just a piece of shit, because I'm going in [assuming] that it's going to be a piece of shit, so anything better than [that], I'm feeling good.

I know the writing's going to be no different than the penciling and the inking. Both of those jobs took me a year or two to feel comfortable with. In a couple of years, when I feel good about my writing, I'll go into coloring or lettering.

AH: Was it hard for you to start writing, then?

TM: The plots aren't that hard, because I think everybody—whether they're a writer or not—always has ideas in the back of their minds. I never really formulated any of the ideas until I decided maybe I should try being the writer.

I blapped out the first four, five issues—the pencils—real quick. Because I was plotting for myself, the plot was mostly in my head.

The way I do a plot now, I write half a sentence for each page, and then my mind finished off the rest. So when I phone up my editor, I fill in all the blanks. Page two might say "Peter and Mary Jane snuggle up," but I might say to my editor, "Well, they're snuggling up, but this is what they're talking about; this is why they're doing it." It doesn't make sense to me to write all that stuff down.

AH: Not if you're doing it all.

TM: As long as my editor feels comfortable with the ideas.

AH: There's only a few people who are doing complete packages like this. Do you just do it all here and then send it in to Marvel completed or—

TM: Yeah, well, I think that's it. They have a certain way of doing things, but you can kinda get around those things on a guy like me who is doing everything. And somebody like Byrne or Miller, who're doing their own packages. Not because they're bigshots, but just because there's no sense in doing it if you're going to be doing it all yourself. There's no sense in me doing tight pencils. There's no sense in me doing a tighter plot, because I'm wasting my time.

AH: Why do you think Spider-Man's such a popular character? What is it about him that appeals to people?

TM: Uh . . . this is where Todd's supposed to get deep, dang it . . . If you want to know why I think that he happens to be popular right now and not why he's popular for the last thirty years, because then I have to get deep and . . . fuck, I don't get deep on things . . .

It's because I think Spider-Man is one of a dozen of what I'd call big superheroes that people, no matter what happens to them, always have a soft spot for.

I'm talking about the Supermans, the Batmans, the Spider-Mans, the Hulks, the Captain America types. The guys that have been around for years and years and years.

AH: So these are the characters that everybody knows, everybody's heard of.

TM: Yeah. The average person on the street has heard of them. Now, again, this is Todd McFarlane's opinion about this, but I think that these guys are so big and so popular, it doesn't take as much effort to get on the bandwagon if something is done to generate some excitement.

So when Byrne took over *Superman*, well, we all go, "Yeah! Superman and Byrne together? Great!" It took Miller a little while on *Daredevil*. Daredevil's a great character, but not quite as big as some of the one I've just mentioned. But Batman? Bammo. He did the book and there was instant recognition.

And Spider-Man, I think, is one of those guys that people, even in the bad times, are going to collect. And I think that's what we owe the popularity to right now. Spider-Man's that big a character and somebody's come along and artistically shook him up a little bit and gave people a reason to read the book before they put it in a plastic bag.

I think you'll find if you talk to most guys that it doesn't really reflect in the sales for a long time. They've been collecting the book for ten years, but now they actually like the book and are looking forward to the next issue.

AH: When you took over *Amazing Spider-Man*, you made a lot of stylistic changes to the characters. I was wondering what the reaction to these changes was from Marvel.

TM: I would say it was lukewarm, really. And I think that you will find that kind of reaction to a lot of people who go in there and mess with something that has established a certain status quo.

That's exactly what I did. Spider-Man looked a certain way for so long that they have a tendency to think that if you mess with it, then the sales might go down.

I can understand that. On a business level it makes sense. You figure that you've been doing it right for fifteen, twenty years and this is how it should be done. But I think the guys like myself that are cocky and uncoachable, we don't really fear getting fired and we don't mind going in and messing something up. Sometimes we succeed and sometimes we fail. I think that's exactly what happened on that book.

I told them, "Hey, if you show me that the sales are going down, I'll stop it in ten seconds." But there was no proof that people didn't like it any more or any less.

My goal is to stay on the book for as long as possible, and the only way I'm going to do that is if I'm happy. Money doesn't motivate me at this point in my career.

AH: Did you have to fight to keep your changes in at the beginning?

TM: Like I said, Spider-Man was their status quo guy. I really didn't look at it as a big deal, because I just made some cosmetic changes with the costume, with the webbing. Mary Jane a little bit. It was kind of like updating him, bringing him into the 1990s. It wouldn't have been such a big deal if they had been updating him every five years, but all of a sudden it looked like I was changing twenty years' worth of stuff. I kind of put in the new 1990s look, mixed with a little bit of the Ditko-era stuff, and made it a hodge-podge of the two.

They assumed that because I didn't want to draw like John Romita that I didn't like John's stuff. Quite the contrary, but I would be a fool to draw John Romita's Spider-Man. It's been done to death. If they want John Romita's Spider-Man, get John. Or there's a hundred guys that are willing to try to do a bad John Romita Spider-Man.

The only thing that's going to make me different from the pack is if I do something different. Even if it's bad different, people tend to notice you more. And the more you get noticed, the better it is for your career.

AH: I'm supposed to ask you about the "big eyes" story.

TM: The "big eyes" story? Oh . . . the "big eyes" story! When I got onto the book, one of the things I wanted to do was play up the word "Spider" in "Spider-Man"—big "Spider," little "Man," and one of the things that I thought would be obvious was bugs have big eyes.

Yeah, you can imagine they had a heart attack with it because all of a sudden the bottom of his eyes was down, tucked into his lips or something. They kind of gave me hell—you know, I'd have to make the eyes smaller . . .

AH: Back to the Romita-sized eyes?

TM: Yeah. The little teardrops. But I'm kind of bad that way, that as soon as somebody tells me no, I tend to go and say the opposite. I actually made them bigger. As a matter of fact, if they hadn't ever said anything, the eyes wouldn't be as big as they are today.

AH: Just to spite them.

TM: Well, yeah. I don't know, I was just at the point that I felt like bugging somebody, I guess. Like I said, I'm just kind of uncoachable and a big dink, anyway. You can put that in quotes. I've told the editors if I ever work for them, this is how I am. I'm not going to listen to them; the book will come out on time and you'll get the best work that I could possibly turn out, but I'm gonna push it and do it my way.

AH: The other big change that took place with the character after you started doing the book was the costume reverted back to the original, from the black suit. Did you have any say in that?

TM: I wasn't interested in doing the black costume. The stuff that I like is the stuff from before I was a professional. It holds sweeter memories for me.

And when I walked in there, I think he said that I could take one of the books, but starting with issue #300 of *Amazing*, they were getting rid of the black costume for some reason—I think it was some merchandising. I had nothing to do with it. But that was what solidified me jumping on the *Amazing Spider-Man* book. He was going back to the costume, so if I made some of these changes, it wouldn't be such a big deal.

AH: Let's move on to some of your earlier work. How did you break into the business?

TM: I was going to school at Eastern Washington University where I was attending on a baseball scholarship, and I was probably the biggest comic book fan you could find. I was reading everything.

At this point, I had figured that if I don't become a major league ball player, I'd better have something to fall back on. So I was sending off packages; I started collecting when I was seventeen so it had only been a couple of years that I had been following the business, and I tend to be obsessive about things. When I put my mind to something, I go totally crazy on stuff. So I was literally sending off hundreds and hundreds of samples over the course of about fourteen months. Probably came to about six hundred packages. And I got, literally, a sacksful of rejection letters. So to some of the people out there who've gotten one or two rejection letters, I'm telling you, I've got hundreds.

AH: You were doing this while you were still a student?

TM: Still a student. And I've got a bag of who's who of "No thanks." I thought, "Wow! I've got all their autographs!" [*Laughter*]

But after doing that for about fourteen months, I did a sample of *Coyote*, which was one of the books that Marvel/Epic was putting out, because at the time I wasn't really hot on the artwork on the book. The way I hear it, one of the packages went off to Ann Nocenti, who was editing *X-Men* at the time.

She passed it on to Mary Jo Duffy, who was doing some editing in the Epic office, and she phoned up Steve Englehart, who was writing *Coyote*. Steve saw it and gave me a phone call. He wanted to know whether I wanted to do a back-up in *Coyote*. It ended up being four issues long before the book was canceled. And that's the way I did it.

The only reason I can see that she passed them on to Epic was because I had done Coyote. So I think it does help for a person to pick a lesser-known character when they're doing their samples because then you're not going to get compared to some of the bigger characters.

AH: But you didn't really get noticed until you took over *Infinity, Inc.* at DC.

TM: Yeah. After doing a couple months on the back-up series in *Coyote*, which I think was #11–14, they phoned me up and told me the book was canceled. But they assured me that it had nothing to do with me! [*Laughs*]

I think most people that are trying to break into the business will tell you that the toughest thing is to get steady work, not getting that first job. That first job is the biggest step, but after you get that, it's to get steady work thereafter. A lot of guys take two years to break in, then three years to get a regular book.

I went through all my rejection letters and one of the sweetest guys on the rejection letters was Roy Thomas. I sent a package off to him, but now I could put "I work for Marvel/Epic" in big bold letters, and all of a sudden the samples go from the bottom of the pile to the top; it's like now you're a "professional," even though you still draw as shitty as you did two months ago.

Don Newton, who had taken over [*Infinity, Inc.*], had just died. It was unexpected and sudden and tragic; he was a very talented guy. But they needed somebody on the book; I mean, really, sometimes that's how breaks are made. I did issue #14, which was a fill-in, and a pinup for issue #13. I was supposed to do issue #14 and #15 as a guest artist, then halfway through issue #15, the guy who was supposed to take over the book decided that he wasn't going to, so they needed somebody again. And since I was drawing it, why not just give it to me regularly?

AH: When you took over *Infinity*, you did some very individualized, stylized page layouts. Did DC encourage you to do this sort of experimentation since it was an offset book?

TM: Yeah, "stylized." In hindsight, they think I'm stylized. It becomes "intrinsically graphic" or something. At the time, it was bullshit. [*Laughs*]

I had just finished University and I had a degree in graphics. I was going into the printing trade. The experience that I had there obviously had something to do with what I did on *Infinity*. But more importantly, the reason I did what I did on *Infinity* was the same thing that I do to this day. Jerry Ordway was the guy who was on before, and he's an outstanding artist. I was a rookie and I'd be an idiot to try and follow Ordway's lead. There was only one thing I could do—go completely to the left so it didn't look like Jerry Ordway and I wouldn't be compared to him. Also, there was a lot of people breaking into comic books, and again, the only way to get anyplace in here is to be noticed.

Luckily, Steve Englehart and Roy Thomas both said, "Yeah, fine." I don't know what would have happened if they had said no; I would have just gone and done the same stuff that you've seen before.

Infinity, Inc. #28, p. 26, July 1986, DC Comics, Fair Use. An example of McFarlane's early "stylized" page layouts on *Infinity, Inc.* that garnered public attention and separated him from many other artists.

In hindsight, it wasn't fair to the writer because it was so artsy-fartsy, so graphic that it interfered with the story.

AH: It certainly stood out as something different from everything else on the stands.

TM: Well, there it is. I accomplished my goal. Even on the *Spider-Man* book, I want to do something different. I'll leave it up to the people who buy it to tell me whether they like it or not.

AH: After *Infinity* you moved on and did one issue of *Spitfire and the Troubleshooters . . .*

TM: Yes!

AH: . . . and that was your first Marvel work.

TM: Yeah. I was contemplating quitting *Infinity* because I was getting tired of drawing nineteen good guys and nineteen bad guys per story, and I haven't done a team book since! So to all you people who want to see me do the X-Men, Roy Thomas has scarred me for life! [*Laughs*]

But Roy Thomas always had so much work for me that if I had quit *Infinity* he would've kept me busy for the next twenty years.

But I didn't know, after two years in the business, whether I was there because Roy Thomas liked my stuff and nobody else did. I was getting to the point where I was trying to find somebody else and see whether there was any validity to what I was doing. So I went over to Marvel and talked to one of the editors, Bob Harras, who was editing *Hulk, G.I. Joe, Spitfire*, and a couple other things. He saw that I was on *Infinity* for two years, and that's one of the big things people don't realize—staying on a book does your career a lot of good.

But they wanted to know whether I could handle Marvel storytelling—straightforward storytelling, if you want to call it that. So I said, "Yeah." It takes less of an effort for me to do standard storytelling than to think up some bizarre artsy-fartsy thing. The artsy-fartsy thing is pretentious and self-gratifying—Todd jerking off on the page—but it takes more thought process. Straightforward storytelling—I can do that in my sleep.

He gave me the book and I told him I could do it in a week, maybe four days. I think I actually phoned him up and told him I wouldn't be able to do it in three days. I can remember Bobbie Chase laughing and saying, "Oh, that's okay. Four or five days, that would be sufficient." I mean, they've got guys that take forty to sixty days, and I'm apologizing that I'm not going to have it done in seventy-two hours . . .

At that point, the *Hulk* book had an opening on it. Anyway, I did one issue of *Spitfire* and the word came down that I was a good "bulk" artist; I could do big things.

AH: Because of the armor?

TM: Because of the armor on Spitfire. So I was off—I could do Hulk now, I could do Transformers, I guess . . . but the only reason they hadn't seen any skinny stuff is because they never asked me to do any skinny guys. That's the other thing that kills me about this business—they want to put you in some kind of hole.

I hate to tell you, I have seen artists who've put the Hulk and Spider-Man next to each other and, other than the coloring, there's not much difference in their size. I'm really big on making sure people know that this guy is this guy and that guy is that guy, even if you put them in silhouette. That's why I do the funky poses on Spider-Man, so you know that it's not some other guy jumping over the rook.

AH: On the *Hulk* did you have any input on the stories you did with Peter David?

TM: No.

AH: He just sent you the plots?

TM: Yeah. They were doing this Rick Jones Hulk when I took over the book. The first issue I did we killed Thunderbolt Ross. That's my claim to fame on *Hulk*—I killed off a major character. But Peter David came up with all the stuff. He took the book off in a direction, and I think it turned out to be one of those ones where nobody was really paying attention to the Hulk and after a while, Peter and I got going on the book. Especially with the Wolverine story, which really brought in a lot of readers. People saw that it wasn't the same Hulk they had been reading for years and years. And I give a lot of credit to Peter for going off in another direction.

Overall in my career, I don't really have that much contact with the writers. Well, now I guess I'll be sleeping with the writer on the new book, but my philosophy's always been "I don't tell you how to write, you don't tell me how to draw, and we'll get along great."

AH: Before you started inking on *Hulk*, there was a number of different people inking your work. How did you feel about the lack of a steady inker? Is this why you started inking yourself?

TM: Well, to tell you the truth, it was frustrating. But being inexperienced, I had to learn the penciling trade before I could get into the inking trade. Actually, it was the final part of "Batman: Year Two" where I did my first inking job. I don't think that there's a penciller out there that doesn't bitch about inkers. Really, pencillers are the biggest dinks. It's like, "Oh, the inkers don't ink good enough and the writers don't write good enough and the coloring sucks and the editor . . ."

Incredible Hulk #344, p. 24, June 1988, Marvel Comics, Credit Marvel Comics. An example of McFarlane's depiction of a bulky Incredible Hulk coupled with a gothic styling.

AH: "But look at those pencils!"

TM: [*Laughter*] We think we can do everything and that we're the greatest. Part of it has to do with when you go to the shows, the artist seems to get the most adulation. Fans tend to forget the other contributions that people have made to the book. That can really blow your head up.

So I was in that thing. You know, "I know how to ink better than anyone else," and so I got the jobs that Alfredo Alcala had done and—

AH: This is on *Batman*?

TM: Yeah. And it just—it was the one that broke me. Alfredo Alcala—and Tony DeZuniga, who inked me on *Infinity*—I love both their stuff when they ink themselves. But there's certain people I just don't feel you put together, and that's one of the biggest gripes about editors—they just don't have a clue about who to put together artistically sometimes. Certain guys need a brush guy, certain guys need a pen guy, certain guys need a guy who's just a laminator, certain guys need somebody who's an artist. I just thought that Alfredo and I sucked.

AH: Yeah. There are a lot of panels in the story that don't look like your art at all.

TM: Yeah, yeah. That's just it. And if you ask a lot of people, they may have loved the story, so I'm not saying that the story wasn't a commercial success. I guess it sold, and they're reprinting it now. I'm just saying that getting my stuff inked like everybody else's drove me nuts. So I ended up inking the last job, even though I had never inked anything in my life. I just got to the point where I said, "I either ink or I walk away from the project," and they said, "Yeah, you can ink it." I inked it with a tool that I've never used again, which is why the inking style's so different from what I do today.

Then I was finishing up. I convinced Bob Harras, that I wanted to take over the inking on *Hulk*. And we were having a tough time getting a steady inker on the book. So they let me take it over and, at that point, you finally get to see Todd McFarlane. Maybe you liked it better before I started inking my stuff. Who knows? To each his own. I'm going to be penciling and inking my own stuff probably until the day I die, so you'll know what the book is going to be. It's never going to be a surprise.

And now that I'm writing, I can't say, "Blame it on the writer." Like I said, being a penciller, I'm a dink. I shouldn't say "we." There are some great pencillers out there.

AH: Are there any inkers you'd still like to work with, or are you happy just to ink your own work now?

TM: Yeah, I am happy to ink my own work. One of the reasons why is because I don't pencil anymore. I don't actually do the drawing until I sit down and ink. Right now, while we're doing the interview and I'm inking here, this is the first time that I'm actually drawing this guy's cape.

But there's a couple of guys I wouldn't mind working with. I like Scott Williams's stuff; it's pretty neat. I've always wanted to work with Terry Austin. It seems like in the four or five things we were supposed to do, something always happens and we can't ever get together. It's disappointing. But other than doing a small thing with Terry, if I don't ink it, I won't do it. I do think—although I haven't had that many people ink my stuff, so it's not really fair to say—that I ink my stuff better than anybody else, and will put in more effort than anybody else because it's my stuff. It's not just another job to me.

AH: So you want the control?

TM: Yeah. For whatever that's worth. I want it to look like what I put on paper.

AH: Getting back to *Batman: Year Two*, how did you end up on it? You came in on the second issue . . .

TM: Yup. Good point. Good observation.

AH: Thanks, Todd.

TM: [*Laughs*] Yeah. "Wow! You looked like Alan Davis in that first issue!"

I was doing two books at a time at that point in my career. I was doing *Hulk* and I had just gotten fired from *GI Joe*—the only thing I ever got fired from . . .

AH: Why were you on *GI Joe*?

TM: Being Todd, being foolish, I figured, "Why do *GI Joe* the way it's been done and the way Hasbro's been selling nineteen trillion of the toys? I'm going to do it my way," and unfortunately—or fortunately, I guess—Hasbro didn't deem that as the way.

And that was the biggest relief off my mind, I've got to tell you. It was just hell; I was only on the book for a few months . . .

AH: Only one issue came out.

TM: But I did tons of redraws and unpublished stuff. It was easily one of the worst experiences I've ever had because you have to conform to this and you have to do that . . .

Larry Hama had his way of doing storytelling that to this day I still disagree with. He took a few chunks out of me, which was okay. I always love the guys like Larry; you might not agree with everything they say, but you do walk away with a couple of new things. You say, "Yeah, I wasn't aware of that." John Romita Sr. is great for that, too. Anybody who goes up to the office, I tell them to go talk to John because he makes you aware of things. It's tough to correct something if you're not aware of it.

Anyway, this is all leading up to how I got on the Batbook . . . [*Laughter*]

AH: I've got a feeling we're going to need more tape for this. . . . [*flips tape over*] Okay, how you got on the Batman . . .

TM: Anyway, I got fired from *GI Joe* at 12:00. I remember because I looked at the clock. At 12:06—no lie—the phone rings. "Pring." And it was Pat Bastienne, who hands out some of the work at DC. And she knew maybe the only thing that would draw me back to DC was to do some Batman stuff. This is pre-Batman-hype stuff. This was years ago.

They told me Alan Davis and Paul Neary had quit the Batman book—I don't know what their reasons were—and they were looking for somebody and would I mind doing Batman?

So I said, "By coincidence, I just quit the *GI Joe* book," not wanting to brag that I'd been fired. I think there was a little bit of misunderstanding that I was going to do more than that . . .

AH: On whose part?

TM: It's always mine, really. My wife will tell you that I'm the worst guy for communication. I don't know how to say no, just "No!"

But no, I never had any intention of doing Batman anymore. That's how I came onto the Spider-Man book. I knew my Batman stint was going to be over after I finished off this last issue, and I was looking for that second book to go along with *Hulk*.

AH: Did you have anything to do with the Batman movie? The production artwork—

TM: Nothing. Nada. Zippo. No.

AH: Okay, it's just that the preproduction artwork—the pieces they were showing around at conventions looked "very influenced" by what you did on *Year Two*.

TM: Yeah, that's true. To tell you the truth, when I saw it, it really bugged my ass; I'm as hotheaded as anybody else. I don't know. It rubbed me wrong.

I talked to several people at DC, and even people at Warner Bros., and they scoffed me . . .

AH: What, they denied it?

TM: No, I don't think they really knew what the full story was. They just knew that somebody else wanted to cash in on the Batman stuff—this is long before the movie came out. And one of the guys at Warner Bros. told me that I was biting off more than I could chew and not to take them on because they would squish me. Which is why I didn't pursue it like maybe I should have. They've got the money; they could bankrupt me.

Detective Comics #577, pp. 1 and 2, August 1987, DC Comics, Fair Use. McFarlane's distinctive rendering of Batman not only added a new styling to the character's cape for added dramatic flair, but would also stand as a precursor to the poses and cape illustrations that would later define *Spawn*.

I told them I thought it was kind of foolish because I didn't want anything monetarily from them. I said, "Why would you even think of fighting me when I don't want any of your money?" To me, that's stupid. The only way you can deal with these guys sometimes is on a business level.

In a weird way, I still think some credit should have been given to me. Whether you just blapped it out on the movie or on some PR thing—anything. That the drawing for the promotional buttons, the drawings for the lithograph that Bob Kane did—that I know he made good money on, and everybody else made good money on—that those are duplicates of my drawings. And in some cases, it looks like the guy used a lightbox and came up with that stuff.

I'm assuming that Warner Bros. knows nothing about comic books, really. So when they hand out money for Bob Kane to do preproduction work, they're assuming that the guy will draw originals. I would take that assumption.

The second thing that got him caught was some of those drawings were sent to DC for approval because Warner knows nothing about the Batman character. And the people at the DC office—some of the people—noticed the similarities, but they kept it hushed. And that it was something that still doesn't really sit that well with me. They knew it wasn't right, and still they did nothing about it.

One of the reasons they did nothing about it was because just previous to that they had gotten called on the carpet—again, this is speculation—for the whole "killing Robin" thing. I don't think they needed another run-in. I had to start thinking about how much of a fight I wanted to get into. I'm thinking, "Fuck it, I'm gonna take on Warner Bros." But then I had to think, did I want to drag my wife into this? There's other things you have to look at.

We got into gray areas. I knew I did not have any rights to the drawings that I did; it was work-for-hire. And I didn't own Batman. I own nothing.

I didn't even care if they wanted to use that image or something that looked like it. They do that with my Spider-Man stuff; it's plastered all over the place and I don't get any money for it. Ninety-nine percent of the time it doesn't even have my name on it, so nobody knows. Fine. I know what the rules are. But what bugged me was that Bob Kane signed his name to what I consider one of my drawings. That was my bone of contention.

I told people, "I don't want any money from you; I just don't want somebody else signing his name to my stuff." I don't think that's being unreasonable. If they did the exact same thing but had no name on it, or to go "Bob Kane," and at the bottom say, "Thanks, Todd." Anything.

AH: Just to acknowledge that you had done the drawing first.

TM: An acknowledgement that the idea was not Bob Kane's. That part of the idea of the cape came from me. There's some things that Bob incorporated into his stuff that hit the movie screens, so inadvertently, I did have something—in a wingy, small way.

On a business level, I know why they did it—Bob Kane created Batman, he's good for promotion. Who the fuck is Todd McFarlane? They orchestrated that movie to perfection and I admire their efforts on it. I just think that somewhere down the line, in some back-alley type of manner, they could have acknowledged something.

I know that Bob Kane made money going to conventions, and on the buttons—they were handing out the buttons everywhere. And he was even selling some of the originals to the lithograph. Literally, $50 to $100,000 for something like that—I hate to say it, but if I had bought that and found out later that it wasn't an original drawing, I wouldn't be too pleased.

Cover of *Comics Scene* #6, illustrated by Bob Kane, February 1989, Starlog Press, Fair Use. An example of Kane's later Batman illustrations that McFarlane believed reflected the influence of his designs for *Batman: Year Two*.

But really, I don't know what I can do at this point. Somebody from the *New York Times* phoned me up and asked me if I wanted to give the story, but I said it's not worth it. That's it.

I don't really have any animosity toward Warner Bros. They got caught in the middle. Some of the people at DC handled things a little differently than I would have handled them, but my biggest bone of contention is with Bob Kane.

AH: Have you talked to Kane about this?

TM: No. I've talked to people about Bob Kane, and from what I understand, he wouldn't acknowledge it even if it was true.

AH: Well, I think there have been other periods where he's had people ghost-painting work for him, and then he signs it and sells it in the galleries.

TM: Yeah. I've heard the stories about what's happened to Jerry Robinson and some of the other people, and if he doesn't even acknowledge their contributions, I'm not going to stand a chance.

So he came up with Batman. I don't think that that gives him the right to swipe other people's Batman.

So, anyway, that's the story.

AH: It's quite a story. Moving along, your last work for DC was *Invasion!* You did two issues of that and then vanished.

TM: Yeah, yeah. Dang it. *Invasion!* was a project where they originally wanted to have a bunch of people working on it.

AH: Everybody would get one chapter to do?

TM: Yeah. You'd have four teams on four chapters. But I figured I could do it all. I always hated these books that had more than one group of artists, anyway. Now, at the same time, they revealed that they were going to put *Spider-Man* biweekly. So all of a sudden, I'm penciling and inking two issues of *Spider-Man* and doing forty pages of pencils for *Invasion!*—and I even inked one of the chapters—all in the same month. I'm doing 100 to 130 pages, depending on the covers. And some people say that like a bragging thing. I say that with a sadness; I have to crank out that much work—and literally, the word is "crank"—and not put my best effort into it.

If I remember correctly, I think I told DC that there was no way I was going to be able to do the whole book. It just blew up in my face. I got in over my head. It came down to if something had to give, it was going to be *Invasion!* because 1) Spider-Man was my normal gig, and 2) Spider-Man was there before.

It was just me totally miscalculating what I thought I could handle. And then, right in the middle of it, while winding it down, there was the tragic death of a friend. This came out of nowhere, and knocked my wife and me for a while, and I needed a breather—to just get away from some of my work.

At that point, I didn't even finish up issue #2. Keith Giffen came and had to salvage it.

It wasn't fair to DC. It bugs me because I like to stand by my commitments, but I got overloaded.

AH: Well, did you at least have a bit of fun working on the DC characters again?

TM: To tell you the truth, I wasn't really paying attention to what I was doing. I was just going at a pace that, when I look at it in hindsight, was unacceptable. I wouldn't do it right now.

AH: You mentioned the biweekly *Amazing Spider-Man* comics. What did you think of that idea?

TM: One of the reasons I quit *Amazing Spider-Man* . . . the biweekly schedule can drive you nuts. I feel, for six issues, you're getting sub-par work out of me.

The book that I'm doing now will not go biweekly. I've told my editor that when they deem that the *Spider-Man* book is going to go biweekly, it will be when I do my last issue on it. That's something I just don't agree with.

AH: Since you've left *Amazing Spider-Man*, you've mostly been doing covers for various other Marvel books. That must be a pleasant change, only having to do one or two big pictures a month instead of twenty-two-page stories.

TM: Yeah, to a certain extent. The majority of the covers are like the *Marvel Tales* covers. The first few issues I put the villain in and action and stuff, but then I just got to the point where I'm basically doing portfolio pieces. [In one issue] I went "Aah, I don't want to do another action one." So I got Colossus on it, and Spider-Man and Nightcrawler on either side of him, having a wrestling match. And I put a big thing where the logo is supposed to go, where Colossus is saying, "Hey, Jim—what the hell has this got to do with the inside?"

But Jim Salicrup is a good enough man that he got the joke.

I just recently handed in a *Wolverine* cover that they rejected, for whatever reason. Nobody ever formally told me. I had to find this out through the grapevine. I'm assuming they rejected it because it didn't have anything to do with the inside, but I told them it wasn't going to have anything to do with the inside. That's another bitch that I have about other editors. The thing I have about other editors. The thing I like about working with Jim [Salicrup] is that if he's got a bitch about my stuff, I'm the first guy he phones up.

AH: Are you enjoying inking other people's covers? You've done some of Rob Liefeld's *New Mutants* covers, and I think a couple of other things.

Marvel Tales #237, Cover, May 1990, Marvel Comics, Fair Use. McFarlane's covers began to detach themselves from the interior stories and began to stand alone as "portfolio pieces," a practice that would later become common during *Spawn*.

TM: Yeah, I've done a couple of Liefeld's and I did a *What If?* Cover over Jim Valentino, and *Guardians of the Galaxy* #5 over Valentino. That one probably won't come out until the *Spider-Man* book's out.

No, to tell you the truth, I don't like inking other people's work. [*Laughs*]

AH: Why are you doing it?

TM: The only guy I'm actually doing is Rob because I get a kick out of him. He's just a funny kid. I like the guy, so it's more like a favor. But it takes me as long to ink his covers as it would for me to pencil and ink it myself. So I could make a lot more money saying no.

I've been isolated since I broke into the business, and I'm not a guy that probably should be working with too many people. [*Laughs*] Just let the Canadian kid sit there on his island and do whatever he wants . . . and for right now, it seems to sell.

I'm saying that tongue-in-cheek. Sometimes when you transcribe these things, if you read those things seriously . . .

AH: The covers. After all these problems you seem to be having with them, are you going to do anymore?

TM: I've already told that *Marvel Tales* covers are no more. I'm winding down all my last commitments. I'm not doing lithographs. I'm not doing portfolios. Maybe the odd poster. I'm doing writing, penciling, and inking. One book's enough.

If I've got any extra time right now, I'd rather spend it with my wife. I'd rather be out there playing ball or soaking up sunshine.

Yeah, it's only one extra cover. But for right now, I want to do my book the way I want to do it.

AH: Who are your influences as an artist? Whose work did you really admire when you were a young kid in university?

TM: Well, I started collecting when I was seventeen so, initially, I wasn't exposed to a lot of stuff. When I started collecting, John Byrne was one of the top guys. George Pérez: I've always admired Pérez's stuff. As the years went by, I saw a lot of merit in Mike Golden's work. I think he's the best of all the . . . if I had to rank them, I'd rank Mike Golden number one. Art Adams came along and really took the comic field by surprise and really added a lot to comic books.

Some of the older guys, Gil Kane. I've always loved Gil Kane's stuff. Not Bob Kane! [*Laughter*] Gil Kane. I love the power of his work. He didn't draw pedestrian stuff. If somebody got slugged, they went flying across the room. And Jack Kirby's stuff. For the storytelling and the power and the majestic feel that he brought to superheroes.

Actually, as a sidebar, I was at the San Diego Convention with my wife, and this was when the heat of the Bob Kane stuff was bugging my ass. Somebody stopped me and introduced me to Gil Kane. And I was with my wife. I exchanged pleasantries for a moment. I said, "It's good to meet you, sir. I've really admired your work and you're a big influence on my stuff." And my wife is standing there with her back turned to him, arms folded, going, "Humph! I'm not saying anything to you!" So we walked away, and then later on in the day she said, "How could you talk to that guy after what he's done?!" I'm standing there . . . "What do you mean?" "That Kane! That Kane guy you talked to!" And I go, "Wanda no. That was Gil Kane, not Bob Kane!" [*Laughter*] She says, "I couldn't believe it. I thought you were being a weasel, sucking up to him . . ."

AH: Any writers who have influenced you?

TM: Any writers? Uh . . . I don't really consider myself a writer, so I don't pay attention to writing. Now I'm sure the people at Marvel won't be too impressed with that statement, but by the time they read it, it'll be too late.

AH: What about writers outside of comics?

TM: None. Definitely, no. Again, that's probably going to kill people. To tell you the truth—I guess I should bare my soul—I don't read. Which is why it's a joke that I'm writing.

I read a sports page. I read statistics up the yang. I can't even remember the last book that I read without pictures. Good thing the *Comics Journal* doesn't ask me what I'm reading this summer. [*Laughter*] I guess I could tell them the 1989 hockey stat guidebook or something . . .

My influences and my energies were going into art. So everything I followed and paid attention to was artistic. I never had any inkling to read. The point I want to make is not that I want to write because I'm a writer. Quite the contrary. I want to write because then I get to draw what I want to draw. So even in the credits in the first five issues, it's going to read "Artist/Writer."

I hate to say it—this is Todd McFarlane on his soapbox again—but I've never been impressed by people who say, "I've studied Shakespeare and Michelangelo paintings in fine art." That's got nothing to do with superhero comic books. It's got something to do with it if you're going to be painting *Black Orchid* or a Sherlock Holmes thing, but superhero comic books? Everything is overexaggerated. It's done for a certain age group in a certain formula.

That's why I drive people crazy when they ask, "How do you be a comic book artist? Do you draw from real—" Wrong. I'll be the first guy to tell you: "Draw from comic books. Then from life." If you think you're going to draw a great

Superman flying across the sky with a twenty-foot cape, and a Spider-Man with big bug eyes, by looking out your window . . . to me, that's a façade.

AH: I was going to say a little earlier that at least you can catch up on your reading now with the *Classics Illustrateds*.

TM: Yeah! They've got pictures! Cool! But that's just it. To tell you the truth, I'm probably an ignorant person.

I don't think if I start reading books . . . it won't hinder me, but I don't think it'll help me. I don't read other comic books, either. But I'm interested in what the readership has to say. I read the letters pages and some of the forums . . .

AH: Do you get your mail?

TM: Yeah.

AH: For Spider-Man?

TM: No, not for Spider-Man. Just the stuff that's to me. Maybe once I start writing the book, there'll be more letters in there that aren't all that positive, and I can maybe pull something out of it.

But the ones that come directly to me—it's kind of like at a convention—a guy's not going to wait in line for an hour to tell you you're an asshole.

AH: You're probably the hottest creator in comics right now—

TM: [*Laughs*]

AH: That's what Fantagraphics is calling you in their order form for the issue, so it must be true. . . . [*Laughter*] Do you think you're at the top of your game?

TM: Artistically, creatively, whatever you want to call it—no. I'd be a fool to think that. I don't think so. I think . . . I was going to say that I've peaked out, but I've got this new book coming out; that isn't going to hurt me. As a matter of fact, it'll probably give me another push.

If you come back in five years, I think you will find that I'm a better writer, better artist; I'm expanding my horizons a little bit more.

There's a lot of guys that I think draw circles around me that deserve a lot more adulation. I'm talking about guys who do superhero stuff. When I compare myself, might as well compare apples to apples. Guys who are doing other stuff, like the Hernandez brothers, as outstanding as that is, I don't really think we deserve to be mixed in the same pool. It's just totally different ballgames. So when I talk about the people that I'm up against, I'm talking about guys who are Marvel and DC "superhero" people.

It's a strange thing. Part of it might have to do with Byrne switching companies, and Pérez gave up the art chores on *Wonder Woman*, and voting came out in *CBG* at a time when maybe some nice issues of *Amazing Spider-Man* came out; a lot has to do with timing and stuff.

AH: Yeah. It's just there are a lot of creators who get to this top position and then they just start to coast . . .

TM: Well, I think if you talk to my wife, she will tell you that I'm a very obsessive type person in that, when I put my nose in a direction, I bury it and go. It almost becomes a sickness with me.

One of my goals was to be one of the guys up there, and I remember they would do John Byrne T-shirts and George Pérez portfolios, and I thought, "Wow! Wouldn't that be great?" And as I've gotten to that point, it's really no big deal. I've climbed the mountain that I set out to climb. There's nothing up there. There's no pot of gold. I guess I didn't really have a goal in mind once I got there. At this point, I'm actually looking forward to sliding.

My wife says, "Why don't you enjoy it for a while?" No, that's not me. I think, "Okay, I've gotten there. People think I'm good at penciling; I'll take over inking. People think I'm good at penciling and inking; what can I do next?"

AH: Is there a downside to being as popular as you are?

TM: Yup. I get locked up in rooms for two hours with geeks like you! [*Laughter*] Nah, we'd better clarify this. Len's doing this conversation; we go back five, six years, so we've both climbed the ladder of success at the same time.

AH: There's a rumor that you don't do sketches at conventions . . .

TM: [*Laughs*] Yeah. To answer that, I don't do sketches because I've got kids standing in front of me that want an autograph, and the $25 I could make doing a sketch in half an hour isn't more important than the kids. As long as the kids stand in front of me with a comic book, I will sign it. I will never draw. Never.

Again, the readers put me where I'm at, and I owe it to them. Which is why I do a monthly comic book. I'm trying to give them back what they've given me. I admire Pérez and Byrne for that exact reason. They could have been doing hardcovers and miniseries, but they didn't. They stuck to the trenches.

Right now, I still feel good about monthly comic books, and I want to stick to the trenches. Maybe in a few years I'll get bored; I'll go for the golden ring then.

AH: But getting back to the rumors . . .

TM: Yeah, they're funny. I take the rumors as success; five years ago, when I was doing *Infinity*, I could have said that anybody was an asshole and nobody would have cared. Now I say, "Well, I don't really like that," and all of a sudden, it's a big scandal.

AH: "Todd McFarlane in the *National Enquirer*."

TM: [*Laughs*] That's it!

I think if you read all my other interviews, this is the only time I've maybe let the leash off my neck a little bit because I'm very polite in my interviews, and I don't think it's fair to bandy names around.

But what I'm saying is, I honestly do live on an island off the west coast of Canada. There's only one comic book store, about forty-five miles away, and I live in the sticks and go in there maybe once every six months. But if I was the ego that some people think, or maybe that this interview makes me come across as—I guarantee it—I wouldn't live on my island where nobody knows where I'm at and nobody here cares what I do.

The neighbors say, "Oh, what do you do for a living?" "I draw Spider-Man." "Aw, isn't that cute?" That's all it is. It's cute to them.

But when you get to the point where I am right now, I find that everybody wants a piece of you. It can get kind of tiresome. Not that many people phone just to shoot the shit; they want to know if you want to do this or that.

Which is why I'm cutting back on the traveling. With the new Spider-Man book, I could probably do a show a weekend for the next six months after the book comes out. But I'll probably do less this year than I've done before just because I've got my priorities, and they are spending time with my wife and playing lots of baseball.

AH: Does it bother you when people copy your style and use your stylistic tricks in their work? I mean, besides Bob Kane . . .

TM: [*Laughs*] It doesn't bother me. To me, it's free advertising. People go, "Oh, that's like a McFarlane-type Spider-Man," or whatever. When I was doing stuff, I was following in the footsteps of Byrne and Pérez and Adams and whoever else.

The only thing that I hope is that after a while they'll get bored of it and say, "Fuck Todd McFarlane." Otherwise, they're just going to look like Todd McFarlane.

Those spaghetti-webbings, though, I didn't invent them; I took them from a drawing Michael Golden did about ten years ago because I'm such a big Golden fan. But now, when people see the spaghetti-webbing, I tend to get credit for it.

I don't think that the next big young kid who comes along—the next big fan fave—is going to be a guy who looks like Byrne or Pérez or McFarlane or Adams or whoever. I think it's going to be a kid who just totally goes off and comes up with something different and new, and everybody goes, "Wow. Why didn't I think of that?"

AH: Do you like seeing your artwork on all the T-shirts and other merchandise?

TM: Well, again, it doesn't hurt. As long as Bob Kane doesn't have his name on it . . .

AH: It's probably a T-shirt a month now.

TM: Yeah. Multiples of it. There's probably twenty to fifty T-shirts out now, and mugs, buttons . . . I've got my own baseball cards. I don't see any money from it, which doesn't bug me. I knew that when I started . . .

AH: Do you at least get copies or samples of the merchandise?

TM: No. [*Laughs*] It's not really as big a deal as you think. You see it and you go, "Eeeh, yeah. So what? The stuff I handed in last week is better than that?" Some guys are not doing as good work today as they were doing years ago, and that will be the day that I quit this business.

AH: When you hit that point?

TM: When I can look at my stuff and say, "This isn't better than what I did last month," that's the time I quit. That means I got to perfection, I guess, in my head, and I can't get any better. And realistically, that should never happen.

AH: What are your interests outside of comics? Obviously, you have a few; you have baseball, your wife . . .

TM: My wife! I've got my wife, number one.

AH: And you still play ball.

TM: Yup. I should play eighty games this year. So that's going to cut back on all my convention trips. I won't be at San Diego Con because I've got a big tournament that weekend.

AH: Is this just a local league?

TM: Yeah. And my wife's going to play some ball. I play in mixed leagues, I play in men's leagues.

And I like to spend time with my wife when she comes home at the end of the day. Instead of doing another cover. Take the dog out for a walk and stuff. Sometimes we try to guess the last time the TV was on.

AH: What about music?

TM: Yeah, we listen to music, but just easy listening, soft rock stuff. No particular thing that we've got to have.

During the summer, we're always playing tennis, going golfing, playing baseball, going camping, visiting people, going to conventions. There's a lot of things. And we own a house, and all of a sudden, a house is like having a baby—you've got to mow the lawn, pull the weeds. That takes time. My days are filled. I don't have extra time on my hands.

The other thing is I now co-own a comic book and sports card shop.

AH: And where's that?

TM: In the state of Washington, in a city of Puyallup, just outside of Tacoma. I saw everybody raising the price of all their Todd McFarlane stuff and thought, "Why don't I do it?" I'll probably get more autographs than anybody else, I bet. [*Laughs*] Plus, I had a collection of about 35,000 comic books—my own personal collection—and so I threw [them] in, and boxes and boxes and boxes of McFarlane Spider-Man stuff and whatever else I've done. And I've collected baseball cards long before I collected comic books. I threw a collection of cards in, and bought some collections from my brother and some other people, and we got a store. It's called The Spider's Web. So that forces me to do Spider-Man for a couple more weeks because otherwise I'd have to change the name to the Batcave. [*Laughter*]

So right now—because I've collected baseball cards since I was about ten—I have more of a fascination with the cards that the comic books. I've been around comic books almost day in and day out for the last four, five years. So now the cards are bringing back childhood memories of when you collected these guys.

[And] if anybody's got some old baseball cards they want to trade for some artwork, send a list to Todd McFarlane, care of Marvel Comics. [*Laughs*]

AH: Back to comics, are you working on any other things besides *Spider-Man*? I know at one point there was talk of a Spider-Man/Batman team-up by you, Frank Miller, and Steve Gerber.

TM: Actually, right now I've cut back on my work. Some of this stuff was committed to a year ago.

AH: Like what?

TM: Like this story right here [*pointing to artwork on drawing board*]. I think it's going to be in the *Spectacular Spider-Man Annual*. I started this last year sometime, and once I'm done with this story, that will be it for anything other than the new book.

The Batman/Spider-Man thing came about . . . the actual idea was Jim Salicrup's. He tossed this idea at me since he knew that I liked Batman, "and we'll get Frank Miller to do it." At that time I didn't really take him seriously. Every editor'll tell you that you're working with Frank Miller and Byrne and Terry Austin will ink it.

But I guess he did actually phone Frank and Steve Gerber and pitched the idea at them, and they both said, "Yeah, sounds good." What was going to end up happening was that Gerber and Frank were going to cowrite it and I would do the artwork.

Marvel and DC were talking about maybe doing three or four other ones, and whoever did the first one, that would be the format for the others.

AH: Did DC know this at the time?

TM: I don't think so. At this point, we were just tossing around ideas.

So we went at it. I had some talks with Steve Gerber; I heard that it was going to be a Batman/Spider-Man play off each other—dark and grim versus nice and funky, I guess. Bruce Wayne and Peter Parker playing off each other—the millionaire and the poor college kid. . . . The two bad guys would be the Kingpin and the Joker, who are outstanding picks, I think. Miller's handling both of them already, and again, he'd be playing them not so much off the superheroes but off each other.

Both these guys are the kingpins of crime in what they do. One guy has done it through strategy and brainwork and a little bit of brawn—that's the Kingpin. And the Joker's done it because he's so psychotic that it's worked. To me, that scares me more, that a psycho can get to that kind of a goal more than a guy who's planned it all out.

Steve and Frank, people were saying, "Why don't they do a Punisher/Batman or a Wolverine/Batman?" I don't think that would interest them because the characters are almost cut out of the same cloth. And the thing that Miller and Gerber have given us over the years is their play on characters. And all the situations—Batman/Spider-Man, Wayne/Parker, Kingpin/Joker—there's a lot of things to play off each other.

So that was the starting point. Frank was writing the screenplay for *Robocop II*, so he wasn't really available at the time, but I thought it would have been a great project. It would have been good for everybody. Something along the lines of *Dark Knight* or *Arkham Asylum*. I don't know what sort of packaging they'd have put on it, but it would have been the hit of the year.

But it just doesn't want to go anywhere. The people at Marvel are dragging their rears; the people at DC are dragging their rears. I made a bunch of phone calls, but I don't think it's up to the creator to try and get these guys together. Timing's everything, too. I think we're at a point where DC's doing okay right now, and they don't really feel that they have to give Batman away. Why give a chunk of all the hard work and popularity and money that they've made off Batman or Marvel?

On the other hand, Marvel knows that I'm content to work for them for a while. Frank hasn't really been all that happy with DC in the recent past. And so if we don't do this, we'll probably just do something for Marvel. [*Laughs*] So why push the matter? There's really no motivation on either side's part to get this project off the ground. Which I think is sad because it would have been a great project to work on.

AH: Do you think fans bothering DC and Marvel to see something like this would get the project going again?

TM: I don't know. Really, I don't know how things like that work. But yeah, maybe if they dialed Jim Galton at Marvel and Jenette Kahn at DC, they'd be cutting through all the red tape.

I did discuss it with one editor at DC who shall remain nameless. And to me, he had the greatest words of advice about it. He said, "Just do it. [*Laughter*] If you could find the time, just do it and bring it in. And if you think Marvel and DC are dumb enough that they wouldn't print this book if you came in with sixty-four pages—complete—a story that's got Miller, McFarlane, Gerber, Batman, Spider, Kingpin, and the Joker . . ." [*Laughs*]

AH: Are you tempted to "just do it"?

TM: Well, I haven't sat down and talked to Steve or Frank. It would be a matter of coordinating our schedules, but it hasn't got past that.

So it's kind of humorous, but it's kind of sad that that's what you've got to do to get through something that should be flying. Will it ever come out? Your guess is as good as mine right now.

AH: That's too bad. I guess we're done, unless there's something else you want to talk about.

TM: Actually, there's something I want to get off my chest. I don't mind doing superhero comic books. There's a lot of griping between different companies, different factions in the comic industry, and I don't really understand why we can't get together as a community and rejoice at the variety of books out there, and the guy who's twenty can get this, the guy who's fifteen can get this, the guy who's eight can get this, the guy who's two can get that. And as we grow, and our minds grow, we can go and get whatever it is that we deem suitable at that time.

AH: So it's not like the old way of thinking where you "outgrow" comics?

TM: No. Even me. If I get tired of superheroes, there's other things I can do right now. But, on the other hand, if a guy wants to read superhero comics until he's a hundred and ten, all the power to him. It doesn't mean he's a mental moron.

AH: As long as he's enjoying himself.

TM: Yeah. I'm not the one to be saying, "Read whatever you want" because I don't read shit. But I'll tell you how many points Gretzky's got. [*Laughter*]

But I don't understand why people have got to bellyache about stuff. I don't understand why a guy who's over twenty and not reading *Love & Rockets* has to be branded a fool and an idiot.

What I do like is if I don't want to read *Superman* or *Spider-Man* anymore, I can go and grab *Love & Rockets*, or I can grab some of the compilations Fantagraphics puts out. And that as an artist and a creator I'm not locked into one genre. I can go and, hopefully, by the time I get bored of superheroes, there'll be even more options available to me.

But for some of the squabbling that goes on, I think it's petty and ridiculous. Superheroes are here to stay, and they're the majority of the sales of comic books. Whether you want to accept it or not, that's the reality.

So why squabble if the stuff's there? Just sit back and enjoy it.

THE LOWDOWN ON FELIX THE CAT

AH: To go off on a bit of a tangent, are you a Felix the Cat fan?

TM: Nope.

AH: So why does Felix appear in your comics?

TM: Dang it, I hate to disappoint people because they send all these nice Felix things, but I'm not really that big of a Felix fan. I don't even know who created that guy.

What happened was there's this guy that I know who's a funny guy . . .

AH: We can name names. He won't mind.

TM: Pat Martin! Pat Martin—are you alive and well?

Anyway, Pat Martin—a mutual friend of everybody that we know here— walks around town almost at all times with a stuffed Felix the Cat toy, and he wasn't really that big of a comic book fan, especially of superhero stuff. I had met him a few times, and wanting to suck another reader into the book I figured, "Hey, there's one way of getting ol' Pat to buy the book; I'll just put Felix into the book."

So the opportunity came up where somebody won a stuffed toy, and I thought, "Well, obviously, it had to be Felix," and after the guy spent $25 winning this toy at the fair, they wouldn't just throw it away, so I kept the Felix doll around in *The Hulk* for a while, and then when I went over to *Spider-Man*, I just continued because Pat was getting such a kick out of it. I just kept putting him in there to the point where it's almost become a trademark now, and if I don't put him in people would be disappointed.

AH: I've noticed that when your Spider-Man books show up one of the first things people do is flip through it and look for Felix . . .

TM: Yeah, two of the things that I think they look for are Felix and the hidden spiders on the cover. Really, it becomes a little bit of a game.

AH: And the little numbers under your name on the covers refer to how many spiders you've got hidden?

TM: Yeah.

Comic Shop News Spotlight: Todd McFarlane

CLIFF BIGGERS / 1992

From *Comic Shop News* 1, no. 257 (1992): 4–7. Reprinted by permission.

Todd McFarlane is one of the outstanding talents in the field of comics today. His ground-breaking new style and innovative approach to storytelling helped to launch a whole new group of artists, and virtually recreated the look of Spider-Man. Now he is about to launch his own new title, *Spawn*, with his own new company, Image, later this month. Todd talked to *CSN* about *Spawn*, Image, and his plans for the future.

Cliff Biggers: Do you see any difference in your creative process since you took your break?

Todd McFarlane: The only thing I can say is that because I took the break to leave *Spider-Man* to spend more time with my daughter, I feel fresh. My head was starting to wander before I left Marvel; if anything, I'm starting to get enthused all over again. I'm mentally ready for comics, and I'm excited again. I feel like I did six years ago when I started into the business. Whether or not that transcends onto the page—well, I'm not really the guy to ask. I either hate everything I do or I love everything I do, so it doesn't matter what I think—it matters what the reader thinks.

I think that you are going to see some similarities in my new work and my old work, but since *Spawn* is a totally different kind of character, there are going to be some differences, too. Whether there is that much of a difference really isn't my call.

Biggers: What can you tell us about *Spawn*?

McFarlane: I don't know if I can pull it off or not. I mean, it will probably take me twenty issues to pull off what Frank Miller could do in two, and I hate myself for that—but Frank isn't available to write the book right now.

I'm trying to make Spawn a kind of sympathetic character in that he is somewhat disturbed. The development of the character, revealing his motivation, is going to be a long slow process of discovery, in that he dies and comes back to life because he wants to see his wife. That's why I would want to come back. I'm trying to get across the idea that he didn't come back for revenge, or for superpowers—he just came back and he wants to see his wife.

Now, part of the deal is that he had to make a bit of a pact with the devil, but he doesn't care just so long as he gets to see his wife. He gets to see her around issue three. When Spawn comes back from the dead, he is shot back five years into the future. He finds that his life is destroyed—but he *does* get to go back and see his wife, so technically the devil has kept his part of the bargain; Spawn just didn't read the fine print of the deal. When he comes back to life, it looks like he won't get his wife back, so he decides that he has no reason to live—and he tries to kill himself again. He finds out that his powers won't let him commit suicide, though, so he has to bottom out and eventually come back up, finding a reason for living. He has powers and he sees that he can use them for good, and that will give him a reason to carry on. After a while, he won't even want to die, so he will just go on with his life.

I didn't initially want to give Spawn a face—just a mask. I didn't do that though, because I feel that it is difficult to relate to someone that you can't see. I did a variation on my original idea: He looks terrible beneath his costume, but he can regenerate his skin; it only lasts about seventy-two hours max, though, and it takes way too much energy for him to regenerate it again and again. He might walk around in the shadows with a trench coat and a hat, and not care how awful he actually looks for much of the book. There might be some sort of "Beauty and the Beast" thing going on, because he does have that horrific look.

Spawn is going to fight bad guys, and he is going to fight demons; the demons are included so that I can show what happened in the deal with the devil and give some of the reasons behind it—like why he makes the deal, why the devil gives him powers, why he gets the costume—things like that. After that, it will turn somewhat pedestrian, because the guy is just going to be a guy. I hope that you're not going to be able to nail a tag on Spawn. I mean, one day he'll be throwing planets—those stories will be few and far between—and another day, he doesn't want to be a hero; he has those powers, however, and one day he'll go walking into the office of a CEO in a Wall Street company who pinches all of his secretaries, and pin him against the wall and make him pay his alimony. His kids are starving and his wife is living in a shack and he's a CEO for this big company. . . . Basically, Spawn's going to be doing the things that I would do if I had superpowers—make guys pay their alimony, make sure people aren't having crack babies, and trying to create world peace.

Biggers: *Spawn* sounds like a very personal book.

McFarlane: Whether the book is right or wrong—it's not like I have the experience to draw on other people's lives. I mean, Spawn used to work for the government, and when he got his tenure with the government, he saw that there were some loopholes being used that he just couldn't stomach. To some degree, the situation parallels my experience in comics. Spawn saw that it was good for a while, and he accepted that—but he saw that the government was doing things that they shouldn't have been doing further down the line. So, does it make it wrong that he enjoyed it at first? No, it just means that his eyes got opened after a while. With his status in the government, Spawn was exposed to more things, and as he was exposed to more, he saw more and more problems in the system: The more he was exposed to it, the less he enjoyed it.

Biggers: Are you going to be working for any other company in the near future?

McFarlane: Not right now. I would like to do some things in the future. I would ultimately like to do a Spawn/Spider-Man crossover. If *Spawn* proves to be successful, it would be kind of neat to come back to the character that I had such a long run on—and that people associate my name with for one reason or another. It would be kinda cool, if for no other reason that that it would be worth doing—but who knows if that will ever come to pass? . . .

When I was working for Marvel I never did anything for DC; when I was working for DC, I never did anything for Marvel. It's not that I have a personal vendetta or anything, but I can only do one book at a time, and right now I'm doing Spawn. If I have time to do something like a poster, it will probably be a Spawn poster. I might do a couple covers—like inking over a Harvey Kurtzman sketch, or something else wacky that would be fun to do. Other than a couple of things like that, I doubt there will be anything outside of *Spawn*.

Biggers: Will Spawn cross over with the other Image titles?

McFarlane: There will be crossovers with the other books—and hopefully with every other company. We at *Image* aren't here to say that we have the answers, we have the characters, we have the players; rather, we are trying to say that the sandbox is big enough for all of us, so let's share the dump truck—why not play together? So, yeah, hopefully you'll see Image/Dark Horse crossovers, or Image/Tundra, or Image/Valiant, or Image/whoever—everybody else. In fact, we would like to try and coordinate tricompany crossovers, things that have never been done. If it would be better to have two companies working together, then why not three? It would be cool to see *Aliens*, *Spawn*, and the *Turtles*. It would be the coolest—if for no other reason than to see what it would look like. I'm just throwing out ideas here—but you need to be able to do that kind of stuff.

Biggers: What is the image of Image?

McFarlane: I think that there is a bit of a misconception on the parts of our peers and critics that if you break away from Marvel and DC, it is almost a sin to do superhero stuff. I *like* to do superhero stuff. You can do it at Marvel and DC, but you can't do them under the conditions that we've got right now at Image. Why should Marvel and DC have the exclusive rights to do superhero stuff? We *love* to do superhero stuff. We *want* to do superhero stuff. But we *couldn't* do it under the system that Marvel and DC had set up; so why should we have to stop? So we went out and created a company for ourselves.

We aren't saying that we are the best guys out there, and we aren't saying that we are going to revolutionize comics—far from it. You are going to see a lot of stuff in our books that could fit right into a Marvel or DC book. What you will also see, though, is a lot of enthusiasm. I've got my mental well-being back. It doesn't matter if I only sell ten thousand copies of *Spawn*, just so long as I have my mental well-being back. I was starting to lose it and complain too much. It became either "shut up or put up." Now I'm not talking so much about my problems; instead, I'm talking about what a neat character I've just come up with. This is what it should have been all along.

We at Image send sketches back and forth to each other, saying, "Cool, now I've got to top that one." The little boyhood-adolescent child is back in us, and I guess that that is good. Marvel paid us money—they gave us *gobs* of money—but that just didn't matter anymore. I can't put a price tag on my mental well-being. I could have stayed doing Marvel Comics and made a good living being a bigshot.

We're not asking people to like our stuff; we just wanted to do this. It's not like we're taking the easy road; the easy road would have been to stay. We're going out on our own, and we just want to be acknowledged. You don't have to like us, or think that we are great—but realize that we are a bunch of guys who had it made and threw caution to the wind. I've never been a guy who has been content—to me, that is a curse word. To just sit content makes me insane; you can't believe how my blood boils on that one. The guys that are throwing daggers right now are the ones who are content, but they aren't going to be content forever.

There really isn't as big a risk factor as I might imply. I was doing a Marvel monthly title, and if I fall flat, I'll go begging back and get another monthly title from DC or Marvel. So, there isn't that big of a risk, because the worst I can end up is doing a monthly book, which is what I was doing for the past six years. Where's the downside of that? I've got nothing to lose and everything to gain. The biggest thing that I am gaining is a personal well-being. When I get on the phone to Rob Liefeld, we shouldn't be talking about how we're having trouble with an editor, we shouldn't be talking about how they are making changes in what we have done in our books, or how we have to get approval for this; because of our problems, our conversations—and I'm just using Rob and me as an example—we're becoming more complaint than creativity. Now, we're on the phone going, "What are you doing in your book? Why don't we do this together? Why don't we call Dark Horse and see if they'll do this? Oh, Robbie, that is so cool. You just did an article with *Time* magazine, and you got to mention your characters."

Whatever we come up with on a given day can be done right then; it doesn't have to go through a committee. Now, 95 percent of our conversation is back to where it should have been, back to that boyhood enthusiasm, and that is what this has gotten us. Whether it is a better book or not, that's the call of the readers—but I know I'll be happier selling ten thousand copies my way than ten million copies somebody else's way.

Biggers: What lies beyond *Spawn*?

McFarlane: I've got a whole stack of characters and ideas, but I'm not quite as productive as Rob or Jim or somebody else who can draw nineteen characters. It might come from all my years on *Spider-Man*, but I like the single guy, and playing with him. I'll keep playing with *Spawn* until I get tired of it—or until the readers get tired of it—and then I'll start playing with the other ideas. Along the way there will be other characters showing up, but that will happen just occasionally. I've got some other ideas—and to tell you the truth, I don't see *Spawn* as my retirement plan; I see something else as my retirement plan. *Spawn* is a good way to see whether we're successful with our plans, and then maybe come in, further down the line, with the character or characters that are going to be my retirement plans. Right now, it's just Todd doing a character that he's had floating around for about ten years, and having a hell of a time doing it.

Biggers: Are you using a new storytelling in your art?

McFarlane: A couple people have said that I've started using a new style. People like Rob and Jim have told me, "Todd, this is some new stuff from you." I'm not that acutely aware of any changes in my art, so if they're there, it's just because the character or the theme or the story just needed that kind of a look.

If the art is slightly different, that wasn't a conscious decision, either. Because I had to get issue two out quicker—or maybe because I did the first issue on much bigger paper—maybe it won't have quite the artsy feel that issue number one has. Once things get settled in and I get into a more regular schedule, things might change. Right now I have time, and I plan everything out so that I make rational decisions about what goes where.

I've had people comment that the first issue doesn't need any words on it; I could put the book in order and you could make perfect sense out of it without one word being added. That is probably because I am an artist first and a writer second. If the art is different and the people notice, that's probably a good thing. Spawn is a guy who runs around mostly at night, so there is a lot of good moody artwork, and that helps. Whether or not people see the subtleties in what I'm trying to do is up to them.

Near the end of my run on *Spider-Man*, the writing was coming to me a little easier. When I took the time out after my daughter was born, I got out of shape. So, I feel like the first couple of issues of *Spawn* are like the first couple issues of *Spider-Man*—I'm kinda dragging here. I feel that by issue seven or eight I should be on a roll and feel comfortable with the characters and know exactly what it is I'm trying to pull off. Part of it is the fact that I've got more ideas than I know what to do with and it's tough to sort them out.

Do I still feel uncomfortable writing? Not really. If I have changed my writing, it is sort of like the manner in which I changed my art. If you change your art style, it often doesn't come about as something conscious, but just from the fact that you draw so much. Hopefully the writing will work the same way. If I just keep writing and writing, then hopefully it will develop into some sort of style the same way. I don't sit and consciously try to accomplish something—I don't think that I have that kind of talent skill right now—I just take it as it comes to me.

Biggers: *Spawn* is a monthly ongoing book; is there an ending in sight?

McFarlane: Not right now. I do have an ending in mind for *Spawn*, and if the book isn't commercial or doesn't work, or I don't like it, or the kids don't like it, or whatever, then I do have an end for the series. It's just a matter of how long we can keep it going. We have a couple of miniseries coming out from Image, but I felt that we should also have something to add stability to the line. I think that Valentino and Silvestri are planning to do monthly books as well.

Eventually, I think that everybody at Image is going to be doing monthly stuff; it's just a matter of some guys wanting to take a break and get their houses in order after leaving Marvel. I didn't want to do a bunch of miniseries, though. I think that there is more of a challenge to selling an issue

Spawn #5, p. 15, October 1992, Image Comics, Fair Use. McFarlane incorporates page design elements similar to his work on *Infinity, Inc.*, but with an updated Spawn-inspired aesthetic solidifying his unique style.

number five than an issue number one. It's not that selling a number one is a bad thing, but I get more of a thrill trying to go what can I do trying to sell issue number five than I get from issue one.

The first issue of *Spawn* is your standard twenty-two-page comic book, and I've thrown in two free pin-ups by George Pérez and Dale Keown. Ken Steacy and I did a free inside poster for the book; since it came out so well, I've hired Ken to paint all of the covers. I've hired Tom Orzechowski to do the lettering because I thought he was the best letterer in the business, and Steve Oliff to color because I thought he was the best. I mean, I'm the boss, so I may as well go after the best. I wanted to put together the best package I could. I really didn't have to worry about issue one or two selling, so I had to come up with something to spur readers on in issue seven and eight—whether that means doing a crossover with *Youngblood*, or *WildC.A.T.s* or *Dragon*, or whatever, or whether that means *Spawn/Aliens*, or killing one of the characters or whatever—I'll do it.

It isn't unlike what they have done in books like *Spider-Man* and *Batman*. Every couple of years, you have to come up with something to spice up the book. For me, right now, the challenge lies in what I can do in issue seven. I take a certain amount of pride in the fact that my last issue of *Spider-Man* was one of the best-selling comics of that month. A year and a half after my start on the book, the kids were still on the bandwagon—I like that. I like the fact that they seem to actually get something out of the book, whatever that may be, and I'm not just giving them a gimmick or something. I hope that people don't think that, just because there is a poster in the first issue, they have to buy two copies—the poster isn't a gimmick, it's a bonus.

I won't be doing any second printings on my books either. I'm not doing this to cut anybody down or anything, because it's money out of my pocket. Rob got 300,000 orders for second printings on *Youngblood*, so I may be throwing away a large print run. My thinking puts me sort of between a rock and a hard place. If you put too many issues out there, it comes back at you—but if you don't put enough out there, then you didn't provide enough copies. If retailers sell out of number one, then it isn't my fault—but more than that, if the book *does* sell through, then it keeps the book's value there. That, in turn, will help with issues nine and ten, because people will realize that they need to order more of a book that they have consistently sold out of, that they need to boost their orders.

My feeling is that I will eventually get back what I didn't get with a second printing. My major concern and plan is to provide a quality book that retailers can sell and collectors want. If retailers see that people are buying the book and the quality is solid on it, then they will keep coming back and we will pick up the occasional new reader. The good thing about the company is that I can do that. If another guy wants to do eight covers, or second printings, then he can—that's great. It isn't for me to tell them what is best for their book, just like they can't tell me what to do on mine. Maybe its suicide for me to turn away a potential 200,000 to 300,000 second printing, but we'll see. All of us here at Image will probably compare notes and to see what worked best when it's all over.

I'm looking to promote the book. I'm open to new ideas. I just finished a poster, but if the retailers don't think that is enough, they should call me up and tell me what they want—what they think will help sell the book. I get to call the shots, and it can be done—I'm looking for feedback. There is only so much you can do in the market. I'm looking to expand outside of the market so people who don't normally come into a comic shop will want to come in and check it out. This is not unlike what the *Batman* movie did; the kids saw the *Batman* movie and then all of a sudden they wanted the *Batman* comic book. They stop at the comic shop and pick up *Batman*, but they also might pick up a couple more titles, and eventually, they are a regular comics customer. We are trying to look at things, whether they be toys, movies, TV, Nintendo, T-shirt deals, whatever; if we can get the characters into the public's eyes, then the people might get excited about coming into comic shops.

One Hell of a Ride: Part One

JOHN RILEY / 1993

From *Amazing Heroes Interviews* 1, no. 1 (1993): 14–27. Reprinted by permission.

Todd McFarlane talks about drawing cool monsters and hearts being ripped out . . . and, oh yeah, Spawn and Image Comics.

Amazing Heroes: First, thanks a lot for talking to me, I appreciate it. I figure a good place to start is with the guest writers on *Spawn* . . . having Alan Moore, Neil Gaiman, Dave Sim, and Frank Miller come in. How did the collaborations begin, how did they come about?

Todd McFarlane: You know, I've been asked that question a lot. There's really no magic to it. It seems more of a mystery and I hate to (almost) give you the truth because it's gonna be kind of boring. I'm the kind of guy that believes that instead of bitching about the boss giving you a raise, you should go in there and ask him for a raise and the worst that he says is "No," and you're still getting the same amount of wages. But if he says yes, then you actually got the raise, you know what I mean?

AH: Yeah.

TM: So, I'm the kind of guy that phones a lot of people, and if I phone Alan Moore and ask him to write me a story and he says "No," then I didn't have him before the phone call, so I'm no worse for wear. And I can be pretty convincing when I get on the phone or whatever. So I just phone people up and it's like, "Hey, you don't know me, I don't know you, but we know each other's work, blah, blah, blah, blah, blah, have I got a proposition for you. I know you like to do this. I think I've got a character that kind of fits into what you do, blah, blah, blah," and I just be a good salesman and they all . . . I mean I had a list of four and I hit four for four.

AH: It's kind of an offer they couldn't refuse.

TM: Yeah, I guess. My attitude when I'm talking to people is that the last topic of conversation is finances, 'cause I don't want a guy to do work for money, I want a guy to do work 'cause he likes it. So when I talk to them I'm like, I know that Alan Moore likes to write some horror stuff and stuff that's a bit off center, so I come at him like, "This is my character, this is what he can do, here's the things that I think would work and I know that you like to write these kinds of stories, but I think that my guy has enough layers involved that I think that there's something there for you to play with, and we'd have a hell of a ride."

AH: That's kind of what I meant. It seems like giving Alan Moore the chance to trace someone's ascent through hell would be pretty much made to order. By the time this sees print, we should have probably read most of them . . . but could you give us a little idea of what we can expect? I mean, it seems Alan Moore and Neil Gaiman are pretty much the same type of writer. Then you go to Dave Sim. It seemed like that was a little bit of a departure in terms of the types of stories.

TM: Yeah, you know, actually once you read the stories, his is the wackiest out of all of them.

AH: Really?

TM: But it's not really very funny, but Dave's Canadian and I'm Canadian, so if nothing else we have to give a fellow Canadian a break there. One of the reasons I talked to Dave, besides that I think that his *Cerebus* is just outstanding, is that he's been one of the guys who's been fighting for independence and creator-owned stuff, you know what I mean? And so it's just like, if I'm gonna go get guys, I want guys who, if nothing else, think on the same level as I do on a lot of things too. Frank Miller has quit Marvel and DC, you know, and Alan Moore has quit, and Dave Sim never really worked for them, and you know Neil was more just because he's just a hell of a talent and stuff like that, but he's done stuff outside the mainstream too. So you know, it wasn't like I was picking, you know, somebody who's just kind of lived and breathed superhero comic books, but Dave, I've just always been an admirer of his spunk more than anything else, so I think he's got a reputation for being a crap disturber himself and I think I do too. So why not work with another fellow crap disturber, you know. At least we know where we're both standing.

AH: *Spawn* #8 took a few people by surprise in that Spawn doesn't really appear in the book.

TM: Right.

AH: Personally, I thought the story was outstanding. I thought the combination of Alan Moore's type of writing with your artwork was really powerful. I know that in *Spawn* #13, Spawn's gonna meet his killer. Are the other stories also somewhat outside of the continuity?

TM: Number 9 is . . . no not really . . . #9 is a good story, a good Spawn story so to speak. There's a bit of a flashback that shows that there's been Spawns in the past. But then it comes back to the present day and our Spawn, the one that was in the first seven issues, gets in a fight and does the comic book thing and whatever. That's one that Neil Gaiman's writing. And then for Neil, that's something that he's not really used to writing, and so it gives him a chance to try something new and different himself. Issue #10, yeah, the Dave Sim one, is just going to be a wacky stand-alone story. And then issue #11, which is Frank's story. Frank's is gonna be as urban and as straightforward a superhero as they get. He's gonna fight gangs in the back alleys so it's gonna be like two out of four. You're gonna get two that are what people are expecting out of *Spawn* and then two of them that are the trip through hell and the other one, the trip through creative hell, I guess if you want to call it something else, Dave's writing. It was a mixture and part of the selling point of getting those guys was that I wouldn't edit them. You know, you give me a story and I'll do it and so you have to have some reason for them to do your book and not somebody else's so . . .

AH: So was the idea of tracing Billy Kincaid's journey through hell then somewhat more Alan's than yours?

TM: I was just heading into issue #5, in which I was gonna have this kid killer, okay. Then Alan said, "Well, I'm gonna have a trip through Hell, you know, of some guy, blah, blah, blah," and it wasn't gonna be Billy Kincaid. It was just gonna be generic, the story was gonna be more of this is what hell is, but he was gonna have this kid killer. He came out with . . . he said kid killer. I go, well by coincidence I've got this story that I've got in the works about a kid killer. So I go why don't we just set it up a little bit so that basically you see him die or you see him dead, you don't see how he dies or anything and I'll just throw it back at you if you wanna show flashbacks of how he actually dies or when he dies or what Spawn did. But I go we have a chance here to make this stuff work out a little smoother, 'cause I know what I'm doing and stuff like that. But that's just part of the comic book process. If Frank doesn't write his issue until the last minute, then he doesn't know what's happening with the Dave Sim issue, and he might be able to pull off an element in that.

AH: The fact that we don't see Billy Kincaid die in an era where we're seeing many exploding heads—I remember the first time that Wolverine killed a character, it was done off panel, whereas now we're deep into the dark age of comics and we're seeing exploding heads, and seeing the bullets going through the bodies is commonplace—what made you decide not to show Billy Kincaid's death?

TM: I guess it's the same silly reason that other people say—I think the mind is a little more scary thing than actually showing it. There's one scene in that issue where he was playing with the girl's finger, which even my wife gave me hell on and thought that was sick. Now, we each have our own threshold of what we consider sick . . . that one in my mind I could have shown him sawing those fingers off or biting them off or whatever, you know what I mean? But all I did was show him getting the girl into the ice cream truck, and then late at night he was playing with her fingers. To me that's more . . . I thought it was subtle, other people thought it was so blatant. So I thought, in a story that was about a guy who ends up getting killed by the good guy, so to speak, and he killed some other children, that book could have been blood and guts, so I thought that I would come in there and do stuff that was more subtle and the point of the story wasn't *how* Spawn kills a guy, 'cause that doesn't really make any difference. The point of the story was that, put in the right situation or the wrong situation, this is a mercenary, he's not a good guy . . . that he would kill in certain situations and to tell you the truth I would have done the same thing. You know what I mean? I've got a baby daughter and if somebody was to take and mutilate my kid, I'd kill the sucker. And I don't even have powers. I'd get the son of a bitch down, I'd spend my ten years in jail and whatever else because he took something, and this guy took twenty-six, you know what I'm saying? So I'm just saying my guy isn't Batman. The point of that story was my guy isn't Batman and he's just not gonna sit there . . .

AH: He was just pushed . . .

TM: And the other thing is, comic books are weird things. We don't want to get too deep into them because otherwise then we'd have to call ourselves a "comics journal," but . . . a character like Batman, to me, is an idiot in that because he plays by the rules, he keeps letting the Joker go to jail, break out, kill two more people, captures him, puts him in jail, he breaks out, kills two more people . . . he's broken out of jail fifty times and killed fifty people . . . if he had killed the son of a bitch the first time around there'd be forty-nine more people alive.

AH: Also, as a character, how does he rationalize, "Well I play by the rules and every time I do so an innocent person dies from it."

TM: He never laments on that. Now maybe he's not aware of it. I don't know, but I'm just saying that, my guy's not there to be a hero really, all that

Spawn #5, p. 9, October 1992, Image Comics, Fair Use. McFarlane's "subtle" illustration of serial killer Billy Kincaid's violence came across as anything but to some readers.

much. But on the other hand too, if push comes to shove he's gonna push back and like I said, I don't want him to be Punisher, I hate Punisher and whatever else. I'm just saying that in certain situations, whether it's you, me, or a hero, we'll push back and that's all that one was. He saw this guy killing kids and he just went, "No more." And that was from a guy who doesn't have kids. I think it's apparent most other people would have made the same decision on some level somewhere along the way, you know. Again, maybe it was just a throwaway story, nobody really paid all that much attention to it and whatever else. But it was there to make a point, and the point was that my guy isn't all that pure and sweet, but on the other hand you know early on in issue #1, when he saw the rapists, he could have done something to them, but he didn't, you know what I mean? Because it was just a bunch of thugs, and he was thinking I'm here to help this lady, and he was more concerned about helping the lady than worrying about beating up on a couple of thugs.

AH: I thought the two issues were very well done. I thought that not showing things . . . for instance, since we're talking about Alan Moore, there's a scene in *Watchmen* where Rorschach finds the bones that the dogs were chewing on, and that's unbelievably horrifying, but everything was only alluded to. I read some previous interviews you did and you were saying that there's comics for all ages at this point, and right now the Image books really have a wide readership and a lot of them are read by little kids. How do you feel about having the Violator holding Spawn's heart on the first page of a book? And knowing that a kid's reading it. Do you think it has any effect? How do you view it?

TM: You know, my first view, as a kid, is "Cool!" If I was eight years old, "How cool! He rips his heart out and he's standing there and it's oozing down his arm, oh cool . . ."

AH: And Spawn's still standing there.

TM: I think most of the kids are saying the exact same thing. The parents get a little bit worked up over it and whatever else, but kids, little boys especially, we like to do stuff that kind of freaks out our sisters by like chasing them with snakes, you know what I mean? "Aw, what are you afraid of? It's just a little snake."

AH: And the Violator is comical to begin with . . .

TM: Yeah, well that's it. And the miniseries I have coming out with Alan Moore writing it . . . I told him, I don't want him to be all that comical, I want it to be more of a nervous laugh, you know what I mean? Because just hard rippin' stuff can be kind of a downer, but if you mix it in there with a little bit of sadistic, black humor, it becomes a nervous laugh and yeah, that's it, the guy's funny, but he's not *funny*, you know? It's my book and I've got to make decisions on it and I make what I consider to be the best decisions. Are they the same you or anybody else would make? Of course not, 'cause you would make your own personal value judgments, you know, so . . . do I think that it's gonna harm the children of the world? Nah. I've argued that with a lot of people, my wife included, but I don't think so, I don't think that we give kids enough credit as to how intelligent they are, you know. They know they're reading a comic book, my God. A seven-foot gila monster that rips out hearts, that thing doesn't exist, you know. I don't think there's a kid out there who thinks that exists. And I don't think there's a kid out there who's gonna grow up and wanna be a Violator. Because first of all he'd have to grow a mouth that's eight feet long. But kids know that it's just a comic book and it's just TV. I used to be twelve, and when I was twelve I used to be insulted that my dad didn't think I could drive a car, you know, 'cause I had to wait four more years. Ten and twelve, you think you know everything as a kid, and part of knowing everything is you know what's right and what's wrong and kids know what's real and what's not real. I mean, if I was dealing with five-year-old kids, I'd still argue the same point, 'cause I still don't think that people give five-year-old kids far enough credit. But we're dealing with, you know, my audience is twelve to sixteen, they know exactly what . . . they're reading comic books for God's sakes, you know, my goodness!

AH: With the string of guest appearances and the *Violator* miniseries coming out, I've heard a few rumors that you're thinking about either having another artist do the book or giving the book over to another creative team or something. Are any of these things gonna happen?

TM: Yep.

AH: It is going to happen. Can you give us an idea . . . ?

TM: Sure, I don't know, it depends. Alan Moore is definitely writing it and so it's just a matter of whether I'm gonna write it with or I'm gonna draw it with Alan. Or after coming off four issues of having writers do the book that I wanna stay on *Spawn* and kind of guide him a little bit, you know what I mean? And say, if I don't draw it then either, you know, Bart Sears or Barry Windsor-Smith's gonna be doing some work for me. So maybe Barry might wanna do it, although he hasn't gotten back to me on exactly what it is that he wants to do, whether he wants to do a solo project or work with somebody or whatever. But my initial plan was I brought Grant Morrison and Bart on, and no matter what happened, I had a back-up plan. So if I took off then this is what's gonna happen and if not, you know, if I wanted to go do the Violator I'd have a good quality team sitting there of Bart Sears and Grant

Morrison to take care of the Spawn, that would do some good work that I could be proud of.

AH: So if Alan Moore is going to be doing a lot of writing, I heard that part of his desire to do 1963 was that he felt he ushered in, or helped to usher in, the dark age with *Watchmen*, about the same time Frank Miller did *Dark Knight*, and that he wanted to try and do some lighter books. Can we expect *Spawn* is still gonna have the dark edge that he's so famous for?

TM: Yeah, I think so. Given that he comes from hell and he kind of lives in the back alleys and stuff, there's a couple elements there that are gonna be tough to get away from. Does it mean that every story's gonna be like that? Nah . . . but on the other hand, I think Image Comics has a lot of daytime heroes, so to speak, that are kind of fun and friendly and, whatever, and I just don't think that there's a lack of good, clean fun superheroes. There's plenty of those books out there, so I'm just trying to give a bit of a different slant on one of the characters that happens to be coming out of Image comic books, 'cause there's no sense in having all our books the same. Now if everybody came up with dark, moody, gritty characters, I'd probably dump the Spawn and go do something lighthearted and fun. It's just a matter of giving variety to the reader, you know?

AH: Do you have any plans on anything beyond the *Violator* miniseries or are you sticking to the "Spawnverse"?

TM: Yeah, pretty much the other Spawn, the Spawnverse. Do I have other ideas? Sure I do, but it's just I don't want to be running around and cheating the public so to speak. They came to the table to see Todd McFarlane who is doing a character called Spawn, and I think I should give them a good dose of it before I decide that I want to go on and do something else.

AH: That's a really good thing because more and more people are becoming interested in *Spawn* every day, which is pretty evident in the demand for the back issues, and I think they'd really hate to see the character just kind of fizzle out and be done away with or put on hiatus . . .

TM: One of the things that I did is I gave him powers that he can be Superman, Batman, or anyone in between, and the reason I did that was because working at Marvel and DC for years, once you got tired of a guy's powers you had to go and quit the book, right? So what I've done is I've essentially given him these powers that he doesn't want to use but he has them, right? 'Cause I used to hate Superman bouncing things off his chest. There was no thrill to that. I always like Batman better. But if I get tired of the Batman riff, so to speak, then I can go and I can do Superman and my guy's got the power that he can go and destroy a building if he wants to, but I've set him up so that he's foolish to use those powers. The day I get bored of doing Spawn crawling around on the tops of buildings and in gutter ways and I just go, "God I need a break." I don't have to need a break and go draw, you know, *Youngblood* or something like that. I can just say, "Ah, I'm gonna do a happy daytime story," and I'm gonna have my guy lift the Empire State Building and I'm gonna do my Superman riff or my Green Lantern riff or my Spider-Man riff or whatever I want.

AH: Actually, just the idea of Spawn running around in the daylight [*laughs*] would be pretty cool.

TM: It would be a new technique. That's right, so I'll use that element when it has its time and purpose. What I want to do is hang with him as long as I can and as long as it's working and there's interest in him, and then as I get bored of him, then kind of use some of the different elements I've laid out there and go, "Ah-ha, I can go do this and then come back." I've tried to set him up so that I won't get bored of him basically and consequently, if I don't get bored of him, I'll stay on it and I'm hoping that some of the elements that make him not boring to me will make him not boring to other people who are basically plunking down their two dollars every month that they get the book.

AH: Let me ask you a question that I've wondered about since I started reading *Spawn*. When you released *Spider-Man* #1, you kind of fueled the whole writer/artist debate. Granted it already existed, but I think people had something to latch on to at that point and the book really was criticized for the writing, and I think you even said that it's going to take you a while to feel comfortable as a writer. With *Spawn*, a lot of people were expecting it to be stylistic, with really great art, but they were wondering what the stories were going to be like, especially if we're not sure what the Image editorial structure is. And I tell you, the stories have been great, they've been really well received, the writing's really strong. Do you feel that you went through some sort of transition in the time in between those titles or was it just kind of a natural thing?

TM: No, I find it humorous when people say that, because when I quit *Spider-Man*, I never really did anything to advance my writing. At the beginning, I took five months off and didn't even look at comic books for five months, so maybe if nothing else, if I was in any kind of bad habits on *Spider-Man*, I maybe forgot what those habits were. But did I sit there and write and hone my ability? Nah, I took five or six months off and I had a baby daughter and I just went out in the sun and played out in the sun, and maybe the answer is the sun makes you a little better creatively. I don't know. But did I do anything intentionally? No, so those are probably the same stories I would have written for *Spider-Man* #17 and onward if I had stayed on there, so it's kind of amusing more than anything else.

Plus, the other thing is that I don't think people quite understand what happened on *Spider-Man*. They were dealing with two different creative people. There was Todd McFarlane the seasoned vet, so to speak, who was doing the artistic chores, and there was Todd McFarlane the rookie, who was writing the book. And unfortunately, the expectations were that Todd McFarlane the writer should be as good as Todd McFarlane the artist. And it gave a lot of people problems that this unknown writer, who just happened to be me, wasn't as good as this guy who had been drawing comic books for the last six years. So if I had written it under the name John Doe, I don't think it would have been as big a deal because then there would be no expectations built up. But the expectations when my name was on the book . . . people expected certain things, they had come to expect things on an artistic level and I think they just transcended that into a writing venue.

Was it the worst stuff that ever came out, I don't know. Was it the best stuff, I don't know. It just was there, you know what I mean? It wasn't the best and it wasn't the worst and I feel the same way with the stuff that we're doing at Image. It's not the greatest writing, but it's not the worst, you know? It's just another comic book product. Now, artistically, I'll argue it differently. I think that we do things that some people can't do, you know, of the super-hero comic genre.

AH: Like what specifically? What do you see that Image is doing that you couldn't have done somewhere else?

TM: I'm not saying that we couldn't have done it someplace else. I'm just saying that from an artistic point of view, the guys that are at Image . . . I'm just saying that there's a reason that Jim Lee has a following, that he has it because he's just a hell of an artist. And so I'll argue why *WildC.A.T.s* is a good-selling book mostly on the merits of the artwork and Jim Lee's name, and the writing is something that's going to have to catch up with it. And then the same thing with *Spider-Man* and with *Spawn*, you know?

AH: You must feel more comfortable as a writer now than a couple of years ago. Do you still feel that people are putting pressure on you, or do you feel that people have accepted you as a writer now?

TM: No way. You know, I can always just cop out and say that I listened to the critics and so I went and got Alan Moore and Frank Miller. So that was part of the joke that I was telling. I was going, "You take the heat off me now." And they'll be going, "How could you, Neil Gaiman, sell yourself out to the devil? Todd McFarlane's evil. What are you doing? Blah, blah, blah." And I go, "You know I need a break. Come on. You guys can come over here and help me."

AH: Fans couldn't wait for stuff like that.

TM: Oh, yeah, yeah. But the funny thing is, the funniest out of this whole thing that I'll be monitoring is, the retailers and the guys like you and I, we remember who Frank Miller is and Alan Moore, but I think there's a lot of kids out there that buy our books who don't know who these guys are: Frank Miller and Alan Moore are rookies. "Who's this new, young buck who writes superhero comic books?" That's an amusing part of the whole thing. I know that retailers ordered a little bit heavy on it but that was because of their personal taste. And I think they're gonna sit there and go, "Holy smoly, that little twelve-year-old kid doesn't really care, so I'm gonna have to try and get rid of these books. And so maybe I better try and promote these books to some of my older clients." And if they promote it to their older clients, then maybe there'll be a couple more people turned onto the Spawn, you know? Because otherwise, Image comic books and *Spawn*, up to that point was, "Oh, here's the latest *Spawn*. Go over there and buy it, it makes me money," you know. But anytime you can get the retailers excited about a product, that's good because then they're going, "Look at this product, look at this product!"

Now, if they're saying look at this product because they ordered twice as many and they're getting stuck with them, then I'm saying I don't care what motivates them really. I'm just glad that they're going, "Look at this product, look at this product!" You know? And maybe it's because they have to get rid of their back stock but they're still doing me a service by saying, "Besides, I can make money off this book. I need a promoter to get rid of it," you know? There's a lot of things that will be learned from this whole experience when it's all said and done.

AH: This is probably a really sore subject, but everyone wants me to ask this question so . . . *Spawn* is now, technically, the oldest title that Image has . . .

TM: I'm the *Action Comics* . . .

AH: Yeah, you're hitting double digits now. And the book really has been shipping pretty much on time, like every month.

TM: Yeah, that's as accurate as we can say: "Pretty much on time."

AH: People are just wondering what makes you different or what's driving you to deliver the books on time when a lot of the Image stuff . . .

TM: You know what's driving me? To tell you the truth? The other books aren't out. If all the other books were out, I'd probably be lazy as crap. But since nobody else is delivering them, I'm just going, "Ah, dang it, somebody's got to come to the forefront here." I go, "Are you gonna do it?" "Nope." "Are *you* gonna do it?" "Nope." "Are *YOU* gonna do it!?" "Nope." I guess I'm the only guy left, I guess I'd better do it. So from the very beginning I thought we needed some monthly comic books or whatever. And everybody else wanted to do miniseries, because some of the guys, Mark [Silvestri] and [Jim] Valentino and even Jim Lee and that . . . there's one thing that I don't think I lack is confidence. So I'm like, "We don't need to come out with miniseries, I mean these books are gonna sell," and they're like, "Well if it doesn't work then we don't have them monthly and we wouldn't be able to go back to Marvel or DC," you know what I'm saying? I'm going, "Are you kidding me? You don't think that a Jim Lee comic book. . . . Goddamn it, *I'll* be your agent, you know? It's gonna work, this is gonna *work*, guys." So I never had any doubts that this wasn't gonna work so I was going, "Well, are you gonna do a monthly?" "Nope," "Are *you* gonna do a monthly?" "Nope, no, no, no." So I just went, aw heck, somebody's got to do a monthly, and I guess since I'm the last guy to ask, then I guess it's gonna be me.

I don't need to do a monthly, I did well on *Spider-Man*, I make a good living. I've got my pennies put away for a rainy day. I don't need to do it, you know what I mean? I'm not doing it for monetary reasons. If anything, I don't like looking at checks because you go, why should I work this week? Because, I mean, what's the point of it? So, I'm trying to still keep the reason I got into comic books, because I like comic books, they're cool, they're hip, they're mod, you know? So what drives me is that I'm just a psycho when it comes down to it. And part of the thing we're doing is, we have to prove that we can succeed, and if proving that we can succeed is putting out product that sells month in and month out, then we have to do that. If part of it means that you can do one-shots and still make a good living, then some of the other guys are taking up that slack. So, we're just trying to do it.

Plus, the other thing is that I know I aggravate people in this business. Not the kids but the peers so to speak. Whether they're businesspeople or comic book peers. From a vantage point of having two brothers that I used to aggravate, there's nothing that aggravates the crap out of people like being there all the time. So the way for me to get my revenge, so to speak, is to keep producing comic books that people buy, 'cause that just drives people nuts. So, while they're going, "They're gonna die, they're gonna go the way of the dinosaur," the best revenge that I can have, instead of sitting and writing a letter column or a "But I Digress" or some stupid thing like that, is to sit there and come up with a comic book and have it sell a half a million to a million comic books like clockwork and just aggravate them by my mere existence.

AH: *Spawn* just seems to gather speed. It just seems to gather steam as it goes.

TM: And I still have a few more rabbits ready to pull out of my hat, so I haven't shown all my tricks. I've still got creative people and just comical stuff, in terms of our business. I've still got aces . . . I haven't even exposed the aces yet.

AH: While we're on Image, there are two things that people wonder about. One, are there any editors, or is it pretty much everyone's on their own and they're responsible for meeting their own deadlines?

TM: Yeah, if you were to do a book for us, and you felt you needed five editors, go ahead. If you felt you needed one, go ahead; if you felt you needed none, go ahead. You own your book, you're the captain of your ship. *I'm* not the captain of your ship; I don't tell you what to do. I mean we've got new people coming on—Mike Grell, Keith Giffen, and Larry Stroman. We don't tell those guys how to do their books, but if they don't do a good job of it, their books aren't gonna sell, so that's their motivation.

Do I have an editor? Hell no! I've got some people that look over my spelling and stuff like that, but there's a lot of people in this business that have jobs that I think are overvalued. Editors are one of them. Do I need somebody to crack the whip if I had five books and tell me to get books out on time and check deadlines and stuff like that? Yeah, but you know, my mom could do that. I could hire my mom to do what most of the editors in this business do.

Editors are glorified babysitters to me—they don't add nothing, they don't do nothing, they get the books out on time and they're traffic managers. Every now and then, just so they can justify their paycheck to the big guys upstairs, they change something. Do they change it for the better? No, they change it for the sake of change. There's no reason behind most of their changes, other than when they get called on the carpet, and somebody says to them, "Why is the sales of *Spider-Man* going up twice as fast?" They can't say, "Well, I've got this creative guy that I don't do nothing with and I just let him do whatever he wants and the sales go up." That doesn't bode well for you when you're starting to meet the people who are signing your checks. So editors are afraid for their jobs and so what they do is they touch stuff so they can say they touched it and that's it. We don't even have enough space for me and my attitudes about editing.

Now, on the other hand, let me say that Jim Salicrup, who's the editor on *Spider-Man*, is the greatest guy I ever dealt with in comic books, bar none. The reason was that he had confidence in me and he had confidence in the people that he hired. When he hired people, he trusted their instincts, and the argument can be made that as an editor, you can't trust everybody 'cause some people need guidance. You know what I mean?

AH: Now I would think that (usually) the sign of a competent individual is someone who surrounds himself with people who are more competent than he is. As an editor I would think that you'd want to be bringing in the really talented people to get the job done. Because if no one can do anything better than you, then you should be doing the whole job yourself.

TM: And that's the point. The point is, and the worst thing about Todd McFarlane is not that he knows everything, it's just that he thinks he does. Which makes me dangerous.

So, the problem that I have in life—and I'm sure you have these same aggravations, 'cause I still get them when I go to rent a car and things don't work out at the rent-a-car—is I hate it when other people are making decisions in my life, because when things blow up, then you gotta pass the buck. And I don't like passing the buck. So if I eliminate all the bucks, then it's like, every morning I get up if there's a problem, it's my problem. If I don't like the way the Spawn looks, change him. If I don't like the way the story reads, change it. If I don't like this, change it. If there's a problem with the comic book itself, I'm the problem, Todd McFarlane's the problem.

You know, I don't even have to phone anybody, I just gotta get out of bed, and before I shave I just gotta reprimand myself. And you know what? I can live with every decision I made on *Spawn*, right or wrong. You can live with personal decisions a lot better when they go sour, than when somebody else makes a decision for you that could go sour. It's just human nature. So I do it just because I don't like to be aggravated and I don't like people telling me how to run my life.

So, I don't tell anybody how to run their life, I just tell myself how to run mine. And so I just do my comic book the way that I see fit. I'm still eight years old inside and I like drawing cool monsters and hearts being ripped out. I think that's cool!

One Hell of a Ride: Part Two

JOHN RILEY / 1993

From *Amazing Heroes Interviews* 1, no. 2 (1993): 6–19. Reprinted by permission.

Our exclusive interview with Todd McFarlane continued.

Amazing Heroes: We were talking about not telling people what to do. I heard that Rob Liefeld publicly stated that as of books solicited in March for May release, that things from Image would be shipping on time from all creators. People are pretty cynical about it, so is that something that you really see is gonna happen? You were saying that you don't tell other people what to do. Is there some point where the originators of Image, the founders, have to say, guys, we have to get together on this?

Todd McFarlane: Umm-hmmm. We see it. We see that the biggest rap against us is not, "We don't like your books," or not that they don't make us money, or not that they're cool or not that they're hip, but where are they? That's it, and so we've heard it over and over and over and over and over, and finally we're trying to do something about it. You know what I mean? If some of it is because they're just aggravated by hearing it, fine. Some of it is because they've heard, "How come *Spawn* somehow seems that it's on time?" And if that's their motivation, because they don't want Todd to steal the thunder, who cares? Anything that motivates us to get our books out on time is a good thing. So, will you see us be better? Yeah. Will you see us be perfect? Nah. Will we be better than last year? Yeah, I think so, because we know that's the rap we've been given, that we can't get the product out.

AH: Is there pressure being put on people by other founders?

TM: By us? Yeah. The new guys coming on? Sure. Every guy that comes on gets to do his three or four issues or whatever else and there's a probation, for lack of a better word, and then if they don't deliver, hell. We don't need guys who do late books. You know why? 'Cause we do those real well. So what we need is guys who actually do the books and have a good attitude and the whole bit. So are the new guys coming on board and will some of them get fired? Yup. The guys who screw up will get fired.

Unfortunately, the founding members can't get fired because we're . . . uh no, we can. We set it up so we can all get fired. But I'm just saying, for the most part, the first firings in our company, so to speak, will be some of the new guys who basically came in, said, "Oh, I want to do this book. I can do this and this and this," and then they didn't deliver. In a weird kind of way, they basically did what we did, you know what I mean? Except there's two sets of rules. There's one for us, the guys who are Image and . . . you know what I mean. And so, is that fair to the people? They have to basically cover our ass 'cause we destroyed the confidence of a lot of people. That's not really fair, but that's just the way it is.

So the people who don't like those rules aren't doing books for us, and the people who can live with those rules are going, "Ah, don't you guys worry about it, I can handle those little . . . ," you know? We've got minimal rules at our company, and one of them right now is we need books out on time. I don't think that's such a bad rule to have. So it's not like we're squelching creative freedom or anything. We're just saying that, you know, we screwed up and we need some of you guys to kind of pick up for our indiscretions.

AH: I see in *Comic Buyer's Guide*, where people are writing letters back and forth about is Image a company, etc. I think it's probably point of view—at this point people are pretty convinced either one way or the other. But how does, for example, Liefeld's Extreme Studios, or Jim Lee's Homage Studios, how does that fit in? There are rumors that they're going to break away and stuff like that. Is that them just setting up their own area for them to be creative within?

TM: Yeah, that's it. You know, I don't call my thing anything, but if you want I'll call it, you know, "Apple Pie Studios" tomorrow if you want. It's just, when you phone me, you're getting me, pretty much, you know? And when you phone them, there's a whole bunch of people working there so you can't really call it Jim Lee's office because it's not really Jim Lee's office . . . there's a lot of people working there, so you might want one of the other nine guys who are working there. So it's just a name. People have been using studio names since I've been collecting comic books. It's not something new.

AH: I was just wondering, because I keep hearing things about, oh, they're gonna break away or something.

TM: No, that's good. See, there's always a new rumor. We get all the new rumors every month and I'm just going, "Ah, cool!" The problem comes when people aren't talking about us. But they're creating rumors about us, and that's good 'cause they're talking about us. Better us than, say, Dark Horse.

AH: That's what they say, the key to success: You know you've made it when people are spreading bad rumors about you.

TM: Any, I don't care—good, bad, or indifferent, we need all the press coverage we can get. Do we get a lot of flak from people? Tons of it. But you know what? Better that they write about us than write about, say, Topps Comics, you know? So, I'm going, I wouldn't want to lose out to Topps Comics. So I'm going, "Aw, cool."

Can we take the criticism? You're darn tooting. We've taken more criticism, both at Image and in our careers. Rob Liefeld and Todd McFarlane . . . probably the two most despised men on the planet of comic books. And you know what? We're still having a ball in our lives, because the people who hate us, we don't give a crap about, because I'm writing a comic book for fifteen to sixteen-year-old kids and some grand poobah who's forty-two years old decides he didn't like the Spawn. Well, you know what? It's like building a tricycle and having some adult say, "It sucks, it doesn't fit me." Well, it's a tricycle, for God's sake! So criticism . . . my mom doesn't like everything I do, my wife doesn't like everything I do. So, if I can still live with the fact that my wife doesn't like everything I do, I could really care less whether John Byrne likes it, you know?

AH: Do you sometimes tone down a page or change something because your wife looks at it and says, "You know, Todd, I just hate that."

TM: No. If you look at the credit pages, my wife was the one who was doing spelling. If you look at the first three issues it says Wanda Kolomyjec, which is my wife's name. And then after issue number three or something, her name's not there 'cause we had a dispute because I didn't pay attention to her. She goes, "Take my name off the credits. If you're not gonna listen to me—if you want me to be your editor, you want me to make suggestions and you're not going to listen to me—then I don't want any pity credit."

So, I'm uncoachable. And that's the thing that you can understand, like am I an idiot that I got peers that hate me 'cause they think that I am a whatever, some weird, wacked out guy, ah yeah, but I'm the same with my wife, so it's like, you know she seems to love me for it. I'm the same with everything. So don't take it personally that I didn't listen to every order I got at Marvel because I don't listen to practically . . . I'm uncoachable. My wife has known that since I was playing baseball, that I'm uncoachable. When I set my mind I don't listen to nobody, because then, if it doesn't work out and I crash and burn, then I can live with it, you know? I can live with failure as long as I'm the one that steered the failure. That I drove it into the tree or I drove the vehicle into the gully. I hate it when somebody else is steering it into that gully.

AH: One of the things I guess people are waiting for . . . we're seeing all kinds of licensing deals, we've got action figures on the rise again and the statues are becoming big deals, like Sandman and the Death and the Batman stuff. I guess we're waiting for Image stuff, and personally I would love to see a Spawn statue—you know, a gothic Spawn statue in the same vein as the Batman one that was released. I just saw that there was a Spawn vinyl model kit released and I was just wondering, can we expect other things? What's in the works?

TM: I don't think . . . the model kit wouldn't be out. There is no Spawn model kit.

AH: Really, because we just saw it in the new Diamond Previews. It solicited for a Spawn vinyl resin model kit.

TM: I'm going to have to take a look at that. Anyway, I'm in negotiations and they sent me the first model kit, but they were reworking it. Part of the thing we get to have is control of the looks and stuff on it. So we kind of rejected the first go-round and we're working on the second one. So, if there's a vinyl kit that comes out, it shouldn't be, but anyway, I think that they just solicited it assuming that they were gonna get approval of the first go-round and they didn't, blah, blah, blah. But there'll be a couple of things out there. You know, I've turned down a lot of things. I'm just looking to kind of throw a few things out at a time to kind of tease people with the product and not to overdo it all in one bunch. So no, I don't have any cards coming out, or anything like that. I had an offer to make some PVC toys and stuff like that, you know, that some of the other guys are making. But I just don't think you can get the detail on them, which is why I went to the vinyl kit, 'cause you can get the lift of the cape and things like that. There will be license stuff. I mean, you're gonna be seeing video games and stuff like that.

AH: But little by little.

TM: As it comes and whatever else. But everybody does it differently. Some guys wanna go and do twenty items. Fine. And some guys want to do two items. Fine. And I'm the conservative licensor. I'll do a little bit here and a little bit there and then see how that works and then go to the next thing. I don't want to throw everything out there right off the bat.

AH: You just mentioned teasing people. Is that the motivation behind the Spawn ring, which is higher priced, limited quantity item? What made you decide to do the ring?

TM: I know the guy who's doing it. He's been a pal for a while, so most of the deals I make actually are with pals. If an unknown guy came with the same thing I probably would have said, "No. Get out of here!" But it was a pal, and I said, "OK. Fine, let's try it." But he did it and I don't think we're going to do any more. I don't like real expensive stuff, but it's a good experiment. I don't want people buying hundred-dollar Spawn items, I want them to be buying two-dollar items. But then you start getting into cheap stuff! So, it's a weird thing to try and figure out right now, what exactly people want, what's too much, what's not enough and whatever else. So it's still a lot of a learning game for us right now. You know Rob is doing his stuff. He's got some cool stuff coming out and I can kind of watch and see how his stuff works, and he can watch how my stuff works, and we can learn from each other's experiments.

AH: One thing that's going to be interesting this summer is you've got a whole bunch of new actual comic lines coming out. We've got Continuity, Dark Horse's superhero line, we've got Vertigo, and Milestone already, there's a lot of stuff. And the market is growing, but it's not growing that fast. How do you think this is going to affect things?

TM: Kabloomo! Kabloomo! How long have you been in comic books?

AH: Twenty years, I've been collecting for twenty years.

TM: Do you remember the black-and-white explosion?

AH: Big time.

TM: This is, in my opinion, the color explosion. This is, everybody's gonna throw their stuff at the wall, their meatballs at the wall, and we're gonna see how many of them are going to stick. And two years from now, half of these lines won't exist. I hope that we're not the half that is not existing, but maybe we will be. Maybe we'll fall to the wayside, other companies will throw out the better and bigger product. The one thing that we're forgetting along the way is the one thing of why we left Marvel Comics. The thing that drives superhero comics is a combination of the characters and the kids are really following the names. This is a name game right now, and you can't just throw out product for the sake of product. It actually, God forbid, would have to be a damn good product, you know what I mean?

So I think that we're getting further and further away from a good product and we're getting more product and that is one of the things that I think is gonna happen to Marvel Comics. I couldn't have written a better destructive course for them because what they're doing, instead of throwing out 130 books and making $130, they're gonna put out 260 books and make $140. And they're gonna make ten more dollars for their shareholders, but it cost them twice as much capital to do it, twice as much product, and the more product you put out there, you know what happens? You water the stuff down.

Now I don't give a crap that you've got twelve Wolverines out there if my mom and dog are drawing them, you know what I'm saying? So tell me who's doing the product. It's gotta be a combination of who's doing the product and what the product is. So, do I like Wolverine? I love him, but if my mom draws him, I don't like him that much. I don't like him enough that you can throw crap at me and I'm gonna still buy it. Then you know what's gonna happen? Work until perfection, they're gonna educate the public—worst thing you can do as somebody who sells a consumer product is get the public knowledgeable, because then they'll stop for a second and they'll go, "Hold a second, what's the best products out there, which ones do I A) enjoy, B) think that I can make an investment on, or whatever their reasoning, and C) da da da da da da." And they're gonna start to say, "I don't give a damn if it's a number one from anybody. It's crap." You know what I mean? And Marvel, tsk, tsk, tsk, tsk. They forgot who brought them to the prom, and you know who got them to the prom? *Captain America, Thor, Daredevil*. All their anchors . . . they're letting go of their anchors. I mean, a couple of years ago you would have never seen the *Avengers* and *Captain America* out of the top twenty-five and now those guys are sitting at number seventy-five, eight, for Christ's sakes. I'm going *Captain America* number eighty? That's a disgrace, you know? Why don't you put your energies into *Captain America* instead of gelling out six new number ones. I'm not saying don't throw the number ones out, because that's good for business, but I'm saying you're forgetting that what made Marvel Marvel was that they had the best quality products. Now, as the years go by, they're gonna have the most products. Not the best, the most.

AH: And the ones that they put their special covers on are the things that move anyway. They add special covers to *Spider-Man*, to *X-Men*, but then *Thor* languishes. Like you're saying, as opposed to helping retailers and helping get people interested in *Captain America* again by putting a good artist on the title and putting some money into it . . . some nice covers to get people reading. Sales get boosted on books that are already big.

TM: I don't know why. Again, I'm pretty ignorant about most of the Marvel products, so bear with me, but I don't know why *Captain America* doesn't sell. I'm not saying that you need a better artist or you need a better writer or whatever. It might be a combination. You might need better stories, you might need a new costume. I don't know why that book isn't selling right now, okay? All I know is that it's not selling. But some of the business decisions don't make sense to me.

There's a book called *Thor* that's dropped from the top twenty to like number seventy-five and they took that same creative team and are bringing them on a book called *Thunderstrike*. Now I'm sure that it'll be double sized with the foil cover or something to hype it all up, and it's short-term profits. Short-term profit's gonna be their death, and it's the same creative team so to me, from a business point of view that's tough to sell. The same team that drove the sales of *Thor* from number twenty-five to number seventy-five is bringing you *Thunderstrike*, you know? I'm going, what's your thinking on this? These are the same people that dropped your sales on the book and you're gonna put them on a number one foil-embossed and get some quick sales, but the same thing is gonna happen. They think the public is stupid. I hate to say it, but that was the one thing that they miscalculated when we left. They think the kids are stupid, that they can just say that this is gonna be the hot character and this is gonna be the hot book and this is the hot writer and the hot artist and they just think that can happen. You can promote *Alpha Flight* all you want, but you know what? The kid is still gonna buy more *WildC.A.T.s.* So I don't care how many ads you put out on it, if my mom draws it, goddamn it, nobody's gonna buy it! And you're forgetting, for the sake of profits right now, they are forgetting what made Marvel Comics Marvel Comics. It was— at one time at least, and I think they're still there right now but if they don't watch themselves they're gonna burn themselves—they used to put out the best comic books in the business. And now they're just gonna be putting out the most. I'm not excited as much about Marvel products as I used to be a couple years ago.

AH: When you released *Spawn*, you said it's not being reprinted at all, and it kind of made a commitment to the people who were buying the book to begin with. We've seen so many superspecial covers and this and that and the hot book of the day kind of thing. Obviously you don't seem to be partaking in any of that. How do you think that bodes for the industry? Are we talking about the black-and-white bust of 1987 all over again? Do you think that we're just adding fuel to the fire?

TM: Uh huh. I think that we're taking something like gimmick covers that might have had a five-year life and we're gonna destroy it in two years. And the only thing that's gonna keep it going for two years is that we're bringing in a lot of card shops now that are starting to collect comic books.

AH: Because they killed the card industry?

TM: Right. All the same things that killed the card business we're emulating now in comic books, and I'm going, "Way to go!" Let's see, put out more product, try to screw the public for freaking overrated rookie cards—but now they're foil-embossed things—and stiff the public and basically get the public turned off to comic books. I'm going, "Way to go, way to do business."

And besides, we're gonna have sharks coming in from the card business. Some of them are good, some of them are bad. We've got Marvel Comics leading the charge by going, "We've gotta make profits so for all intents and purpose we don't give a crap about the product anymore," and if they argue it the other way, then I've got enough ears up in that business that I know that's not true. Their arguments right now have to do with profits, end of the conversation. You know, I don't give a crap if I make a nickel off *Spawn*. Would I like to? Yeah, 'cause I need to pay the bills, but you know what? I don't need to pay as many bills as Marvel Comics does. So I can still continue to say next issue, issue #9, I'm going up to higher grade paper, the paper that we used on *Youngblood* #4. We're gonna dub it "Youngblood paper." *Youngblood* #4, if you saw it, was a beautiful-looking book.

AH: It was sharp.

TM: Beautiful. Okay now, *Youngblood*'s always been solicited at $2.50, but we're going to that *Youngblood* paper, 'cause Rob's book looked so beautiful, but the price ain't going up. You know Marvel Comics is going to be squeezing profits. They're looking at the opposite, they're looking at how can they get a cheaper paper and keep the same price. Or better yet, how can they get a cheaper paper and raise the price?

Somewhere along the line you get educated, you're gonna see that I wasn't one of the guys that was screwing you, you know what I mean? I'm giving you a $1.95 book. I'm gonna put the computer coloring in it. Does it cost me more than anyone else in the business? You're damn right. Do I pay the letterer more than any of the other guys? You're damn right. Do I have the most expensive paper? You're damn right, you know. Am I raising the price because of all that? Heck no! I'm here 'cause you guys have given me a good living and I'm gonna give some of it back to you. I'm not here to worry about some stockbroker's commission or some guy making a profit.

Unfortunately, the same cannot be said about my good friends at Marvel Comics. They're neglecting the product, and that's what frustrates me right now. They're neglecting the product, and when the burn comes down and people start going, "Screw comic books, you just get burned in that business from collecting," they're burning me with them. And that's why I get aggravated and I get hot because it's like don't' take me down with you. So all I can do is go, "Listen, I can only lead by example, like a good little parent would do with their kid." I can lead by example by saying, "I'm selling a million comic books, I've never fallen out of the top ten at any of the distributors and I haven't put one friggin' foil on my comic book." Do you wanna know what? I'd probably sell two million if I put foil on there, but you know what? I'm not that greedy so I'll just be content with the million 'cause that's a pretty damn good number anyway. I'll save the foil for when I've got nothing to say and I'm desperate, and at this point in the game I'm not desperate. On the other hand, some of the boys at Image are doing it so. . . . I'm not saying that it's right or wrong, I'm just giving you my opinion why I don't do it. Some of the other guys are doing it for their reasons and their reasons are just as valid as anybody else's. But I don't agree with the fancy cover crap right now.

AH: I was reading one of your past interviews in which you said that you always want to bring your art to the next level. It sounds to me now that you're concerned with bringing the book, the whole book, to the next level, to create as high-quality a package as possible.

TM: That's it, you hit the point. We're missing the word that used to be synonymous with a lot of books: try to bring a quality product to the table. Now, I've had people say to me, if you can imagine, and I'm just like wow, where have we stooped or what? You're bringing in Alan Moore and you're bringing in Frank Miller and that's your gimmick and you've got the sales boost 'cause you're bringing in these fancy writers, well you know that's what you're doing. And I'm going, wow, where have we stooped in our business when we bring in good freaking writers and it's called a gimmick? Years ago it used to be called quality, you know what I mean? Years ago it used to be a hell of a story, a hell of a read. You know: "Aw, cool!" But today, I think we're so cynical that I bring in Frank Miller to do something and they think that Frank Miller's my gimmick? Well, if Frank Miller's my gimmick, then damn right I'm going to be gimmicking my books, because I'm going to be doing a lot of quality stuff, and if that's called a gimmick then I'm gimmicking my way through the books.

AH: And it's kind of scary that there are people who think that way. That you can associate Alan Moore or Frank Miller or Dave Sim with the word "gimmick."

TM: Well, that's it. I keep saying to those guys, when I was hiring them, I go, "Guys, I need foil but I hate foil. I want you guys to be my foil." You know what I mean? I think Dave Sim is better than foil, I think Frank Miller is better than a trading card polybag. And I think Alan Moore is better than embossed covers. Take that.

And so, if I sell a million, thank you. I'm glad we did it, because I sent the message that, you know what, you don't need to put foil on the books to sell a million copies. You need to put good people on the book, goddamn it. So you sold a million copies of *Morbius* or whatever your latest book was that had foil on it, I don't care. Take a look at issue number, see again I'm looking at this for long-term stuff. I don't think that when you're looking at profits you're looking at long term; you're looking at short-term crap. I don't want to sell ten million *Spawn* #1s 'cause I had a poly-bagged double, triple whatever in there, and then fall to number twenty-two in the top one hundred for issue #2 and fall to number thirty-five for issue #3. What I want to do is come in at number five for issue #1, and then go to number seven for issue #2, and down to number nine for issue #3, and then I've got the death of so and so, and then come back up to number four, you know what I'm saying? I want to be in the top ten every month, and if I just cheat people, I don't think that's going to work, and so take a look at where *Bloodshot* is for Valiant. It went from number one to number twenty-seven on the top one hundred. That's not my business there. I don't want to go from one to twenty-seven but I made so much goddamn money off number one, 'cause that's short term, goddamn it. I'm looking for *Spawn* to be on the stand by issue #50, and so the only way that's gonna happen is I either put out a lot of foil covers and people will get bored, or I try to come up with twists and turns and put out a quality product. That will keep the book out there for fifty issues or a hundred or a hundred fifty, I don't care.

AH: It surprises me that people haven't hit on the concept, which seems to be at the core of comics, that the comic is supposed to be fun. And *Spawn* is a fun book to read. Granted it's dark, but it's a really enjoyable read. And a lot of the books now, they're just not that much fun. They have foil covers all over the place, and cut outs and holes drilled through it and this and that, but they're not fun to read.

TM: I'm not saying that. Some of them are. Here's where I stand with the fancy covers, and I've said it in my letter column: If you would buy that book, rip that cover off it. If you still would have bought that comic book, then you got a bonus, you got this cool cover. So it's a bonus. Although if they have to raise the freaking price a lot, I think they're cheating you. If I ever put foil on my comic book, I won't raise it a nickel, 'cause why do I want to cheat the public?

And here's the stupid thing about some of that stuff: If you do a cover that costs you 20 cents and you sell your book at 60 percent off to the distributors, you have to raise your price 50 cents because you're going to have 60 percent off of 50 cents is 20 cents. So just to break even—not to make a penny, to break even—on a 20-cent gimmick cover, you have to raise the price 50 cents, okay? So, if I wanted to make the exact same amount of money and put a foil on it, I would have to raise the price 50 cents to break even, okay? So who's paying for that cover? Guys, we're not giving you a foil cover 'cause we like you, we're giving you a foil cover and stiffing you for 50 cents. We're not doing it out of the goodness of our hearts, you know. We have to raise the price. So I'm going, if I can come up with a gimmick and not raise the price, like putting in better paper, I'll do it. If I can come up with foil and not raise the price, I'll maybe do it, I don't know. But to do it and raise the price . . . no way, not me. I'm not gonna be caught up. When this whole thing blows up in our face, I'm not gonna be one of the guys that they can point to going, "That two-bit whore." No way. I want to be clean when this thing happens and goes down.

AH: Do you think it's going to happen soon?

TM: No, because we've got the card guys coming in, and unfortunately the card guys, the collectors and the new retailers are ignorant of the process, so to speak, so they have to get educated. So, if it was just the comic book people, yeah, I think it'd go down faster, but we're bringing in a whole new brand of people who don't really know they're getting stiffed. And so it's lucky for Marvel and DC and whoever else that this fancy cover thing is going to have longer legs than people probably think it's gonna have, because there's too many new people in the business that don't know they're getting shafted. You know we're just gonna have to play it nice and slow and easy and just go out there and whatever. Nah, I'm not cynical that it's gonna happen in six weeks or anything like that.

AH: Where do you see yourself, Image, *Spawn* in the next five years? Or are you even thinking that far ahead?

TM: Not really, but we'll still be someplace and we'll be someplace because we're rabble rousers, and if we're not in comic books being rabble rousers, then we'll be somewhere else being rabble rousers. And that might be in Hollywood, that might be in film making, that might be in TV, that might be, I don't care which. If we're not in comic books, you can count on it that we're still out there being jerks. But I would like to think that we'll still be in business and we'll still be doing well, and the reason I would like to think that is that means that I have five more years of aggravating those people that think that we should have gone down with the ship like five years earlier—we're never gonna succeed, we're fly-by-night, we're this, we're this, we're this. That means for five years they've had that pit in their stomach called Image Comics, just eating away at them, and somewhere along the line, maybe by the twentieth year of our existence, they might even actually go, "Gee I don't think these guys are going away." I'm here to aggravate, and if that means sticking around for five years to aggravate, I'll stick around for five years.

AH: The crowd around the Image booth at comics conventions gets to be pretty out of control. I mean, it gets really deep and really packed in.

TM: It's a mania.

AH: Are you gonna do anything special for future signings? Are you planning that everyone has to get in line or anything?

TM: Yeah. Unfortunately, there's a rule, I guess if you want to call it that, of how to get signatures, and that started when I was on Spider-Man, the Spidermania, and the McSpideymania and the McFarlane mania, so I've been at this now for three or four years, so there's actually a system that works, if you get the cooperation of the organizers and it actually works. And I've explained it to the guy who's going to be doing this and he's fully aware of what has to be done. So we'll make sure that people don't go home pissed off, 'cause I don't need that, they don't need that and the promoters don't need that . . . nobody needs that. It doesn't serve any purpose, so there are ways of organizing. Will we be organized? Yep. Will we be doing stuff that's a little bit different than most guys? Yeah, we will.

AH: That's cool. I was outside the Image booth at one convention and you couldn't get within ten people of the booth. And some of the little kids were in there and I thought, wow the little kids shouldn't be in the middle of that crowd.

TM: And that's . . . it just is. People get mad at us for having those crowds sometimes, which again is like, we don't tell these people to get in line. We just show up, we don't beg these people to do this, they just do it. I mean, people think that we go around the country and force a million people to buy our books every month. No, we just turn out the products, stay home and people do it voluntarily. But again, critics say the people buy it because it's crap and they don't know any better, because our public is too dense to actually know what's good for their life and we need other people to run it. But things get taken care of and we try to do the best we can. Sometimes we fail and sometimes it works, but it's tough . . . you know, the grass is greener on the other side.

And to all those people who wish that they could have what we have, it's not all fun and games. There's a lot of a downside to it. And then part of it is, you know that the crowds are so big that you don't have any personal contact with them anymore, and there's not really all that much fun at conventions, you know. You just kind of sign all day long and whatever so. . . . We'll work on it. You watch me, I'll rock and roll.

Todd McFarlane

JIM SALICRUP / 1993

From *Comics Interview* 1, no. 119 (1993): 6–13. Reprinted by permission of Jennifer Bush-Kraft, administrator, estate of David Anthony Kraft.

Jim Salicrup has known Todd for a long time—having edited McFarlane on *Amazing Spider-Man* at Marvel and unleashing him to write and draw the all-new adjective-less *Spider-Man* series that set sales records and ushered in, for lack of a better term, what we'll call the Image Era of creator-driven megamillion-selling comics. Now Jim's at Topps Comics and Todd's one of the kingpins at the new, Malibu-free Image, so let's listen in between the static and feedback of Salicrup's speaker phone to hear what's in the works from the big hot Toddy himself . . .

Todd McFarlane: Is this going to be one of those high intellectual pooh pooh ones? [*Laughter*]

Jim Salicrup: Well, speaking of which, why the hell did you ever do that interview with Gary Groth?

McFarlane: [*Laughter*] For two reasons: Number one, I could say stuff in there that I could never say in the *Wizard*; and number two, I knew that every one of my peers was going to be reading it. So, all the guys who *hate* me, I gave them a *reason* to hate me.

Salicrup: [*Laughter*] Why is that, Todd?

McFarlane: I'm getting *tired* of fucking people *hating* me for no reason. After all, I'm not doing nothing to aggravate these people, so fuck it! If they're going to hate me, give them a reason. So I just go, "I'm gonna do an interview that pisses everybody off." The guys that get the joke will be able to see that the whole interview is like a joke, but the guys that take this business too seriously will go, "That transient homosexual!" [*Laughter*]

Salicrup: So, now Gary's going after poor Dave Sim.

McFarlane: Look, see, I don't got a problem with Gary Groth because Gary Groth thinks the opposite of me, you know what I mean.

Salicrup: I think he would be flattered to hear that.

McFarlane: Well, I've *told* Gary all he needs is a date. Fuck, he just needs a date and to coach a baseball team and he'd be normal. [*Laughter*] But, see, Gary Groth is like . . . it's like me being an atheist and him being, you know—

Salicrup: A religious fanatic?

McFarlane: Whatever, I don't care. I'm just saying that if I say one thing and he says the opposite, it's because of his *beliefs*, you know. The guys that astound me are my fellow peers that do superhero comic books, that are basically *more* fanatical than Gary as far as I'm concerned, that do the same thing I do! Those are the guys that boggle my mind. That Gary Groth says black when I say white doesn't bother me. That my fellow superhero peers say black when I say white, that one stuns me more than anything.

Salicrup: Well, how are you and Dave Sim getting along?

McFarlane: Oh, I just got his script for #10 [of *Spawn*]; it's the coolest! It's the coolest! It's twenty-two pages of a political soapbox for Dave. It works! It's too funny; this is too cool. It's got Wonder Woman in it, it's got Batman, it's got the Thing—it's got *everybody* in it. It's a keeper for the ages.

Salicrup: What made you include Dave?

McFarlane: What made me include Dave? Two reasons: Number one, he's Canadian; and number two, he's always been a fuck and I kind of *admire* guys like him.

Salicrup: How about the other issues? How are they? How's Alan Moore?

McFarlane: As we're talking I'm just finishing up the last couple of pages on it. You know, the stuff with the other writers, I'm *hoping* that people don't think that Alan Moore is going to do *Watchmen* in twenty-two pages, you know. In fact, it's twenty-four pages; he wants to expand it. But you know what I mean, I hope people aren't going, "Okay, give us that great, deep, philosophical story in twenty-four pages." It's not going to be that. Even though the story takes place in hell, it's kind of a funny story I think, and it's weird and whacked and stuff. What Alan and Neil Gaiman have done so far, and Dave, it's just one issue each, take it for what it's worth and enjoy it for twenty minutes then leave it at that. Don't try to read anything deep into it.

Salicrup: Why'd you get these guys in the first place, need I ask?

McFarlane: Why did I get them? I couldn't take my critics saying I couldn't write. I finally caved in. [*Laughter*] It's *not* the critics! No. You know me, Jim, long enough to know that whenever anybody goes left, I go

Spawn #10, p. 6, May 1993, Image Comics, Fair Use. With guest writer Dave Sim, McFarlane depicts perhaps the most allegorical story of Image Comics, one that shows Spawn's freedom in comparison to the many imprisoned characters cut off from their creators.

right. So, right now everybody seems to be selling comic books on covers and not content, so being that everybody's doing it *that* way, I decided to try a different angle, which is trying to sell it on the content. I'm not saying one is better than the other—I'll argue which one is—but I'm just saying if tomorrow everybody tried to sell on content, I'd probably try and sell it on cover. I got to where I am by doing the opposite of everybody; it doesn't mean that I think it's *better*, it's just whenever you do something *different* it seems to sell.

Plus, I think we're getting a little bit away from what used to sell comic books, too. My attitude is . . . like people go, "Oh, Todd, your gimmick is you're bringing on the writers." At what point are we at in comic books right now that because I decide to bring on quality writers it's considered a gimmick? [*Laughter*] Years ago it used to be because it was a hell of a book.

Salicrup: What did you think of Sim having to defend his decision to write *Spawn* in *Comics Buyer's Guide*?

McFarlane: Whatever. I mean, look, I don't have control over anybody. I've been blasted enough in the press and I never answer any of that, but I'm not gonna tell anybody else not to. Dave, I guess, feels that when he reads that stuff, he wants . . . if it's erroneous he just wants to defend his honor. I can live with it, you know. Even to the fact that, if he says something that's really not even that correct, I don't even correct Dave. I don't correct Dave, I don't correct the critics, I don't correct anybody. Let 'em do whatever; the more talk about it, the better it is.

Salicrup: Well, let me see if I can find the quote here.

McFarlane: I didn't let a little thing like not being able to write stop me; is that the one you're going to throw at me?

Salicrup: No, not that one. This is Dave: "Image, as Todd explains it, is just that little 'i' logo on the cover which creators who are invited to join their loose-knit coalition are welcome to use. I even asked Todd on a recent visit to his home, 'If one of the creators decided to move from Malibu to another company or, you know me, self-publish, can they take the "i" logo with them?' His answer was an unequivocal yes. Sounds like freedom to me." Then Gary asks you about this and you said, "No, no. Dave's full of shit."

McFarlane: I said he was full of *fucking* shit! [*Laughter*] I'm sure I said that. It's pretty funny because Gary quoted me all the way up to . . . he didn't quote me on that one, you know. Whatever. I mean, I talk a lot and I cuss a lot, but it's hard to figure—even out of context—how he would have gotten that. Gary decided to try and get me in trouble, so that's okay.

Salicrup: [*Laughter*] Well, what is the deal? Can—

McFarlane: No. As soon as I saw that—it was like, "Ah, Dave!" Either I didn't express myself correctly or he misinterpreted—either way, I didn't go and correct him. What I meant to say, or what I *thought* I said, was that anybody at Image, whatever they *create*, whatever they *do*, they *own*. If they decide to leave they can take every and anything *with* them. If they've created the Baxter Building, they can pull it right out of the Image Universe and we're going to have to go, "Uh oh, we've got a hole in the middle of Manhattan." They can take everything with them *except* the "i" logo.

Salicrup: A-ha! Okay.

McFarlane: It's a minor point, but it was a *big* minor point. [*Laughter*] Gary phoned me as soon as that letter came out. That issue came out and the phone rang and Gary was like, "I thought you told me that you couldn't take the 'i' with you!" I apologize, Gary. Fuck it.

Salicrup: So, you're saying if you wanted to quit Image, or say you got disgusted with Image and you took all their top artists and you left [*laughter*], you couldn't call it Image; you'd have to come up with another name?

McFarlane: Yeah. But I could take *Spawn* and all the background; I could take everything I've created. I couldn't call it Image, though, because otherwise we'd have twenty Images after a while.

Salicrup: What about the guest writers? Who owns their stuff? Are they working work-for-hire? What's the deal?

McFarlane: Well, I haven't made them sign contracts or anything, so I guess they could . . .

Salicrup: Oops. Todd?

McFarlane: . . .

Salicrup: You're breaking up a little bit.

McFarlane: It's not me. It's at your end.

Salicrup: It's the speaker phone. You're going in and out a little bit. But we'll keep going and let the poor transcriber worry about it.

McFarlane: Essentially, the way that I'm working is something like this: I divide the money up between the guy who writes, pencils, inks it, and the guy who created it, you know what I mean. And the guy who created it gets basically the least amount of it. So, if anybody decides to do an issue of *Spawn*, then I get a little piece just because of advertising, and I laid the groundwork, and I did the first twelve issues. I got . . .

Salicrup: There you go again.

McFarlane: . . . but other than that, you know, this isn't about money, it's about keeping the legend going.

Salicrup: What's in store in the future for Spawn? Isn't there a big project you're going to be doing and taking off a few issues?

McFarlane: I haven't, I'm, mmm—it depends on how things go. Originally, my game plan was to do, like, as close to twelve issues a year as possible. But that never meant that they'd all be *Spawn*, okay. *Spawn* is still my ace up my sleeve, but if I decide I want to go do a Violator miniseries I'll just take a couple of months off *Spawn*—but *I'll* be producing *work!* In other words, in April and May, instead of getting two issues of *Spawn*, you get two issues of something else, so essentially you'll still get twelve issues of McFarlane, it just might not be twelve issues of *Spawn* by McFarlane.

So, right now, I've got Alan Moore lined up to write a three-issue *Violator* miniseries, then it's just a matter of deciding whether I'm gonna go and do the artwork on that, and if I do that, then Bart Sears is going to take over *Spawn*. Instead of shutting down *Spawn*. . . . And if I decide that I want to stick on *Spawn*, then Bart will probably do the miniseries with Alan.

Salicrup: Well, why would you . . . why not shut down *Spawn*?

McFarlane: Why not shut down *Spawn*? I could. I probably would if I hadn't found people that I think can carry it on and not disrupt the flow of it. I've got Bart and I've got Grant, and I think the two of those guys doing a weird story for a couple of months isn't really going to affect the sales . . .

Salicrup: There you go again. [*Hits phone repeatedly*] Todd? Hold on.

McFarlane: I don't think it's going to hurt the sales, or the legend of it or something like that. So I'm *hoping* by the time I end up doing *The Violator*, if I decide to take off, the kids are going to want to still see *Spawn*, you know what I mean. My goal in breaking away isn't to be "Famous Amos" Todd McFarlane, I had enough of that on *Spider-Man*. My goal is to create characters that become bigger than me. So, if I can get to the point where if I leave *Spawn* for a couple of months and the book still does good, then that means they're buying it for *more* than just because Todd McFarlane's on it. They actually like the character. That's, in my point of view, what this whole game is all about right now; trying to come up with characters that sustain readers—then maybe I won't have to draw them for the rest of my life. [*Laughter*]

Salicrup: Was that always the game plan?

McFarlane: Well, I mean, we each have our own game plan, but *part* of the game plan was creating the next Superman, Batman, Mickey Mouse, you know. But *we'd* own it! Some of those guys have been around for fifty years, have long legs blah blah blah blah, but the guys who actually created those books aren't prospering, you know. If I create the next Mickey Mouse I'm going to profit, not no fucking . . .

Salicrup: There you go again. Hold on. Sorry about this. I don't know why my phone's acting up. [*Hits phone repeatedly*] I'll pound it into submission! Todd?

McFarlane: Hello, Dad! [*Laughter*]

Salicrup: Hey, Todd. How is the whole break from Malibu? Now in addition to writer, creator, penciller, inker, et cetera, you're also the publisher, right?

McFarlane: Not me personally, but Image Comics, yes.

Salicrup: Well technically, isn't that you?

McFarlane: I guess so, yeah, in a roundabout way. I'm *part* of it.

Salicrup: Well, I mean, you're going to be publishing some issues of *Spawn* that you're not doing. In a sense you've become the editor-publisher.

McFarlane: You betcha!

Salicrup: Owner. [*Laughter*]

McFarlane: You betcha!

Salicrup: How is the transition?

McFarlane: You know how I edit! [*Laughter*] I edit just like my good pal Jim Salicrup. I edit with *confidence* in my creative crew.

Salicrup: Well, then you won't have a long career, let me tell you.

McFarlane: What do you mean? You were there for a long time. [*Laughter*]

Salicrup: Well, tell me, what's going on now that you're on your own?

McFarlane: Now that I'm on my own there isn't a day that I don't thank my lucky stars. Things are *happening*! We've got deals upon deals, we've got freedom, we've got the most *fun* in the business! We are just having a big party over here. I've got total control over it, I'm working with some of the best guys in the business, we're just rockin' and rollin'! I just put to bed another big comic book deal that'll be announced here in about a week, so we're *killin'* 'em!

Salicrup: You can tell us. We won't tell anyone. This won't come out in a week.

McFarlane: I know, but if I tell you—I mean, it can't get out period.

Salicrup: Just tell us and it'll come out after it comes out anyway.

McFarlane: There's no loose lips in that office of yours?

Salicrup: Nope.

McFarlane: I just put together a *Batman and Spawn* team-up. The better part of it is the issue that I do, which doesn't tie into their issue. . . . Here's what the deal is: They get Spawn for one issue and they keep all of it; I get Batman for one issue and I keep all of it. For the first time in fifty years, Warner Bros. has allowed Batman to go outside DC's door and they don't get a penny for it.

Salicrup: Well, I can think of a card company that has the rights on the Batman cards.

McFarlane: That's the thing that I think is going to get complicated, is how do we handle the merchandise, how do we handle the rights of each character . . .

Salicrup: Todd? Hold on. [*Hits phone*]

McFarlane: I'm here.

Salicrup: Well, that's exciting. How did that come about?

McFarlane: It came about. . . . Since the Image group is a competitive lot, Rob and Jim are doing their crossover with Valiant, well the big Toddy couldn't stand still and just let them steal all the thunder now! No way! But on the other hand, I don't want to step on their toes, so basically they'll do their crossover and just when that's starting to fade from memory *Kaboomo!* Another big crossover with the name Image on it. So, we're going to be in the public eye here for the whole summer.

Salicrup: Okay!

The Peter David-Todd McFarlane Debate

GARY ST. LAWRENCE / 1993

From *Comics Buyer's Guide* 1, no. 1044 (November 1993): 92, 98, 102, 108, 113, 116. Reprinted by permission.

TOPIC: HAS IMAGE COMICS/TODD McFARLANE BEEN TREATED FAIRLY BY THE MEDIA?

Prologue: Moderator George Pérez (who filled in at the last minute for the ailing Don Thompson) dictated the rules of the debate as they applied to the debaters—and the rules for the audience against disruption, interruption, and behavior. Introducing the debaters to the standing-room-only crowd, Pérez explained the history behind the organization of the debate, events which led to it, and the format for the debate.

George Pérez: One thing I'd like to note is that I was asked to be the moderator for this debate, because Don Thompson, who was originally scheduled to be here, couldn't make it because of illness. For those of you who don't know who I am, my name is George Pérez. [*Audience applause*] I was asked to be the moderator from a list provided by Todd McFarlane which Peter David OK'd, as were the three judges who will be presiding over this debate.

This is a debate. It's not an audience participation sound-off. The reason I was asked to be here was to try to keep it as much like a debate. There is some flexibility that has been agreed to by both sides. Any time that you in the audience take away from the people who are answering their questions is irretrievable to them. And if somebody's heckling another person, that person will be ejected. We have people here around the room who will eject anyone disrupting the debate. People came here to hear two creators who've had disagreements in other forums who want to set the record straight.

95

There will be three questions provided by each of the debaters. Each of them was submitted to me. They were supposed to be submitted twenty-four hours in advance. Unfortunately, in the case of Mr. McFarlane, I just received his questions when I checked in today. [*Audience laughter*] So there may be a little bit of a slight rewording, but the questions have been OK'd.

Now, the first question will be addressed from Todd McFarlane to Peter David, who will be allowed three minutes to respond, timed from the moment he begins speaking. Then Mr. McFarlane will have two minutes for rebuttal. And Mr. David will have one minute to reply and summarize. Then the next question will be addressed from Peter David to Todd, and the same rules will apply. In all cases, I will be the one asking the actual questions for each of the respective debaters.

After the actual debate, there will be closing statements at three minutes apiece. The first speaker will be Peter David and then Todd McFarlane. Now, one of the concessions made is that, during the answers to the questions, it's fairly no-holds-barred. How the question is to be answered, whether it be verbally [or with] visual aids is strictly up to the debaters.

But, again, because it is the debaters who are rebutting, I don't want the response to be from the audience. If the response causes people in the audience to go crazy, the time is going to be taken away from the person who is speaking. So you won't have accomplished anything as far as getting the debate going, and you'll have basically ruined the debate as far as being a debate. I don't want this to be a circus.

When I took on this responsibility, it was reluctantly. It was kind of a sting to think of a convention appearance of getting a lot of people coming to a convention thinking they're going to see a bloodbath. This is a convention: Ostensibly we love the comics, we love the media that we're all in, and we're all trying to produce something that we like. There are bound to be disagreements. There's no reason for it to become a riot.

So, with that said, I'd like to introduce our three judges. As far as what the judges are going to do—to tell you the truth, I'm not sure and I don't know if they are, either. The judges are: from Wizard Press, William Christensen; from *Hero Illustrated*, John Danovich; and from *Comics Buyer's Guide*, Maggie Thompson.

As if you don't know who they are, I'll introduce our two debaters. [*Throughout the introduction, McFarlane is visibly undressing behind his podium and donning yellow boxer shorts and a bathrobe, slinging a towel so that it completely covers his head and shoulders.*] I'll do it alphabetically. He is the writer of *The Incredible Hulk* and *Sachs & Violens* and, more germane to this particular debate, the writer of the regular weekly column in *Comics Buyer's Guide*, *But I Digress*, Mr. Peter David. [*Audience ovation*]

And [*Pérez eyes McFarlane's new state of dress, including covered face.*]—this isn't a rebuttal yet! This wasn't the three minutes you were talking about, are they, Mr. McFarlane? [*McFarlane doesn't respond.*] And, if words don't fail me now, I guess visuals will have to. OK, the creator of *Spawn* and cofounder of Image Comics, and easily one of the more influential people in this business, Mr. Todd McFarlane. [*McFarlane turns on a boom box, which fails to play. He sits back down, without a word.*]

OK, now, there will be opening statements by the two debaters to discuss the question at hand to be debated: "Image/Todd McFarlane: Have they received fair treatment from the media?" That is the topic to be discussed. The opening statements will be five minutes apiece again, pretty much to be done with as the debater wishes. First up will be Mr. Peter David.

Peter David: Hi, thanks a lot for coming. Sorry about the game last night. Better luck next time.

Image Comics/Todd McFarlane: Have they received a fair shake from the media? Hell, no. Because "fair" means even-handed, fifty-fifty. The fact is that the vast, vast publicity about Image Comics has been uniformly positive, ranging from blurbs saying that the next Image book is going to be a hot collectible, to press releases or interviews originating from the Image creators.

And then there is my column, *But I Digress*—a column that was started by fan request, a column that readers have been following and trusting for over three years. And that is the reason I'm here today. Because I didn't want Todd McFarlane's posturing or insinuations to give anyone out there the thought that I was betraying that trust.

I do not consider trust to be silly. I don't think of it as humorous. And I don't think of it as something to be disposed of when you no longer need it. Now, out of 175 columns I have written, how many have focused on Image and Image personnel? The answer is, less than 4 percent. And some of it was positive. But it was this minuscule negative coverage, this one dot in the vast Seurat painting that is the Image bandwagon, that is being challenged here today. Because any negative viewpoint must be found and squashed immediately.

Now, I have watched Todd work audiences, and he is good. He is very, very good. Today *he* might go for the humble approach: [*Imitating McFarlane*] "Hey, we're just out to produce Image Comics and do the best comics we can, and what's wrong with that?" As if having good intentions means that. criticism is never fair or warranted. That line never works for Tom DeFalco [*Audience erupts in laughter*], never works for Bill Clinton. It's not going to work for Todd.

He may just try to annoy me. Now, the man who quit Marvel Comics because [*imitating Rodney Dangerfield*] he don't get no respect, is well-known for pushing and shoving people and calling them condescending little nicknames like "Petey" or "Johnny" and so on. Now, if you think that's funny, go ahead and laugh. Oh, and if you *also* think it's funny when he slams creators who trusted Image to do right by them, laugh at that, too, if you're not uncomfortable with it.

Or he may just say whatever it takes to make me look bad. In the most recent *Comics Buyer's Guide*, he warned me ungrammatically, "You aren't going to control this event the way you did during our year-and-a-half on *The Incredible Hulk*. Sorry, but I don't have to listen to your orders any longer." Now, you can ignore the mangled syntax, but you cannot ignore the insinuation. But if you're not going to ignore that, you should also not ignore what he told *Comics Journal* several years ago, and I apologize for the language. Quote: "The first time you accept any advice or criticism or whatever I have about your writing, I have to reciprocate and say that you can now change my artwork. And unfortunately, I'm not big enough of a man to have some [*expletive deleted*] writer change my artwork. So I go, no, I don't tell you how to write, and I'll be [*expletive deleted*] if you tell me to redraw a panel. And it worked. It worked for two years with Roy Thomas and for two years with Peter David."

Oh, and he also told *Comics Interview* that writers always came to him for opinions.

Those are the kind of facts that Todd is going to do everything he can—tricks, bells, whistles, props, whatever—to get you to ignore.

But here are three facts that I would like you to remember:

Number One: I have criticized Marvel and DC as frequently as I have Image. So any contention that I have singled Image out, for whatever nonsensical reason they will fabricate, is completely ridiculous.

Number Two: Todd implied that it takes no bravery to write an opinion column. Hey, I criticized my bosses, in print, where I know they'll read it! Todd and his brass band waited until they were gone from Marvel before bravely striking out at their former employers. Or at least writing critical essays and having the guts to sign their names to them. [*Audience ooohs and aaahs*]

Third: Todd has questioned the sources for my columns. Who have my sources been? Todd McFarlane, Rob Liefeld, Erik Larsen. All I did was hold up a mirror to them and they didn't like the image they saw. [*Audience ooohs and aaahs*] Their own words have made them look bad.

Now, if they don't like how they're coming across in public, then may I humbly suggest that they try giving some thought to what they say? And if they can't do their readers and their fans that small service, then maybe they might do us all a favor and shut the hell up. [*Audience ovation*]

Pérez: And now to open with his opening salvo, Mr. Todd McFarlane. [*Audience applause, Image-contracted Dallas Cowgirl cheerleaders cheering*]

Todd McFarlane: OK, let's dispel the first rule here. First off, Peter's gonna beat me to death here that I'm not a writer and that I don't know how to put syntax and grammar together and whatever else. That's not much of a debate, I don't think, and it's not much of an argument on his point. That'd be like me being a [base]ball player and Peter being a football player and me debating that he can't hit a curve ball as well as I do.

I'm an artist first. I'm a husband, you know, a friend to people, and a writer. Of all the things I do, I don't think that maybe my writing will ever catch up to where my art *has* maybe brought me to at this point. I think people have a little bit of a tough time separating Todd McFarlane the writer and Todd McFarlane the artist. But we are, in essence, two separate people.

Todd McFarlane, the guy who does *Spawn* comic books, is also different from Todd McFarlane who is a cofounder of Image Comics.

There seems to be a misconception about how Image Comics is run. When I talk in the public, I talk—unless the question is directly asked about Image Comics—I'm giving a Todd McFarlane response to the question. I'm not speaking for Image Comics. I don't have the *right* to speak for Image Comics. I can give my opinion, if I was in charge of Image Comics. But, ultimately, I'm just giving my opinion on what I have to say.

That I present it in an overzealous way—Yes, what the hell. I'm standing here in my shorts. Now, that doesn't mean that what I have to say has no value.

But let me also tell you this, I'll also dispel the biggest thing right now. Some of the interviews that he pulled out, the *Comics Journal* one, those are ghost personas that I put out there. [*David raises an eyebrow and shakes his head in his hand.*] I don't think that Peter was gullible enough to buy that, that there's two or three personas of Todd McFarlane out there and I'm amused at the professional community—not my young crowd out there that buys it, nor the young at heart, but *at the* professional community—who have not been able to decipher that the kid is just a freak of nature.

He's A) a hambone; B) he just likes to have fun up there; or C) he's just mentally deranged up there.

I'm telling you right now: I've been in this business now for almost ten years—I am doing exactly what I set out to do. When I broke into comic books, when I was twenty-three-years old, I said I want to get in because I like superhero comics and I want to have a hell of a time. And you know what? I still do superhero comics and I'm still having a hell of a time.

And you know what the problem is—the problem is that we as an industry have forgotten to laugh at ourselves. We're concerned about market shares. There's an explosion. There's a glut of stuff out there. We've got stock markets to answer to. We've got so many things to answer out there that people are not laughing at themselves anymore.

And if I've got to be the example out there, guys, if I've got to stand out here and tell you guys we've got to keep laughing—and if we *still* don't get it, you know what? The kids are getting it, because the kids are laughing along with me. And if I don't sign my name to an opinion column, well, if Petey—excuse me, Peter—if Peter had done his homework and had not just—

My biggest gripe with Peter is that he doesn't phone us. He has never once informed us or me personally on an opinion about Image. He hasn't phoned the office. I find it rather amusing that a professional journalist can do a story and not actually contact the sources themselves and ask them a direct question. That, that, I'm out there:

Yes people, I'm sorry that I'm a little bit arrogant at times. Maybe I'm a little bit crazy, whatever. But you know what? The people who say yes in this world do not change the system.

Now, whether you agree whether the system has been changed, there is free envy right now. There are new companies out there that are giving chances to Peter and many other people because, in a small way, of the existence of Image Comics.

Image Comics would not exist, if I'd said yes, if I'd played the way I was supposed to, if I'd dressed the way I was supposed to, if I drew the way I was supposed to. When I started Spider-Man, they beat me down because I had to conform to the look of that book. And I said, "No, fire me before I change that to the way that you want me to do it." But I've said no my whole life. I'm gonna continue to say no.

Now, I'm a crazy and I'm a kid. Go ask my kindergarten teacher. She'll tell you that I was a crazy kid and a hyperactive kid, too. But I want to tell you right now, I'm here and ready to debate Peter on whatever question he wants to give. But I'll tell you right now: I have a passion for comic books. I believe in comic books.

Is this to draw attention? No, this is for the good of comic books. We have a lot of panels and a lot of comics conventions out here. They're boring. I'm sorry, a lot of them are boring, if you've been to them. We've got a full room. We've got cameras here over a debate.

You know what? I don't see that that's a bad problem. And I'm gonna continue to keep doing that. Thank you.

Pérez: [*Repeating debate notes*] Now, these questions are provided, as I said before, are provided by the debaters themselves. And the first question will be from Todd McFarlane to Peter David, and he will have three minutes to respond. And then, as I mentioned, two minutes for rebuttal for Mr. McFarlane and then final reply and summarization from Mr. David. And the question, from Mr. McFarlane: How do you get your information as media, and do you contact the people you write about?

David: What I write is an *opinion* column. *But I Digress* has been and always will be something that is purely reactive. I see something that's out there and I comment on it.

Now, when Image put forward an opinion, what I'm doing is responding to that opinion. When they say, "We're going to do this," then I say, "If this, then that." When Erik Larsen writes, "Well, up until now, we've been holding back," I'm perfectly free to write a column that says, "What the hell do you mean by that? What have you been doing up until now, dogging it?"

Now, since I'm an opinion columnist and not a news writer, there's no onus upon me to pick up a phone and say, "You know, Erik, this makes no sense. Would you care to explain what the hell you meant?" No, the people who wrote the press releases for them should have done that. *Erik* should have done that.

What I do is I see the public face that they are presenting and I interpret it and I try to see if it holds up under logical scrutiny, which I'm sure is unfortunately what has probably confused my esteemed opponent. [*Audience laughter*]

Now, when Image first came out, the thing that they would all have you forget, is that when there was a gap in my knowledge about Image, namely the deal that was set up between them and Malibu, I called Dave Olbrich. I had a half-hour phone conversation with him to make sure that I got everything right, and I quoted him extensively, attributing it all to Dave. That is one of the, as I said, less than 4 percent of columns that I've written about them. Everything else is stuff that was taken from their own words. That is pretty much all I have to say on that, because I'd like to think that that is something which you can pretty much all grasp. It seems fairly straightforward to me.

McFarlane: You know, Peter, I don't really care that you want to put your opinions out there. We all give our opinions, some of us a little louder and some of us a little more helter skelter. [*David laughs mockingly*]

What I have a problem with is that some of the opinions, from my perspective, are lies. So that, if we don't check with our sources and we don't have to see if any of the stuff is right and we can hide behind the skirt that it was just an opinion, then what's the point of that opinion column, anyway? If you're gonna give an opinion of whether you like the Mets, then I think that's a solid opinion. But if you're gonna give an opinion on Doc Gooden, then somewhere along the line, you have to assimilate some of that information.

In the beginning of your column here—I didn't have to do that much research in some of your stuff because you, in your last couple of columns to the [*Comics Buyer's Guide*], you open up saying, "It would appear that I, who should have known better, have made the same foolish mistake that so many others have—I took Todd McFarlane at his word."

Now, maybe I'm a little simple and I might have read too much into this. But I read that as that you're calling me a liar. You're saying that I've out and out lied to people in this business.

Now, again, there is miscommunication on every level, and depending on what we say, there is two sides to the story. Unfortunately, whoever I've lied to, you obviously haven't got the other side of the story, or I've just out and out lied.

Now, what's today, Friday or something like that? OK, here's what I'm gonna do Petey—excuse me, Peter—I'm gonna go on record, we've got the cameras here: I'll put down $5,000 that'll go to the [Comic Book] Legal Defense Fund, so it'll go to a good charity here, if, other than Larry Stroman, who I had to tell a little fib to, if you can bring somebody in the next seven days that I've lied to in this business—boldface lied to, then you can take collect that $10,000 and give it to the Legal Defense Fund [*Audience laughter*]—What'd I say? Who?—$5,000, what the hell.

You bring that person, you let me give the other side, and if it comes up that I straight-out lied to that guy, you can have the money, because, you know what? I didn't lie to anybody out here. And if you can show them, that if, that if I—I got a problem with the way you word your opinion. So if we're just gonna start to give opinions. [*Pérez intervenes, as time has expired.*]

Pérez: Peter, obviously you have extra time to make your reply.

David: When I'm talking about telling lies—and, by the way, I should note that the piece that you're talking about in *CBG* ran *after* you issued the challenge for the lies I'd supposedly been telling. So I find it interesting that the best evidence you can pull out is something that happened *after* the challenge had already been issued.

In terms of lies, what I'm essentially referring to is—oh, let's see, for example, Todd McFarlane and his description of what he wants from life and what he expects out of comics. This, I would tend to think, relates to what the noncreators—nonoriginators, I should say—of Image heard when they got their books.

In *Comics Journal*, Todd said, "All I have to do is sell 5,000 copies of a comic and I would be happy because I'm doing comics." In *Hero Illustrated* #1, Todd said, "I knew we only had to sell 30,000 copies and we'd make a living." *Wizard* #27, "I'd rather have 100,000 copies of the books put into the right hands than have a million copies in the wrong people's hands." The numbers start to escalate, and yet, mysteriously, at the Chicago Comic-Con, when asked about the criteria for the reason those guys were let go, he stated, "We set a standard for ourselves in that the books had to sell 150,000 copies. And you know what? That's a great-selling book for any other company. We don't want their books."

Which brings us full circle to his *Comics Journal* question posed by Gary Groth: How do you measure success? And he responded, "It ain't in the number of copies I sell, I guarantee you."

I'm talking about internal logic. [*Audience ovation, whistles, etc.*]

Pérez: The next question is from Mr. David to Mr. McFarlane, which basically is going to follow the discussion we just had here. Mr. McFarlane, please tell us your definition of a lie, as opposed to an opinion you don't agree with, giving one example of each from *But I Digress* to illustrate.

McFarlane: My definition of a lie is probably not that far from most of the people in here, that a lie is the deliberate—the deliberate telling of something else that's not the truth.

Now, do people word things sometimes differently than they should? Yes. Is there mass miscommunication in *the* world? On every level.

That a person intentionally knows that the color of something is blue and goes out of his way to tell somebody that that's red: that's what I consider a lie.

If you want an example from *But I Digress*—because obviously I carry them on me at all times [*Audience laughs as David holds up several of his columns, offering them to McFarlane, who ignores him.*]—I'll see if I can pull it out right here, because I actually have them in memory.

You made mention that the way we let go of the people, and more importantly, our reasons for letting go of those people. One of the reasons why we let go of those people, and one of the reasons why we banded together, was over the issue of money. Now, I'm here to tell you people, whether you want to believe it or not—which is fine because, I mean, I've got a clear conscience—what I did and how I left Marvel comic books and what we do, it has nothing to do with money.

You know why? Because when I quit Marvel comic books, I'm telling you right now, I was the best-paid guy in this country. Now, if it was money, the stupidity of it would say: Why would the guy making the most money leave? Now he's saying the reason that we left Marvel comic books was over money and saying that we got dissed by Marvel Comics to the tune of six figures.

His attitude says that, because the world pays you a lot of money, you should take it. And I'm telling you: I don't care how much money they pay you; you don't have to take it. And you know what? Michael Jordan just proved that to me the other day. They paid him $26 million over the next three years, and it wasn't enough for him.

So, from your opinion of that we left for the money, I don't know where you based any of that, but I consider that a lie and not an opinion. Thank you.

David: I would really not want my esteemed opponent to go to the grave believing that—umm—

How many people have seen *The Fugitive*? Remember when Kimble says, "I didn't kill my wife," and Gerard says, "I don't care!" Todd has frequently, over and over again, stated that they didn't leave Marvel Comics for the money. *I don't care.* I have never said that you left purely because of money. Maybe in the Bizarro World column, I said it [*audience laughs*], but not in this one.

And to those of you who have been genuinely paying attention and have realized that what Todd said, in fact, made little to no sense, I can cite specific lies that Todd has said about me:

Number one: He said that I've been spreading lies about him. That's not true.

Number two: He stated that John Byrne and I were psychotic. [*Audience laughter*] Now, I assume that he could try and have lots of factual evidence to back this up, but I tend to think not.

If you're gonna slam people with psychological terms, here's the kind of thing you should do: Paralogical thinking—paralogia: false, illogical thinking found particularly in schizophrenic reactions. Paralogical thinking may take many forms. A patient who is preoccupied with his own subjective thoughts and fantasies may give answers to questions that are either wrong or beside the point. [*Audience erupts in hysterical laughter*] His interest in intentional analogous thinking becomes unrealistic and restricted.

Another characteristic of paralogia is its false, dream-like logic. In his study of schizophrenic thinking, Mueller, 1911, cited a patient who was convinced that he was Switzerland. [*Audience erupts in laughter again*] Such a false logic could not be entertained by the normal mind. But this patient's thinking followed the line: Switzerland loves freedom. I love freedom. I am Switzerland.

Ladies and gentlemen [*pointing to McFarlane*]—Switzerland! [*Audience roars with laughter*]

Pérez: [*Suppressing his laughter*] Mr. McFarlane?

McFarlane: He's good. [*Audience laughs*] Not even Rob Liefeld would have had a better chance.

David: Don't worry. He could've just repeated what you were saying . . . [*Pérez interrupts David, reminding him of the rules.*]

McFarlane: I don't know where you got that I said John Byrne or Peter David was psychotic. Obviously you're misreading into something or looking a little bit deeper. Every person that's named Petey or Johnny—obviously, you're paying far too close attention to what I'm doing out there. If you want to call me the psychotic, I'll be the psychotic. I'll be the bad guy in this. I'll be the guy who can't write. I'll be the guy who doesn't stand up for what he believes in. I'll be whatever you want me to be, Peter.

But I'm just saying that, in a crowd of a lot of professionals right now, you're standing here at a table with a guy that was at least stupid enough, I guess is the word, to debate somebody who I knew was gonna he able to use $5 words that probably I wouldn't be able to understand half of them. I mean, talk about *me* being able to play the audience; you're doing a great job, buddy.

And then, I'm just—I feel that I will put my neck out at any time when, as a company person, you can't. I think somewhere along the line, we have to acknowledge that at least, where we stand, and where I stand right now, I can at least give an opinion, even though I'm part of a company, where a lot of people right now are not entitled to that. But because of that, I'm allowed to be attacked. And I enjoy it. I bring it upon myself, and I thank you for disseminating what you have to the crowd.

Pérez: The following question is from Mr. McFarlane to Mr. David. This should be interesting [*audience laughs*]: What changes could Image, and, more importantly and specifically, Todd McFarlane personally, can they do today to satisfy you? *Keep* in mind that Image and Todd McFarlane are two different entities.

David: In order to satisfy me, make sense.

Thank you.

No. If you're waiting for me to put forward a list of things: Ship books on time; do this; do that; do the other thing, it's not for me to say. That is not what *But I Digress* is about. And since I'm here supposedly doing a column of *But I Digress* because Todd said he wanted this to be one of my columns, it's not for me to tell you guys what to do. What it *is* for me to do is wait and see what you do and then react to it and say this sounds cool or this doesn't . . .

However, I would really, strongly suggest, as I said in my opening statements, that what you try and do is give thought to what you're saying. Give thought to the way people are going to be reading it.

And try this: When you talk, or I should say *before* you talk, picture in your mind what it's going to look like on paper. And take it along those lines.

I learned this ten years ago when I was sales manager at Marvel, where I made a thoughtless remark about retailers that sounded OK when I said it, but I got pilloried in *CBG*. And I said, "Oh, God, I better not do that anymore."

Now, I've been pointing out that Image has been saying dumb things for a year and a half now, close to two years, and you still haven't gotten the hint. Now, if you wish to separate it, fine. I've criticized Todd. I've criticized Rob. I've criticized Erik. I never took a shot at Jim Lee. Why? *He didn't say anything dumb!*

Try it! Thank you. [*Audience laughs and applauds*]

Pérez: Gee, this is turning out to be more fun than I thought it was going to be. [*Audience laughs*] Mr. McFarlane, your reply now?

McFarlane: In terms of Jim Lee, may I tell you that all the rest of us ride Jim pretty much on a weekly basis, because he is so liked in this industry. We don't feel that to break out and to change the rules and to stand against a lot of the things that the system stands for, that they should actually *like* you. I don't think you're doing your job if the system that you hate now, that you want to break down and you want to change completely from head to toe, likes you.

He doesn't have to, really, for the most part, because he knows that, when we go to conventions, that Todd for the most part will go up there and make an idiot of himself, or Rob will make an idiot of himself, or somebody else. So he can stand it. That's his prerogative. He at least stands behind the convictions that we have and behind the opinions that we have.

Now, do you want me to get the books out on time? I don't have control over those books, Peter. I have control over *my* book. Is my book perfectly on time? No, I've never stated that it was.

Would I *like* to see those books out on time? Sure, I would. Would I like to see fifteen books or hardly any late books? Sure I would.

But, unfortunately, again the misconception is that Todd McFarlane has some kind of muscle pull on Image Comics. I have muscle pull on the *Spawn* comic and that's all that I can control. I can't control the other stuff.

But I can now be a better human being and present myself in a better way? Peter, I'm never going to do that. I say no to everything, and it's a bad attitude on my part. But it's probably I don't have that many people surrounding me.

One of the reasons why I didn't expand and I've only got *Spawn* and not twelve spinoffs [is that] I know my own idiosyncrasies and I've accepted those idiosyncrasies. But given that I know that I can't huddle around the people, I've been able to come up with enough friends around me that will stand by and say that the system that we fight against should not like us, and I hope the system never does like me, because then I know that I'm doing my *job*. [*Audience applause*]

David: Ahh, the cuckoo clocks are chiming in Switzerland. Only at Image could being liked be something that's a downer.

Possibly the reason that Jim is liked by the people is because he's courteous. Courteous does not require being an idiot.

You're not a fool, if you're not nasty to people. It's not that people react badly to Rob Liefeld and Todd McFarlane and Erik because they're saying no and taking strides and that kind of thing. They're reacting that way because you're saying and doing things that show a complete and total arrogance and disregard for anyone who is not you. And *that* is what is annoying people and *that* is what is upsetting people. You might try acting with that thing which you so stridently said in *CBG* that you believe in— *respect*. Thank you.

Pérez: The following question is from Mr. David to Mr. McFarlane: Please explain what you expected from the nonfounder titles, the Image nonfounder titles, in terms of quality and sales.

McFarlane: Uhh, we expected from them, the nonfounders—our satellite books or what did you mean?

Pérez: The ones done by the artists that weren't the actual founders of Image: Jerry Ordway, Larry Stroman, Mike Grell—

McFarlane: What we expected was, we started out a company and we took on all the responsibilities, and whether that was right or wrong, that was a lot for us to handle. That our books started coming out late, and that people started going off in different directions, was just part of the process. Some of us reacted a little better than others, but for the most part, we all had troubles.

What we expected when we hired these people was that they'd come in there and be the anchors, because nobody was putting down any anchors for the company. We were floating around. We were putting out a miniseries here and something out there and trying to feel our way around. We knew that we couldn't do it at that time, because we were trying to handle the whole publishing, printing, advertising, and everything else.

We then said we have to bring in a couple of books that will then anchor us down and at least be, quote unquote, our Iron Mans, Captain Americas, and Thors. What we wanted from them was not just good-looking books. What we wanted from them was *on-time* books, because, as we told them, we turn out, I feel, some of the best *late* books in the business. So we don't need any more good-looking late books. We do plenty of those books.

We expected on-time performance from them and we expected a certain sales level, and, from nonfounder books—

(Because, unfortunately, can Todd McFarlane still sell 5,000 and not get fired? Yes. You know why? Because unfortunately, Peter, in most businesses, the bosses can't get fired. We own the company. We can't fire ourselves. We've now just recently put in rules where we *can* fire ourselves. [*Audience laughs*] So, you know, stay calm, because we now feel that it's somewhat hypocritical that we should be attentive.)

But there are different rules to us. But they also have a bad attitude? I don't care if they have a bad attitude and they sell a million comic books, I will not put up with a guy out there who's using our name, ruins our reputation, as good or bad as it is and sitting there saying we're going to take your cash, we're gonna take everything you've done. You guys stuck out your neck, and, but we're not gonna perform. We're gonna promise you a monthly book, but we're not gonna do it. We're gonna promise you this, and we're not gonna do it.

We had to lay some ground rules, and the people who didn't fit in the ground rules, unfortunately, got the axe. I'm sorry, but they didn't follow the rules. They got the axe.

Pérez: Mr. David?

David: You said that a number of times in past meetings that you did this, and you produce late books, and that's easy. You know. So why do you need these guys to do it for?

The thing that you were missing, Todd, is that you sent a message, a signal, a sign, to fellow creators in the industry. What you said to you was: At Image Comics, we will take our time to get the books right. That was the message you sent to them. It doesn't matter at this point whether late books are good or bad. Nobody's going to say late books are good. But you have to take responsibility for having sent that message out to the creators.

And they take Image, believing that they were going to get the same kind of equal treatment that they were going to be promised by you guys. They thought that your respect column applied to them, and it didn't. You didn't just fire them, Todd. You *betrayed* them.

McFarlane: Peter, I see it, see, but, you're, you're not there, and that's your opinion and I appreciate that.

But I see it quite the opposite. We put the word out that we wanted people to come. The people who said, "Todd, we want to do a miniseries and it'd take us ninety days between each issue." A) They either, we said, "Yeah, good. You got ninety days. We'll hold it back." Or B) we go, "No, ninety days isn't good enough. We want to try and get monthly."

So the people whose stuff we accepted didn't come to us saying, "Todd, you just want to put out a book; let us print it." They came up to us promising they would turn out regular monthly books. That's the promise they made to us.

Once they made that promise to us, we told them even—because we are pretty tough guys—between monthly books, you have forty-two days between monthly books to get in the next issue. So we gave them six weeks to hand in a monthly book. Again, all of them failed to do that.

Did we do that? Yes, like I said, we just laid in the rules to be able to start to fire us. But they were the first ones who came to us who said, "We will give you a monthly book. We will do this. Let us join." And, when we let them join, *they* were the ones who betrayed us, because they didn't come and give us what we contracted out to them to do, which was a book and a book on a monthly basis.

And, when they didn't give it to us and they went past the forty-two days, we got rid of them. I don't see where that's betrayal. I see that as they promised us something and they didn't deliver. [*Audience applauds*]

Pérez: This question is from Mr. McFarlane to Mr. David. I'm going to have to alter it a little. Otherwise it's going to be a little hard to get out. What is wrong with the writing of Todd McFarlane and with *Spawn* in general that you would suggest be changed?

David: I'm not quite sure what the hell this even remotely has to do with whether Image has received fair treatment or not. But, since you asked, I don't generally read *Spawn*.

Now, you will notice that never in my columns have I criticized *Spawn*. I think that Todd's writing, based on what he did in *Spider-Man*, was fairly poor. I base that on several combinations of structure and characterization.

If I'm really going to talk about writing, I do seminars that run about three to four hours. Three to four minutes is not going to cover it.

What I would like to see in Todd's work, should I ever really sit down and read it again, is story structure having to do with first- and second-act turning points, having hills and valleys, and building ideally to a climax with the concept of what anticlimax is like.

I'd like to see characters that ring true, that build some sort of central core, that relate to the real world and relate to me, that I care about.

Now, unfortunately, I'm not Todd's target audience. Because Todd's target audience is twelve- to fourteen-year-olds. This is not a slam. This is what he said, and that's fine. Anybody can write to a particular target audience. However, I think even twelve- to fourteen-year-olds certainly have the right to well-constructed stories.

I really don't want to stand here and describe the Peter David way of writing. I certainly would like to see more of a sense of humor. I would like to see a sense of things being thought out properly. Things never seem to be, in a lot of comic books, really thought out.

It really puts me in the mind of a book that Scott McCloud did some years back called *Destroy!* How many people remember that one? Now, *Destroy!* was this great big book involving this great big character who smashes everything in sight until the book ends.

When it first came out, this was funny! Now *it's typical*.

Everybody's going "Oooooh." This isn't particularly aimed just at Image. That is aimed at the vast majority of stuff that we see coming out. Quality story lines that really hang together, that have a beginning, middle, and end, are too few and far between.

It can be done! Superman's line has certainly proven that. It can be done. I would just like to see it done a little *bit more*. I'd like to see more thought and more intelligence put into things. That's pretty much *it*. [*David begins to sit, but stands again.*]

Oh, I'm sorry. I should have mentioned this, also: And *read!* I see people who say they want to be writers, and they don't read. I'm not just talking about reading comic books. I'm talking about reading books, novels, histories, anthologies, biographies—things to be drawn from the real world. That's at least how I would do it. Because once you bring that real-world feeling to a comic book, it then rings true to the reader and makes them more involved in what's going on. It feels right.

McFarlane: OK, Pete. I'm going to do all that and then we'll be going head to head in the *CBG* awards for the writers. Thanks, you just gave it to me. That's all I *need*. [*Audience laughs*]

The writing part that I do, again, like I said, is, it was a trial period for me to do. Now, I guess it can be argued, and I've heard it stated before by you, that if you then, were to become an artist, you'd have to hand in art samples. It only follows logic then, that as a writer, you should have to hand in writing samples.

I ended up building a bit of a reputation with my editor, Jim Salicrup, on *Spider-Man* and, through the years that I spent with him and discussing ideas back and forth, he was willing to give me a chance to try and prove whether I could do something. That it wasn't so much that I thought that I could write the books *per se*. But it was that I wanted to visually draw the stories that I had in my head.

Now, we did go back and forth saying, "Todd, why don't you just plot them, and why don't we get a scripter in there?" We thought about that long and hard, and for a short time there was actually going to be a scripter on the

Spider-Man stuff. The only reason we didn't go to it was, again, because knowing my idiosyncrasies I knew that, after five or six months, I was going to get frustrated again.

Whether that was the writer's fault or that was my fault, I would sit there and go, "Awww, I would've put this. I would've put that. Duh duh duh duh duh."

So Jim and I then came to the conclusion that the best thing to do was cut out the middle step. He gave me a ball and he said, "Here it is. Go play with it. And I hope that you bounce it the right way."

I tried, at the beginning—and, yes, it was a weak effort from the very beginning. But I think that, again, maybe you should go and read some of the comic books that I've done. I don't think, I don't think that, that the opinion you probably heard, from the peers, that it's actually the worst comic book out there. I don't think it's the best. But I think it's probably somewhere in between.

If you guys was to give me a little bit of insight, instead of just saying, "Todd, why don't you do this? Why don't you do that?" I'm always open. But one of the things that never happened at Marvel or from any of my peers isn't, "Todd, as a writer, why don't I give you some advice?"

Me, as an artist, when I have people coming up to me, showing me their portfolios, I'm always giving artistic opinions. I'm always trying to help people on how to do something and giving them an opinion. But I've yet to have a writer come up to me, though, and say, "Todd, as a friend to you, let me see if we can't correct some of this." Some of the writers I've worked with on *Spawn*, luckily, have done that. And I'm hoping to improve on this. Thank you.

David: Well, Todd, considering that at several times in several different places you've said repeatedly that you don't want people telling you what to do—Now, I don't know whether that was the "Ghost Todd" or the "Real Todd" or the "Space Todd" or whatever it is we're dealing with.

The problem is that you've gone on record as saying that, "I didn't let a little thing like not being able to write stop me." Now, this doesn't set up a tremendous venue in terms of an exchange of ideas. You have said repeatedly that that's not the help you want.

As a matter of fact, you said that, after three issues of *Spawn*, your wife quit as editor because you wouldn't listen to what *she* said. [Unless] you really will take from what I have to say more strongly than [from your] wife, I think we have a slight problem. Thank you.

Pérez: We're getting a little short on time. So we're going to get a little more strict on the time limits here. OK, the question from Peter David to Todd McFarlane: How do you claim the moral high ground in your landmark column about respect? Please explain how the treatment of freelancers by Image is appreciably superior to that of Marvel. [*Audience ooohs and aaahs*]

McFarlane: If you read the column and read my opinions on why I quit Marvel Comics, I'm gonna tell you guys right here, because, again, obviously, you've missed the point. It wasn't money.

As a creative person, you want to create. You want to do comic books and you see them in a vision of your own. When you start to get people around you all of a sudden saying, "Todd, here. Or Bill, here. Or John, here. Here's a book. It's not selling very well. Go and do whatever you want." There's minimal amount of interference on that book. Because as creative people, we like to take an underdog approach.

So we take a book and, as we build the momentum on the book, at some point, the companies want to jump on and start to guide that train. It was only going five miles an hour when you jumped on it. They didn't care about it. But as soon as you get it going up to a hundred miles an hour, all of a sudden they want to become the conductor. That's why I ended up quitting.

The *Spider-Man*, the popularity of *Spider-Man became* the status quo. Don't mess with it. You can't do this with it. You might offend people.

Your audience is so big now, Todd, that you might say something wrong. So that, all of a sudden, I have to be guilty of my *success*. [*David, Pérez, and much of the audience look extremely confused.*]

The people who were coming up to Image Comics, I can guarantee you to the person: Jerry Ordway? I've never had one conversation with the man to tell him anything about how to do his work. We said, "Here's your deadline. Here's the book. Here's where the printer's gotta be. We've gotta get the book." I've never given him one word to say this is how you have to draw. This is how you have to fit into Image. This is how you've gotta do that,

Al Gordon—not one.

Bill Loebs—not one.

Sam Kieth—not one.

What we have given is not a haven to run helter-skelter on deadline. But a haven for those who will play and have a bit of an attitude and have a good attitude about it—is a haven to create as you see fit completely, from beginning to end, on that book, that fits into the Image universe, and, as a book that we don't have a problem with.

And we're never going to tell you, Peter, if you do a book for Image, how to do anything on your book, other than to get it on time. Thank you.

David: What is really kind of unfortunate, in my opinion, about the way Image is set up is that you've totally dismissed the notion that perhaps an outside eye or another opinion can sometimes improve a book. Not always. It's a system that cuts both ways. Sometimes it can hurt a book, as well. But a certain amount is owed to the readers, to try to get the best product out there as possible.

Now, the problem is that you can say as much as you want, "Oh, we won't tell people how to do a book." That's great. That's fine. Sometimes, they might need the help. But even so, if they don't, that's fine, too. They should feel bound to do whatever they want, within limits. And, apparently, the limits you have set are within the confines of the Image universe.

I'm sorry, but I find that to be slightly contradictory: that, if you're going to say to someone, "You can do whatever you want," then let them do whatever they want. If you're going to say, "You can do whatever you want, within the confines of the Image universe," you're not allowing them the freedom they're entitled to as creators. You can't have it both ways.

McFarlane: Peter, we never asked for it to be both ways, bud. We've opened up the doors, even to Mr. Pérez here. We made the offer to him long ago. And one of his reasons for not joining Image was he wanted to be able to blow up the planet.

Nobody has come up to us—[*Pérez mugs to the audience, eliciting laughter*]. We wanted him to be able to blow up the plane, but not kill our guys. And our response was back then, as it is ultimately, was you can blow up the planet. *Legends* is now doing that. You can have your own little universe. What we're looking for is that little emblem up in the corner.

What ended up happening wasn't so much that people were going, "I don't want to play *in* my own universe," and now all of a sudden, we're saying, "No, you've got to play in the universe": They came to us specifically saying, "We will do a monthly book, and we want to interact with *WildC.A.T.s*. We want to interact with *Spawn*. And we want to interact with this stuff."

Getting into the book, all of a sudden, they started going into different directions—and, actually, it wasn't even so much the content again, Peter. It came down to the promise they made to us of bringing an anchor to us and giving us some stability that they reneged on.

Pérez: Thank you. Now we're going to have the closing statements from each of the debaters. I want to thank the audience for really showing *an incredible* amount of control [*audience laughter*] and to the two debaters who actually did keep this running smoothly and within the confines of a debate, with a few little flourishes added in to make it nice and spicy.

The first closing statement will be from Mr. Peter David.

David: *Sachs & Violens* #2 is going to be a couple of weeks late. [*Audience roars with laughter*]

Now, George and I signed a contract with Marvel Comics and Epic. They didn't take us to the cleaners. They could cancel the book. They could demand money back. They could do all kinds of horrible things to us. Instead, what Marie Jenkins said to us was, "Look, just get the book out as soon as you can. We believe in the quality of the book, and we want to see the best job possible. And, if it takes an additional week or two or three, get it done, and have it come out when it's ready."

That is the cherished respect for freelancers that Todd McFarlane put forward so many months ago in *CBG* and which, to a very large extent, Image has not really been able to live up to.

They may have set goals that were too high for themselves. That's not a crime. There's no crime in that.

What *is* a crime is to state that I have been putting forward lies and rumors about them and, when asked point-blank to name one, ultimately, Todd couldn't. That is what you should be concentrating on here today: that the reason for this debate is a nonexistent one. There is no reason for everyone to be here.

I'm glad that you had a good time. I'm glad you enjoyed it. But I, personally, don't like having my veracity put on the line, in print, and then, when asked to present any serious challenge to it, we get *nothing*.

Nothing.

I, personally, am just a touch offended by that.

I would also like to thank the judges for showing up and doing this silly job. And George Pérez for standing in at the last moment. And all of you. I certainly hope that the Phillies do the job for you.

OK, seventh game of the championship series, bottom of the ninth, four to three, Phillies down, Dykstra at the plate, bases loaded, two outs, three and two, pitch in the dirt. Dykstra swings at it. [*Audience laughs*]

Now, do you sit there in the audience and say, "Well, you know, he had really had good intentions"?

Or do you say, "Dykstra, *you moron!*"

And—if he's there in the evening on the TV news saying, "You know, I really went out there and I had the best of intentions, and it's tough out there and—Gee, I don't see why everyone's picking on me"—would you say, "He's got a point"?

Or would you say, "My heavens, what a mewling, spewing little crybaby"?

Thank you. [*Audience ovation*]

Pérez: I had no idea where he was going with that.

And now, for the last words: Todd McFarlane.

McFarlane: OK, using the Lenny Dykstra.

OK, we'll be Lenny Dykstra and we swing at the ball in the dirt. But the point is: At least we got to the point where we're in the playoffs.

Now, I find that what happened was, when I first started to think about Image Comics with Rob Liefeld and Erik Larsen, we were the three spearheads. My idea was that we wanted to have a union. I just felt that the working conditions, in terms of both pay, the way that we were giving information to the companies, the way that they asked for information from us, was not right.

When we went into the office with Terry Stewart that fateful day in December to quit, his opinion and his quote to us was, "It's an entertainment business, and this is how it's always been. We exploit you and it will always be that we will exploit you." And for Tom DeFalco, "What was good enough for me, why shouldn't it be good enough for you?"

Using that mentality, folks, we would still have people of the black persuasion in the back of the bus. You know why? Because it would have been easy for us to say, "That's the way it is. That's the way it's always gonna be."

Well, I'm here to say that that's wrong. That we can do things, and justify them on a business means, is completely wrong. That we now exist, and we are open now to criticism. We're opened up to criticism, first and foremost, that we should at least have an acknowledgment that we even exist. That, that, there's the respect now that they get to hand out their books two weeks late?

I feel that, in some small way, is because of the response of the other companies—Defiant and Valiant and Image Comics and Legend and Dark Horse, that have now come out, and the Ultraverse—and have now ruined it for staying the same, that the creative people can now take back what is now rightfully theirs.

As far as some of the opinions that I give, and provement of your lies, Peter, you and your *CBG* columns (I don't carry those *CBG* columns, excuse me, I don't carry those *CBG* columns with me), that I am afraid, and shunned down on people who give their opinions and won't sign their names to it—if you'd made a phone call, you would see that I now have a column in the *Wizard* that's an opinion column not unlike your own. So that thing that you say that I dislike so much has now become something that I now do. So, once again, you jumped the gun without checking the facts, of telling me, "Todd, this is what you do," without ever checking exactly what it is that Todd McFarlane does.

As far as Image Comic books, from the union point of view: You know what, folks? The creative people, we found out, they didn't want to be saved. They were afraid. They believed the lies. They were brainwashed.

Come on, you *can* come out. You can come out of the game and survive. No, we don't want to come. We don't want to do it. We want *you* guys to go out there, stick your necks out, do it, see if you can survive, see if you get chopped or just get mildly bloody. And then, if you guys still survive, we would then love to come and join you.

Well, you know what? We're having a good time right now and we're not inclined now to slow down for those guys who didn't have the guts to come out and join us.

Some of the fringe players, like the Alan Moores and the Frank Millers, they've always been fighting for those rights. We have a good time and we see on the same level of trying to expand the market in terms of books like the *Legends* and having books that have their own copyright. And from that point of view, we have to acknowledge that the existence of our company now, Peter, has done the creative company that seemed to hate us more than anybody, a little bit of good in the free agent market.

Thank you.

Pérez: I'd like to thank Todd McFarlane and Peter David. Now, as was discussed in the organizing of the debate, we have three judges. Truth to tell, neither the judges nor I realize what the judges were supposed to do. So, by discussing with them, it's going to be very brief, and each judge has a statement to make, and from that I guess the consensus will be made. Since I introduced them alphabetically, I'll start backwards alphabetically, and I know Maggie hates that—Maggie Thompson of *CBG*.

Thompson: OK, we've heard two creators with different skills. They're both obviously entertainers. They've both obviously entertained us. We had a wonderful time. All the judges want to thank them for these great seats. [*Audience laughs*]

The question was whether the media have treated Image and Todd fairly, and I think the media provide an ongoing process and this event is one of those processes. I think they've presented themselves the way they wish to be presented, and so that's fair.

Pérez: Now, you're going second, no matter how it's handled, John Danovich, from *Hero Illustrated*.

Danovich: Unlike Maggie, I can't say I appreciated the *view*. [*He sat directly behind George Pérez throughout the debate. Audience laughs; Pérez scowls.*]

What we had here was a debate based on opinion for the most part. And opinion cannot be wrong. It is merely opinion. Peter's opinion cannot be wrong in the fact that it's his opinion. It can be misguided. It might be misinformed. Nonetheless, it's opinion.

On the other hand, a book like *Sachs & Violens* getting the respect that wasn't there in the past is due in part to what Todd and Image have accomplished.

In this debate, I'd like to use Peter's example of the Phillies down, four to three, bottom of the ninth, Dykstra at bat, three-two count, pitch is in the dirt, and Dykstra swings.

Only in baseball, you can advance to first, the runner scores. It's a tie game.

Pérez: And to answer the question of have they received fair treatment from the media? [*Audience laughs*]

David: Looks like the catcher picked up the ball and threw to first. [*Audience roars*]

Danovich: The media [are] not being represented by an opinion column. If you're talking about the media and the facts, that is not what's been debated here. It's a tie; there is no winner.

Pérez: William Christensen from the Wizard Press.

William Christensen: See, I came very unprepared for this. I was expecting the steel cage bloodmatch. And I came primarily to see Peter donning the shorts and gloves.

Pérez: Only Todd would really have looked good in the shorts. [*Audience roars*]

David: Glass houses, sweetheart! [*More laughter*]

Christensen: In terms of the media and whether they've treated Image, and Todd especially, fairly: Clearly, they've gotten lots of media coverage. And one of the best things about columns like Peter's is that we can see sometimes what is not necessarily clear to both sides. We get to see what other people think of what Image is actually doing. Part of that fairness is making sure that everyone knows everything they can about Image, and all the pros and cons, and what they're doing, is that we have people who will stand up and say, "Look, I don't like this and I think this is wrong."

And I think that Image has been treated fairly. And I think that part of that is due to people like Peter, who will stand up and put their neck out on the chopping block, like was done here today, and say that they think Image was wrong in something.

Pérez: Basically, if we are to rely on the opinions of the judges, and that's what this whole thing was about, we'll have to agree that your opinion will always be your opinion.

You may think this was all a waste of time.

You may have had your opinions set before it started. You may have changed them, you may not have. That's your prerogative.

If we have to make any kind of judgment call, two out of three judges say that there has been fair treatment, because there has been both positive and negative treatment of Image in the media, of which the *But I Digress* column is [representative of] but one of many, many periodicals that are out there.

And, thus, media cannot be described or measured just by one column. And if you're going to be talking about the media, the consensus is "fair."

Again, thank you all for your decorum. Thank you all for making this debate a success.

Peter David, Todd McFarlane, and George Pérez all shook hands and mugged for cameras after the debate.

McFarlane Speaks Out

ROBERT J. SODARO / 1993

From *Hero Illustrated* 1, no. 1 (July 1993): 44–47. Reprinted by permission.

From his early days on Spider-Man *to his megastar as Image Comics' cofounder and all-around hot shot, the awesome creator of Spawn gives* Hero *readers his insight into the comics industry.*

Today it is difficult to have a discussion in this industry, with fans or pros, where the name Image doesn't come up.

McFarlane has his own, rather boisterous views on the subject, and he recently expounded on them at length in this exclusive interview. One thing is certain. You don't have to like him, his comic, or even the company they own, but you have to give credit where credit is due. Image has forever changed the way the comic book industry works. They have not only proven that the creators are every bit as important to the fans as the creations, but they proved that there is a market for superheroes not associated with Marvel or DC. They turned the entire industry on its collective ear, and made everyone sit up and take notice of what they are doing.

Hero Illustrated: Were you surprised by the phenomenal success of *Spawn* and Image? Can you honestly say, "Yes, I expected to be this big," or is it even bigger than you thought it was going to be?

Todd McFarlane: I think what surprised me is the across-the-board success of it. I had a certain reputation, and if anything, I'm probably too overconfident. I didn't have any problems thinking I could sell a comic book. I guess what surprises me is that people are buying the entire line now. They are buying other guys who maybe didn't get the chance to establish themselves quite as well as we did before they jumped ship, so to speak.

Hero: When you guys started out, you were all considered hot-shot, snot-nosed, punk kids. All ego. All flash, and no form. Style over substance. Now you have Alan Moore, Steve Bissette, Dave Gibbons, Mike Grell, Jerry Ordway, you've got established guys who have been doing this years and years.

McFarlane: The reality of it is that those guys will never carry the line for us, so we do a lot of flash, you're right, we do a lot of that. Unfortunately, it's what sells comic books today. Do I think Alan Moore is a better writer than me? Sure I do.

We're trying to bring the guys on, given that push comes to shove and we have to put out another flashy comic book to keep the line going. God forbid, if it ever got to that point, we would take the flash, because the flash would sell. I know what you're trying to get at . . . and it's kind of frustrating . . . those guys don't sell as well or better than us so that critics could basically show that we're frauds.

Hero: Do you think that attracting those people to the Image banner has given you credibility with professionals?

McFarlane: I think it's given us credibility amongst some of our peers and some of the critics, but ultimately, screw our peers and screw the critics. We didn't bring those guys in so the guys who hate us would like us. I don't care about that. I didn't get Alan Moore because of the guys who were writing rumors about us. I got Alan Moore because he's a good writer. We got Mike Grell because I like his work. There wasn't any, "This is the right guy to get because he's critically acclaimed." We just got people who we thought would do good comic books for us. Some of them don't do the same exact stuff we do, but it wasn't really that deep of a thought process, to tell the truth.

Hero: These guys are proven quantities, but isn't it cool that you can hire someone who you respect, and you get to send them a big check?

McFarlane: I take pride in the fact that, to the critics or whoever is bellyaching about the flash and substance, I go, "Guys, there's a character called Spider-Man, and Batman, and Wolverine, and Superman, and all the big guys—four writers that I put together—*those four guys have never done one character.*" Somewhere along the line, either I just happened to be the nicest guy on the planet, or they saw something in the character, or hopefully, it was a bit of both. They kind of liked me, they saw a little bit in the character. I'm proud of the fact that I could attract those guys to this character, more than anything else.

Hero: There's a perception that when someone got into comics, they got work at an independent and then graduated to DC. Then, if you were really good, you got to work at Marvel. The way you guys have been raiding artists over at Marvel, it's like Marvel is your farm team.

McFarlane: In all honesty, I think anybody who does an Image book and then has to go someplace else is going backwards. In terms of getting the quality paperwork and printing and computer-generated colors, in terms of getting as wide an audience as possible, in terms of getting a financial reward for the work you put in from nine to five, nobody can beat us. So if greater freedom and quality of printing and getting a decent paycheck mean anything, which I hope is somewhat part of why most of us are doing it, nobody can beat us. I think we are the major leagues and with any other company, you have to take less. Any one of those three objects or in most cases, all three of them. Less freedom, less quality in the actual product, in terms of the reproduction, and less in terms of a paycheck. You're going down on all of those.

Hero: As much as someone might like doing a particular character, it's gonna come to a point in time, where a creator is going to have to say, "Yes, I like doing this guy but if I go over here and do this, I'm gonna make more money." After all, we're all in business to make money.

McFarlane: I guess so, except for the one misconception about us, is when I quit Marvel, without a doubt, I was the best-paid guy in the country. Now why would I leave if I was the best-paid guy in the country? People think we want to do this because we're money-grubbers, if anybody had a reason to stay, it was me. I'm the king. I'm the king at least at counting how many zeroes come in on the paycheck. I quit because I couldn't take it creatively. I think that creative people get to the point where they're just fed up with the system and want to go and do creative stuff their own way. I don't care if anyone agrees with what he puts on paper. Personally he would be happier, and if he made a quarter of what he was making elsewhere, it would be irrelevant. Did I think we'd be selling a zillion copies every single month? Nah. I knew that we only had to sell 30,000 copies and we'd make a living. I was so frustrated with the system at that point, that to me, I'd rather sell 30,000 books and put some fun back into my job, because they sucked the energy out of me. The money was irrelevant; I couldn't spend what they were giving me. We are successful, and money is irrelevant. I couldn't stress that more, because every time I get on the phone with somebody, they think that's why we left. If they took every single dollar I've ever made, and every single interview, and all the fame and all the fortune, if I just became Todd the shmoe again, I still would be doing comic books. If you were doing the exact same job tomorrow, and it was selling fifty-two million copies, and all of a sudden you got a big paycheck, they think that you're doing something different.

Hero: So what you're saying is, "Doing what I'm doing and getting well-paid for it, is not selling out, it's just doing what I'm doing?"

McFarlane: That's the American way.

HERO EXCLUSIVE! SPAWN BATMAN CROSSOVER!

During the course of this interview Todd let it slip that he is working on what could ultimately prove to be one of the hottest crossovers of all time . . . *Spawn/Batman*!

The excitement generated by the crossover between the dark one and the Dark Knight will undoubtedly have the entire comics world buzzing in the months to come—but *Hero* has the exclusive now!

Both Todd and DC are decidedly tight-lipped about the specifics of the project, but they are more than willing to let people get excited about the possibilities and potential of the crossover.

Although it couldn't be confirmed at press time, it appears that McFarlane may be given complete creative control over the project to ensure that his vision is properly rendered in the final product.

Will we see Batman tracking down Spawn? Maybe the Caped Crusader will find himself in the middle of a battle between Spawn and other characters that inhabit the Image universe! Whatever the circumstances, this one is going to sizzle mucho big time!

Todd McFarlane

MARK LUCAS / 1994

From *Comics Interview* 1, no. 129 (1994): 28–51. Reprinted by permission of Jennifer Bush-Kraft, administrator, estate of David Anthony Kraft.

Ask a comics fan who the current "hot" creators are and he'll undoubtedly name Todd McFarlane almost immediately. As one of the industry's most outspoken figures, Todd is also one of the industry's most influential talents, an individual who's risen to heights of superstardom in the comics industry undreamt of just a few years ago. From his early work on Batman to his redefining role on Spider-Man to his current efforts with his own creation, Spawn, McFarlane has steadily built a large fan following with his own individual style. Nevertheless, he's been consistently criticized for his public statements and actions. Todd sat down with us to set the record straight, to discuss his public image, the state of the comics industry, the future of Spawn, and the upcoming *Spawn/Batman* crossover he's working on with Frank Miller . . .

Mark Lucas: *Spawn/Batman*—why this project? Why now?

Todd McFarlane: At the first San Diego Con after I left Marvel, I remember some of the guys at Image and Bob Wayne at DC announced an Image/DC crossover coming. This was three years ago. I was the only guy out of the group going. "I'm not going to do no crossovers," because when we broke away [from Marvel], I was pretty militant. I wasn't going to work for anybody, no how, no way. I'm going to stay here. Later on, the guys at Image did some stuff with Valiant, which was the *Deathmate* crossover. They wanted me to do that one too and, again, I was, "I'm not going to work for anybody else. Why would I want to put money in anybody else's pocket?" About the time that *Deathmate* got rolling along, I had a conversation with Neal Adams. Neal in some respects fought for some of the same things that I did, told me that, when he was trying to start his union years ago (he was somewhat "militant" too), he passed up opportunities to do stuff. Forget where the money was going to, forget who he worked for, it would have been creatively kind of cool to do it. He said he passed up some fun projects. This from a guy now saying that in hindsight. I was thinking, "Hmmm. Good working advice." I'd hate to be there forty years old one day going, "I could have done all these cool things." At that time I said, "Okay, I can do the Valiant thing." But it was already underway, so I went to find something that would be more to my liking anyway. The Valiant characters I know nothing about. The obvious choice at that point was to go for somebody big. I knew Marvel wasn't really in the mood to talk to me. The only other character I'd have an interest in doing was Batman. So, I went for the jugular. If you're going to crossover, crossover big.

Lucas: Did you approach them or they approach you?

McFarlane: I phoned them up with a deal that, basically, they do a book, they get Spawn, they get to do whatever they want, and advertise it however they want. Have their cake. And I do a book that's unrelated to theirs and I get to have Batman. I get to promote it however I want with whoever I want on the book. Basically, it was like a foot race. You get a book with these two characters. I get a book with these two characters. The story isn't connected. Let's see who puts out the best product. I think I'll put out the best product. I hope they think they'll put out the best one. But, again, being a little bit competitive, I think it'll raise the level of both books so that both books will be good for the kids.

Lucas: What's the story of your *Spawn/Batman*. What happens in it?

McFarlane: It's not going to be fire and brimstone or anything like that. It's going to be as down-to-earth as it can be considering that it's a comic book. Spawn has a history of being a military commando. And Batman's pretty urbane. So, we're going to try to keep it as urban as possible given we're mixing the element of some winos who are being experimented on and turned into cyborgs. But it's going to have more of a military slant to it. There isn't going to be a Joker or a Penguin or a Violator or any of that.

Lucas: How did Frank Miller become involved?

McFarlane: He's actually been involved for a long time. We just both kept it a secret. I think that he finally said he'd do it seven to eight months ago. The one good thing about being where I'm at right now with Image comics is that I get to control my own destiny. Part of the destiny is that I get to control marketing. I knew that if I said, "Spawn! Batman! McFarlane!" that people would be interested in that. They'd buy it. They'd get excited. So, I let that trickle out, but I had Frank on it at that point. Frank and I thought we'd hold off on his name so that, why give them all the information right now? If I were to announce Frank when I got him . . . you know the attention span of readers and dealers and distributors. You're better off to give them information as close to ordering as possible. When you drag it out, they get excited, but they don't get excited for eight months. I had a plan that I'd put out the book with three pieces of information, which I thought was enough. Get people excited. Again, they think, "Yeah, this is cool." But, just before the ordering comes out, and just before all the distributors produce their catalogues, drop the one piece of information that I neglected to tell everybody that was a calculated neglect. "Oh, by the way, since you're excited up to a level of three, let me pop it up to a level of six here. I forgot to mention that the guy who did *Dark Knight* and who basically established a lot of new things for Batman is going to do the Batman character." Plus, it gives Frank a chance to come back to the character he's always loved, and he doesn't have to work with DC, technically. I phoned him up and go, "If I can get you to write Batman, and you don't have to work for DC, would you do it?" "Uh, how you going to do that, Todd?" "Aw, just watch me!"

Lucas: What can you tell us about the DC edition? There's been very little publicity on their book.

McFarlane: From what I know, the writers are going to be Doug Moench, Alan Grant, and Chuck Dixon. I think they're the three guys who are doing the Batman books right now. I think Denny O'Neill wanted to keep a core group of people who are familiar with Batman right now and (let them do it) as a gesture of loyalty. The book's forty-five pages and they split each guy up fifteen pages, though it's not three chapters—it's going to be written seamlessly. The artwork is going to be pencils and inks by Klaus Janson. In a roundabout way, it's a connection to *Dark Knight Returns*.

Lucas: How does it feel loaning out your character, your "baby" to other people?

McFarlane: If it was in context with the continuity of *Spawn*, then I'd have a lot bigger problem with it. So, while I'm doing the *Spawn/Batman*, I have Greg Capullo and Grant Morrison working on the *Spawn* book. I'm more concerned about that because it ties directly into the momentum of *Spawn*, the comic book. Essentially, because the book of theirs is not really related to *Spawn*, the regular book, and it's not related to my book, I don't see where, good or bad, it's going to have any lasting effect. So, I can feel more lax about it, too. If anything, I think they're getting the short end of the stick. I can theoretically read seven hundred issues of *Batman* comics and try to figure out something cool about Batman, whereas they only have ten issues of *Spawn* to work from, so they're working from less information than I am. But I'm sure they're not going to do anything stupid. I've seen the story. I know they haven't. I'm relaxed. They're professional.

Lucas: How was it returning to Batman, a character you probably haven't done in six to seven years?

McFarlane: It took a while to get into him and figure out exactly what way I wanted to play him. However, since Frank's handling the story, I just need to figure out a way to deal with the graphics of him. How can I make his cape have a different personality than the cape of Spawn? How menacing do I want to present him? How much do I want to have him in the shadows? I just want to go for those cool visual effects and try to give the people a book with the same coloring that they're used to [on *Spawn*]. In terms of getting into him, I'm not nervous. I've been doing capes now for the last couple of years. I've got enough on that. I think he's a cool character, given all the characters out there. If anything, the only challenge I'll have is trying to fit those two guys with their capes on the same page and not make it look too complicated.

Lucas: The battle of the dueling capes.

McFarlane: Yeah. Technically, I'm going to try and give each cape a personality of its own. Spawn's, I've drawn it so it's always shooting out, the wind's always blowing at it. It's a majestic cape. Batman's, I'll make more so it's coming down to the ground before it actually starts to come back up. If they're both shooting up in the air majestically, we're going to have trouble. So, I'll probably have Batman's cape more creepy, coming down, slithering on the ground, and shooting back up. Of course, when he's up in the air, I'll have it all over the place.

Lucas: Do you foresee doing any more crossovers like this?

McFarlane: We'll see how it goes. I've talked to Paul Levitz. Depending on the success of this book, there'd be a lot of factors. Does it sell? Yeah, it's going to sell. That's not even a given right now. More importantly, do all the parties get along at the end of it. Is there any resentment? If it goes over, I don't see a reason why we couldn't do a Spawn/Batman kind of annual event where I take a couple of issues of *Spawn*. I wouldn't mind doing a Spawn/Spider-Man one day. Go back home, being that I could still draw that character.

Lucas: Before you left Marvel, you were rumored to be doing a Batman/Lobo project. Whatever became of this?

McFarlane: I was the first guy to quit out of the core seven of the Image group. I knew that I was quitting *Spider-Man* when my first child was born. I was biding my time until they were ready. We'd always been talking, and I'd been pushing people. My philosophy was, when I quit, I couldn't quit

Spawn/Batman, p. 33, 1994, Image Comics, Fair Use. Through McFarlane's depictions of capes, he's able to contrast the stark and serious Batman with the more casual Spawn.

alone. Neal Adams has done it. Frank Miller's done it. Alan Moore's done it. Jack Kirby's done it. Steve Ditko's done it. I could go on and on. The only difference between what we did and what they did—we're not any more talented—is that I figured there was strength in numbers. I went, "Guys, if those guys couldn't quit and establish something on their own singularly . . . I'm talking about to change the industry, not to succeed in this industry. They're not going to care if Todd McFarlane leaves. They're not going to care if you and that other guy leaves. They'll care if we leave as a unit." So, since every guy was committed to other projects, I was going to bide my time. I was talking about a possible Venom miniseries. I talked to them about that because I wasn't able to do Venom when I was doing *Spider-Man*, the book that I was writing. Then I went over to DC and see if we could do their two hottest characters at the time: Batman and Lobo. It would've worked. But some of the other guys ended up quitting a little bit quicker than I thought they would, jumping on board faster, so I didn't have to do a "bide my time" project.

Lucas: Let's move on to *Spawn*. You'll be returning with issue #19. What do you have planned? What do we have to look forward to?

McFarlane: Issue #19 is going to be about a guy who thinks he's a hero, and Spawn thinks he's a hero because he doesn't have the information. But he's actually a psycho with multiple personalities. Issue #20 is an issue that's told from the "evil entity" or devil (the guy who made the deal with Al Simmons) and we get a little more information on how he made the deal. There's still a lot of stuff I've been ambiguous about that a lot of twelve-year-old kids write in asking, what does this or that mean. So, I'll have to spell out a few more things in that issue. After that, I want to bring in a couple of major bad guys. I've also been playing with the plot threads right now. The CIA thinks that Al Simmons's buddy is the one that's been disrupting several things because all the clues lead to his buddy. Nobody would think that a dead man's doing all this stuff, which is Spawn's greatest ally right now. Nobody would think that a guy returning from the dead is the one causing all the crap. I have a couple of detectives hounding him down. The mafia is going to get back on his trail. As well as the CIA people. I'm going to try to pull off a semicomplicated three- to four-part story where all those things come into play, along with the safety of his wife and her child, and get into a big, convoluted story that has to be sorted out. At the end of it, somebody might actually know he's alive and back from the dead.

Lucas: When is Spawn going to confront his ex-wife?

McFarlane: I don't know right now. Again, what he's found out so far is that his wife is happy. She's happily married to Al Simmons's best friend. I try to project this stuff on me. If I came back from something and my wife thought I was dead but she's married to my best friend . . . I'm thinking, if anybody else other than me is going to be around my wife to make sure somebody's there, I would want it to be my best friend. So, she's married to a good guy. It's not like she's married to his killer or something out of Hollywood. And he wasn't ever able to give her children (I haven't played it up that big but it's an important part). He wasn't able to give her children, and children were a big part of what she wanted. They tried when they were married. But now when he comes back, she's remarried to a good guy and she has a child, the thing that was important to her. So, he has to make the decision that now he can't turn back into what he was (he looks like a burnt hamburger). The best he could do is put some skin on himself and look like a white Beach Boy. But I haven't got to this point: That skin rots like every forty-eight hours, which is why he keeps living in the alleyways. I'm surprised more people haven't asked why he just doesn't convert to the white guy and go get a job. He can't because he actually rots. With all those things there, he has to stand there and decide, would you go and disrupt your wife's life at this point? For all intents and purposes, she's over your death. And she's happy. What would it accomplish at this point other than you wanting her back to tell her you're alive. It would just mess up her life. Spawn has to come to grips with that answer. I don't know what the final answer is. Maybe I'll have a story where he gets her back or at least tells her he's alive. But there's nothing in the cards right now. He has to figure it all out as much as you do. What can he do to solve this and not injure anybody?

Lucas: Realistically, how long do you foresee doing *Spawn*?

McFarlane: That's a tough question. A lot of people have asked me that. I'd like to do *Spawn* for a hundred issues, really. The realistic part of me says, though, that with all of the things that I've got going on in the back room, my attention might get diverted more and more, and at some point, I might have to make a decision on where I'm going to put the majority of my energies. One of the things I wanted to accomplish when I quit was that I wanted to see if somebody could create the next Mickey Mouse or the next Superman. The only way you can do that is to get out, not only to the masses but to the world. I've got plans going on now that will get it out to the world. At that point, you have to manage that character out across the world. I'd like to say that I'll be good enough that I'll have a management team behind me making sure that everything's taken care of so I can concentrate solely on the comic book, but I don't know if that's going to be true. I've always been a kind of control freak, and I always like or need to do everything myself. So, I'll keep going as long as it doesn't interfere with anything else and I'm having a good time drawing. I've got other ideas too that I'd like to draw. But those other ideas aren't superhero ideas. They're kiddie/toon stuff. If I'm going to do superheroes, I'll be doing Spawn. Spawn's my man.

Lucas: So, Spawn's this character you're talking about as the next Mickey Mouse or Superman?

McFarlane: Mickey Mouse. I'd compare him more to Mickey Mouse, not in terms of cuteness or accessibility, but in terms of management: Marvel and DC, when I was working for them, they just licensed out those characters, as long as the logo was right, it didn't really matter what they manufactured. So, you'll get these bad versions of Batman, drawings on lunch pail boxes, or a bad version of a Spider-Man Gumby doll. The only thing that would let you know it was Spider-Man or Superman was that there was an "S" on his chest or that the cape was red. Walt Disney does things like, if you want to license Mickey Mouse, when you come back with that product it better look like fucking Mickey Mouse. They don't sit there and go, "Aw, as long as it's kind of like a rat with big ears, that's close enough." That's what we've been doing on the superhero end. "That's close enough. The costume's right." I say to all the people I'm talking to that whatever design is on the shirt better look like the comic book, and whatever's on the shirt better also look like the video game. And the video game better look like the comic book that looks like the shirt. And the shirt better look like the toys that look like the video game that look like . . . etc. So, every time they pick up something that's Spawn, it looks the same. There's reinforcement of the look of the character and not so much the logo. Otherwise, at that point, the only thing I'm selling is the logo. The downside is that, being around fifty years, there's no definitive Batman look. There's no definitive Superman look. But, like I tell everyone I deal with, there's only been one guy that's been drawing Spawn. Take a look at the book. The only look is mine. When you go do something or even contemplate doing something, it better look like this book—it's the look. It's not like four hundred artists have interpreted Spawn. There's only been one, and Greg Capullo now. For the most part, there is a definitive Spawn look. That's where my Mickey Mouse mentality comes in.

Lucas: Should we look forward to Spawn cartoons, video games, movies, TV shows, etc.?

McFarlane: Yeah. I'd like to see them all. Again, as long as I can maintain control over some of them. Some of those deals are done. Now's not the time to tell you which ones. Part of marketing is keeping an interest in your character. Right now we're talking about *Spawn/Batman*. Okay! Let's talk about Frank Miller and Batman and Spawn and cool books. Then, in two months, if there's a lull in the Spawn, "Oh, here's a piece of information I forgot to tell you." Now's the time to bring that out. Now is the time to bring up Frank's name. If I told you five months ago, "I got Frank! I got these five deals done," I've just blown my whole wad. I have nothing to tell you for the next year. But, if I only put out that information every two to three months, then I've got something to tell you for the next year. And, if I have something to tell you for the next year, then hopefully that will keep interest in my character for the next year.

Lucas: So, why are you doing comic books and not marketing? It sounds like you'd be good at it.

McFarlane: In a roundabout way, I guess I am doing marketing. I'm out there with six hundred other products, so to speak. Image Comics works in such a way that Image doesn't promote *Spawn*, I do. I'm a co-owner of Image. Image just takes in the number of how many books are ordered. But each of us promotes our books differently. If anything, I've been a frustration to the retailers. Why do books from Extreme do this and why do books from Jim Lee do this? Why does Todd do that? There's no consistency to the line. That's because we're each allowed to push and market and do what we want with our own books. When I go to shows, I have this funny car, the Spawnmobile. People ask why I have a funny car. Nobody else does. Because I can. In terms of marketing, if everybody had a funny car, I'd put my logo on the side of an elephant because nobody would have an elephant. I have my logo on a sixteen-foot car that has two different paint jobs on it. They have to look at the car twice as long, hence they're looking at the logo twice as long. We just made a Hot Wheels of that car, I can sell the little Hot Wheels. I have big signs. Even in terms of marketing—bringing on Frank Miller—that's a way to help market the book. A few months back, when everybody was doing foil and all the graphic covers, I said fuck foil, I'm going to get Alan Moore. Technically, I market every day of my life. That's the only way I'm going to stay up in the sales, keep coming up with things that keep people interested, or more importantly keep people's habits in mind. So, if a kid is into video games, and I go, "We have a video game coming out," they might go, "Cool! I like video games. And I like Spawn." So, they'll continue to buy *Spawn* until the video game comes out. Once the video game comes out, they might go, "This sucks.

Spawn sucks," and quit. But I think if you can always have something for them to be looking forward to, it only reinforces their buying habit. If nothing else, it seems to be working anyway. *Spawn*'s always been in the top ten since it debuted. Over the last six months, it's either been number one or number two. It seems to be working. No tricks. $1.95. Just give them a good product.

Lucas: Do you think people are buying *Spawn* or buying Todd McFarlane? Do you think if you did, say, *Transformers*, that they'd buy it just because it's Todd McFarlane?

McFarlane: Yeah, I think so. One of the goals I had when I left . . . I had a handful of them: crack the establishment, go show that the Cinderella stories exist. One of the other things that I wanted to do in connection with trying to get the product out to the world is to get them to care about that product. So, you don't go out selling Bob Kane. You go out there selling Batman. You don't go selling Peter Laird. You go out and sell the Teenage Mutant Turtles. There are a lot of eight-year-old kids who don't know who Peter Laird is, or Kevin Eastman. But they know who the Turtles are. My goal is to get it out to the point where Todd McFarlane becomes irrelevant, eventually, to the whole process. Todd McFarlane was necessary in the beginning to get the attention and to get the sales. But issues #16, #17, and #18 I had nothing to do with besides owning the copyright of the character. Issue #16 came in second in the country in terms of volume sales. Issue #17 came in first for total sales in the country. And issue #18 came in second, but just by a little. So, those books were either number one or number two for three consecutive months when I wasn't even on the book! At that point, that is encouraging. At one point, I've made myself redundant, and yet a lot of people are still looking for me to come back on the book. On the other hand, they care enough about the Spawn character that they're still buying that book. They're not going, "Aw, Todd's not writing or drawing it—I quit." They're going, "I like Spawn. He's cool." If I had done this on issues #4, #5, and #6, it might not have worked. But, again, I'm doing this on issues #16, #17, and #18, so they have a year and a half of books already. They've made a decision. As you know as a collector, once you get up to issue #15, you've either A) made a decision that it sucks and you're never going to buy it, or B) you're in for the long haul, so to speak. As a matter of fact, it doesn't even take fifteen issues. The people who didn't like *Spawn* dumped it after issue #4. I've got a faithful following right now. Now it's a matter of taking that core and using that core to then jump to the next level, which is mass media.

Lucas: Do you see the comics artist or creator as almost a "rock god"? He's mobbed everywhere he goes. You go to conventions and can't walk around. You're stuck behind a table for six to seven hours.

McFarlane: From the outside looking in, I still don't get it. There's a mania there. The mania started on *Amazing Spider-Man*. Then, when I went to the new *Spider-Man*, when Marvel promoted it and did those multiple books, it jumped up to another level because they were able to pull in the public at that point. They sent some stuff out to the *LA Times*, the *New York Times*, etc. It just doesn't seem to go away. *Spawn* is a big seller consistently. It's a weird thing. The downside of it is that I limit people to one autograph per person when I go to shows, because I can do 2,100 signatures a day (300 an hour for 7 hours). We hand out 2,100 tickets and I sign 2,100 books. But you don't get to talk to the fans anymore, which is why you try to take time out to have a panel or something so you can say something more than just thank you. On the other hand, some kids get a thrill out of standing in line. There's something weird and magical to them that they can say they stood in line for five hours and they finally got the autograph. It becomes an event to them. In terms of why me, I don't know. I can give you a list of twenty guys who I think should be mobbed. But I think right now Todd McFarlane mania, the whole is better than the parts. They're not coming because Todd McFarlane is a good penciller anymore. They're coming because Todd McFarlane's a whacky guy. He says a lot of outrageous stuff. He's in control of his destiny. He puts out a pretty good book. He's got some great coloring in it. He has a cool funny car with him. He's going to be doing these neat toys. He has a guy walking around in costume. It's a whole big package now they're buying into. It's not just Todd McFarlane they're buying into. It's not like Joe Quesada who they're buying just because he's a good penciller. They're buying into this big schtick of mine now.

Lucas: That's one thing Image Comics helped do, they helped to make comics an event again. What other things do you think Image has accomplished?

McFarlane: What have we done? We've created free agency. We've created a better work environment. That's 100 percent true. There are a lot of guys out there who think we suck and that we're their enemies. But I can probably give you a list of two hundred to four hundred guys right now who are getting a better deal, at least financially, than they would have gotten had we never existed. We cracked the door open. Suddenly, Valiant had to up the stakes, and DC had to up the stakes. Marvel just gave a raise to everybody. Malibu's doing a good job treating creators fair. Dark Horse, too. There're spin-off companies now: Defiant and the Legends imprint and stuff. All of a sudden, where there used to be only two opportunities, Marvel and DC, if you weren't working for them, you were working at some real backwater place. We've kicked open the door. When we kicked open the door, we never said you had to follow us now that we're out and we're free. You don't have to follow our path. But we're saying that now we've helped to give you a choice of paths to pick. Whether you like us or not is irrelevant. Whether you like our books or think we can write or not, who cares? You're going to have to accept that Image Comics opened up the waters and created free agency. There are people who have prospered, even those that didn't leave. The major companies had to up their ante to keep the people, the people who didn't leave or never wanted to leave, that are now getting a better deal in terms of creativity and in terms of finances. To me, that's what I'm most proud of, that there are a lot of people doing a hell of a lot better today. If they want to argue that point, come in my direction and we'll argue it.

Lucas: What do you foresee for the next five to ten years in the industry?

McFarlane: The first thing I see is a bit of leveling off. The one concept that I think people are missing—even six months ago, the retailers and the buyers to a certain extent were missing—is that just because you create free agency and just because you come up with twenty new companies doesn't mean that twenty new companies will be good. I see this as no different from any other entertainment or sports. There are twenty baseball teams out there. If you expand to sixty teams, that doesn't mean that they'll all be great baseball teams. You'll have a bunch of sucky ones. It's going to water down the product. Just because you go, "I'm going to create fifty new books, like Marvel," doesn't mean you can find fifty good creators. If anything, if you take a good look at their product, you'll see *they* didn't. You'll have to go after a lot of young kids that weren't quite ready or are still diamonds in the rough. I hope a couple of those kids turn out to be the next big shots in the business. The product then becomes watered down because you don't have "established professional" people ready to jump on these books anymore so you start putting out product for the sake of product. I think there's a finite amount of talent out there. You can't just keep expanding and not expect the quality of all the products to go down a certain level. The one thing that will help us at Image and *Spawn* is that I put top-flight letterers and colorists on there (Steve Oliff and Tom Orzechowski), and I use top-flight paper. I pencil and ink as good as I can do. But all that stuff . . . a lot of books can't compete with that. A lot of books can't get that kind of paper and can't get that kind of coloring or lettering. Maybe I draw a little bit better than some people, so I can put a package together that may look a little bit better and, as you water down the whole line, the ones that are decent go from being decent to pretty damn good. When I took over *Amazing Spider-Man*, I was following six fill-in issues in a row. I was on it for a few months and people started paying attention. I think they started paying attention because I did three issues in a row more than anything else. But I've often said that if I'd followed John Byrne or George Pérez or Art Adams on *Amazing Spider-Man* and they'd done twenty issues in a row, I would probably have been a dead man. Nobody would have cared about me. If anything, they would have said, "You suck." Luckily, I was coming at a time when the Spider-Man books were on a downswing. If they want to start putting out more books in the next few years, and everyone comes up with their own universes and companies, they're just going to make my book look better. That's a plus side for me on that.

Lucas: Where do you see yourself in five years?

McFarlane: I don't know. I'm asking that same question. I see one of two things because I'm an extremist. In five years, I can see me still hunched over the board doing a monthly comic and screwing all the rest (Hollywood, toy deals, T-shirt deals, animation). Or, I'll have jumped full steam into that stuff and be running the Spawn Empire, so to speak. I'm one or the other; I'm not good at being somewhere in-between. The challenge of Hollywood for me is that it's virgin territory. One of the reasons I act and say and do a lot of the stuff I do in comic books is because (I hate to say it) sometimes I get bored. What can I do? I'm going to put out *Spawn/Batman*. Cool. I have to get some kind of creative juices out of that. I will because Frank's a cool guy and I'll be drawing it. However, in terms of, if you put out this book and you'll be number one, well I've been number one plenty of times in terms of sales. You'll be number one in the hot artist list. Well, I've done that for twenty consecutive months. You'll get a mania if you go to the conventions. I get that. You'll get a big paycheck. I get that. You know what I mean? There's a lot of things I've accomplished. It can get kind of boring, so to speak, at the top. I hope that doesn't sound egotistical. I get more of a thrill that Greg Capullo and Grant Morrison's *Spawn* #17 came in number one. That's cool because I never would have expected that. I get my thrills in weird ways now. In terms of trying to keep myself enthused in comic books becomes tougher and tougher every day. That's why I come up with these crazy stunts or say stupid stuff, if nothing else to get people crazy about me so I have something to talk about. But, in Hollywood, it's a whole new game. It's Marvel Comics all over again. They think they know what they're doing. They think they have all the answers. If you try to do anything a little bit different, you're going to get kicked and slapped around. I've fought against the changes on *Spider-Man* and I've fought against being able to be a writer on the book, and I fought against leaving the company. To tell you the truth, if I wanted to, I could do the exact same thing in Hollywood, try to unionize the frigging place and go crazy on it. Again, because I've found creative people are kind of weird since leaving Marvel and trying to unionize, all I can do is go into uncharted territories. You may think I'm crazy and I'm going on a suicide trip and you think I shouldn't be doing this . . . fuck you. I'm going to do it my way. Even if it doesn't work. That's the greatest thing about taking a suicide trip, which I'm always so amazed that people are so afraid to take. If you take the suicide trip and you die, you were supposed to! Nobody gave you any chances of living. If you pull it off, in the one in a million chance you pull it off, you'll look like a genius and they'll trumpet you for the next ten years because you pulled it off against the odds. That's always been the path that I love to take. Could I have sold this *Spawn* movie to the big studios and had the big directors and stars? Yeah. I had that offer a couple of times. But all they want are the Spawn rights and then they want to spit me out in the streets. I've told them, fuck yourselves. There are some big studios that aren't quite too happy with me, but . . . no. Would it be a better movie? Yeah. Would it gross a lot of money? Would a lot of people see it? Yeah. But I also have to come to grips with something like my dad coming up to me one day and saying, "Todd, I just saw that *Spawn* movie. That was cool. What did you do?" "Cashed the paycheck." "And what else?" "Nothing." I'm not going to have that. If you don't like that movie, I can't say I'm going to pass the buck ("I had nothing to do with it"). If you loved it, I can't take any other praise than I owned the copyright on it. No, no, I want to be involved in the movie so that I can say I had something to do with the movie. If you dislike it, you'd better talk to me. It's my problem. If you like it, then you have to talk to me again because I had something to do with it. I won't allow my "baby" . . . I keep telling them that this is my child. How dare they try to adopt my child and not give me visitation rights? Screw you. I'd rather make no movie than do that. They're in the movie business. They have to make movies. I don't have to. I make a good living as it is without movies. I'll get the other deal, guaranteed.

Lucas: Moviemaking is a lot more of a collaborative process as opposed to comics, where you can do it all yourself. Are you willing to accede that type of control?

McFarlane: At the beginning, yes. I've always been able to accede any kind of control that I don't think I can do a better job on. When I get in a plane, I don't want to pilot it. If I took pilot lessons and I studied piloting and I thought I could fly the plane, I'd go and pilot the thing myself or at least go buy my own plane and pilot on the weekend. So, have I ever directed a movie? Nope. Have I ever written a screenplay? Nope. Have I ever done this or that? Nope. But can I help on the visual end of it? Technically, I direct in my mind. So, can I maybe sit there and give some suggestions? The point isn't that they even listen to me, the point is that they just acknowledge my existence in the first place. It's a weird thing, but that's all I'm looking for.

Lucas: So you want to be heard. You want to have your opinion acknowledged.

McFarlane: That's it! Acknowledged to the point that they go, "That's stupid." Okay. But at least they took ten seconds to say, "Todd, you're here on the set. What do you think about this?" That's enough for me. It's not that I actually want them to do what I say, I just want them to acknowledge that the guy who created what it is they're working on, they have respect to turn to me and ask what I think on this. On the making on *Jurassic Park*, the guy who wrote that book, Michael Crichton sold the rights and got himself a nice chunk of change. They gave it to Universal and Spielberg makes a movie. Spielberg wanted to keep these dinosaurs as secretive as possible. He did a good job, because some of the people that I know were working on *Jurassic*, and I was surprised at how many people in Hollywood knew nothing about *Jurassic*. Six months before that movie came out, I knew that Spielberg wanted to make this the biggest movie in history, and nobody really knew what *Jurassic Park* was until you started seeing the trailers. Because of that secretiveness, the guy who wrote the book wasn't allowed on the set, and they wouldn't allow him on the set. Now, I think there's a certain level of secrecy, but to me that's crazy. That makes me mad. That's the story I always use when I'm in Hollywood. I get fucking angry when I tell that story. They see the redness in my face. How dare anybody! I created the Spawn. I wrote the Spawn. And somebody's going to buy that thing from me and is going to create a movie that's going to make $600 million. The studio is going to make money and everybody famous off this thing. Everybody's talking about it. But the guy who planted the seed—the guy who wrote the book—wasn't allowed on the fucking set. He didn't want to direct it. He just wanted to see the dinosaurs. And they wouldn't even allow him the courtesy of being on the set. Fuck Hollywood then at that point. I can make that deal in ten seconds. But I won't make that deal. If somebody else wants to at Image or some other company, God bless them. The important thing to me is that at least the guy who controls that character gets to make the decision. Dave Sim says, "I don't want to sell nothing. I don't want to make any licensing stuff." Good for Dave Sim. He gets to make the decision. Somebody else says, "I'm going to sell my soul. I'm going to take my character down and sell it to Showtime." Fine. You do it. Take it in the shorts. But at least the creative person got to make the decision. My decision is that I will not allow myself to be locked out of this process. I don't need this. I don't need Hollywood that badly. I'm making a good life as it is. I'm happy with my life as it is. If I can't get what I need out of Hollywood, then I'm not going to get Hollywood.

Lucas: How would you like to be remembered, then?

McFarlane: As a guy who made some modifications to Spider-Man that had some lasting impact. They're still doing the big eyes and spaghetti webbing. I created a potential new character like Spawn. I was able to show the Cinderella story there, that you can create something that will get out to the masses. And, more importantly, as a guy who fights for his convictions, whether it was the popular vote or not. I get crazy when the answer to the question is, "Because that's the way it is." That's not an answer to me. So, I fight for that. If I was born forty years earlier, I'd be fighting for the rights of Blacks or for the freedom of women to vote fifty years before that. Just because women hadn't voted doesn't mean that they weren't entitled to vote. That would have been my argument in 1910. Just because the Blacks have always sat in the back of the bus doesn't fucking make it right. Do you understand? That's the mentality I've got from comic books. I'm overstating the problem. But that mentality leads to these kinds of decisions in the world. Why is it that you don't treat your creative people this way? Their answer is because this is the way we've always treated them. That doesn't mean it makes it right. I've been telling you that you've been treating them wrong for fifty years. Screw you. If I can do anything to buck the system, and I can do anything to persuade people . . . in a small way, they've had to up their ante and had to pay these guys they've been paying shit wages to another $5 a page so that they can put food on the table. I guarantee that the CEO's at Marvel and DC Comics are eating steak every night. They're not worried about where the next paycheck is coming from. So, if I'm a bane to the existence of others, then hallelujah. Do I care that people hate me in comic books? I could give a crap. If I have one guy who hates me that buys my comic book, then that's stupid. The people who hate me are executives, creative people, editors, jealous peers, whatever. But, if I told them all to go fuck themselves tomorrow (which I wouldn't because I like most of them), I'd lose maybe two sales. I don't really care that somebody who has a personal grudge against me is mad at me because it doesn't affect my life. Now, if a twelve-year-old kid came up to me and said, "Todd, I don't think you should have said that," I'd go, "Oh, sorry about that." That's an important guy to me, that twelve-year-old kid with his $2 in his hand. I could give a shit about the rest of them. If they like me, beauty! If they dislike me, beauty. That everybody likes me in the world doesn't change how much love my wife gives me. That they all dislike me doesn't change how much my little kid calls me Dad at the end of the day and gives me a big hug. To tell you the truth, I have more fun with those that hate me, because I don't care that they hate me. But they're not used to being on the receiving end, so I can actually poke fun at more people and instigate them. That's how I have my fun. I bring it on myself. But, in a twisted way, that's the way I entertain myself. My book's selling number one. I'm famous. I'm rich. What can I do? I know! Let's see if I can get John Byrne pissed off today. I do stupid stuff. Am I immature? Yeah, I can be immature.

Lucas: Speaking of people you pissed off, you recently debated Peter David in Philadelphia.

McFarlane: Let me tell you this. I didn't really make the point there (in Philadelphia). You know the title of the debate? I didn't give a fuck what the title of the debate was. When we were trying to put this together, Peter said that there had to be a title to a debate. I couldn't give a shit. You can call it "Mom's apple pie," and I would have said, "Okay." That was Peter's title. Whatever Peter's title was, I didn't care. Essentially, I wasn't even here to argue that point. My whole thing was that I wanted to go there. I couldn't care what this was about. I was here to tell Peter blah blah blah. But, as it got further and further down the line, I could see that people on certain ends were taking this thing far too seriously. They actually wanted an "official" debate, to the point that once I got going at the debate I rolled over and realized, "You don't want to have any fun." My whole point of that debate was basically to tell people that no one's laughing in this industry anymore. Nobody wants to have a joke. Nobody wants to smile. Everybody's worried about the glut and diminishing returns. Everybody's such a tight ass. But, again, nobody wanted to have any fun. So, if they wanted to have a serious debate, then fine. Let's have a "serious" debate. Here's a Rhodes scholar sitting talking to some moron, and he's going to beat him to a pulp. If you guys get some kind of charge out of that, that's perfect. But it kind of worked, because a lot of my enemies were sitting in the stands, and they loved that I got the shit kicked out of me. And he killed me. I'll go on record as saying Peter gutted me from ear to ear. The people sitting in the stands felt good about that. I did bring some joy that day, because the world was now put back into perspective to these people. "Good! Image Comics took a shellacking. Todd McFarlane, that schmo, took a shellacking. The world is brighter now." These are the kind of people we're dealing with, so . . . whatever. I thought we could have had a lot more fun with it. I had four costume changes, which they said they wouldn't allow me to do, or some people had strong reservations about. I hope Peter takes it and does a continuation of that. However, the actual topic of whether Image gets a fair shake or not, I don't think about that. I just worry about *Spawn* and try to look out for Image. I can't control the media in any way whatsoever. I can only control my destiny in getting the books to the kids.

Lucas: You have a column in *Wizard*. Do you think your opinions influence the readers or the industry?

McFarlane: I hope not. I think the kids don't care about my opinions. The kids don't read those columns. They don't pay attention to any of that. They just care whether I turn out a *Spawn* comic book when they come into the store. Do my opinions count to the people I aggravate? Yeah, they do. In that column I can say and do stuff that will aggravate people. They'll write back and shoot back their little venomous letters. It's the way I have my entertainment.

Lucas: You've added a sense of showmanship to comics that didn't exist for the personalities/creators before. Would you want to see more of this?

McFarlane: Oh, yeah. But it becomes a personality trait. I've been a hambone since I was five years old. I was always the kid that had to give the right answer when they asked what two plus two was. I was always the kid that bucked the system from grade one to grade twelve and through college. The funny thing is that people think you just turned into an asshole in the last two years since you happened to get a few extra bucks in your pocket. No. If anyone's actually stopped and done their homework on Todd McFarlane, they'll see that Todd McFarlane is the same out-of-control, spaz, immature little punk that he's always been since day one. That's the thing that's always amazed me. I'm doing nothing different today that I was doing even five years ago when I first broke into the business. But the only difference is that nobody listened to me five to six years ago. I can tell you hours and hours about how I sat with the other creative people and said, "The system's wrong. I think they're not treating us right. I think that somebody's got to unionize and break away from this." I've been saying the same thing for years. I guess it had just fallen on deaf ears. Selling a lot of comic books means people listen to you. Somehow, someway, I guess I've helped change this industry, broke some of the rules that exist because they exist, nobody knows why.

Lucas: Do you think that this creator's "union" that the people behind Pro/Con are discussing is an answer?

McFarlane: I don't know that we could ever unionize. I would like to think so, but that's a full-time job. I'm the kind of guy that, if that was my major goal in life, I would quit doing everything else and unionize this business or die trying. I think the business could be unionized. But you get to the point where you deal with a lot of people who don't want to have the freedom that I'm looking for. In other words, I have to come to grips with, "Todd, why should you push your influence on other people? If other people are content to work at Marvel, that's fine. If other people are content to work on a creator-owned book, but don't want to publish their own books, that's fine. If other people want to do kiddie comics or adult comics, that's fine. If other people want to do this or that, that's fine." I have to sit there and take a step back and ask, do I want to start something like this because I want to put my opinion on everybody or do I think it's good for the industry? Right now, I've come to a happy medium, that Image Comics becomes an example. I'm not talking in terms of the quality of the product. I'm talking of an example to show that creative people can leave the barn and go and survive. Maybe you can argue whether we're surviving good, bad, or indifferent. But that's irrelevant. I'm just saying that we're surviving, period, which wasn't a big thing two to three years ago. If you want to follow, there are new examples out there (Legends imprint, Malibu's Bravura). There are things out there now where you can take another path down the road. Whether they pick the example is not really my fight anymore.

Lucas: As one of the most visible and influential people in the industry, what are you doing and what can you do to aid new talent or creators?

McFarlane: Good one. Open the doors again. Open the doors so that there are more doors there. When I broke in, there was just Marvel, DC, and a couple smaller companies. There was just a finite number of places you could sell yourself to. But now there are a lot more places where people can get work to start with. In terms of me personally, I try to go over people's portfolios at conventions, as I don't really have the time to go over kids' stuff as much as possible. If I'm lacking in something, this is probably an area I could do better in. I'm not putting as much effort into trying to get kids into the business as I should be. Rob Liefeld and Jim Lee hire ten new guys a year. I'll have to figure something out.

Lucas: It seems that, if you want to break into the industry, you'll have to work at a Marvel or DC or Valiant.

McFarlane: I'd like to be able to give some guidance. But I also have the attitude of when I broke in. I kicked and screamed and clawed my way to the top. I like to see people who are hungry. I don't want to see people coming to me saying, "Hey, you're Todd McFarlane, can you put in a good word for me?" I never expected any of that when I got into the business. I expected my work would do the talking for me.

Lucas: A lot has been written about your recent achievements, but how did you actually get your start in comics? How did you break in?

McFarlane: The same way everybody else does—send your samples off for a year and a half and then finally somebody gives you a call and goes, "This ain't that shitty. We can give you a couple pages of work." Mine was in a back-up story in Steve Englehart's *Coyote* book for Epic in 1984. One thing leads to another. Once you get your first gig, it's always easier to get your second gig and your third and your fourth. You just climb the ladder. It's like starting in the mail room and moving yourself, keep getting promotions. Again, I sent out 1,400 packages. I have, like, 700 rejection letters. I still keep them. I should take them around with me so when the kids go, "I sent out two letters and I don't know what the problem is." I can dump a bagful of rejection letters. People who write rejection letters are actually very nice about it. The people who think your work sucks just throw your stuff in the trash and never respond.

Lucas: Dave Sim seems to think the answer is just to self-publish. Would you recommend some new creator to self-publish something?

McFarlane: It depends on what their motivation is. If you want to do superhero stuff, I would take the route I took. Go out there, work on a book, and make it so the day you quit . . . the longer I stayed on *Spider-Man*, the longer you stay on any book, the better it makes it when you do your self-publishing book. I always knew that, even though I wanted to self-publish four years earlier, the longer I hung around, the better I'd be in the long run for it. Learn your trade, and when you leave, you've a built-in audience going with you.

Lucas: Let's go back to Spawn for a moment. Do you have a definite ending to Spawn like Dave Sim does for *Cerebus*?

McFarlane: Yeah, in my mind I do. He has a finite amount of power. Those numbers in that power meter of his keep going down. Could I technically give him more energy points? Yeah, I guess, but that's cheating the public, too. Maybe in twelve years when he's down to zero, I might go, he's pretty popular. He's like Mickey Mouse now. It would be a shame to kill him. Then, maybe, I'd have to go back and keep him around. But, for right now, someday I could see him running out of power when I want to go on to something else.

Lucas: Do you want to globalize the character, have him appear in Europe, Russia, Japan?

McFarlane: Actually, we have a deal with Italy, France, and Spain right now. They're being published over there right now. I think all of globalization will go in part and parcel in getting him out to the world. Once you get out to the world, someone, somewhere always wants to do something with your character somehow, someway.

Lucas: A Violator miniseries is set for 1994.

McFarlane: It's being drawn right now by Bart Sears and being inked by Mark Pennington and written by Alan Moore. When I left Marvel, I had a character I helped in the creation of, Venom. I never really got to play with him. When I got to do my own Spidey book, I kept asking for Venom and he was always tied up. So, when I left, I wanted to come up with something I could play with. I've always liked monsters. If you actually look at that whole run on *Spider-Man*, it was nothing but monsters: the Lizard, Sasquatch, Morbius, Hobgoblin, and Ghost Rider. I like drawing cool fangs. The Violator is my attempt to come up with another major villain. If I come up with a storyline, at the end of this I want to make him the baddest, toughest on Earth. Right now he's tied to hell. So, I have to figure out a storyline that puts him back on Earth permanently. That's what I told Alan Moore. He has to be stuck on Earth after his miniseries is over. That's all I asked for. I want to then make it so he can appear anytime. It doesn't have to have some kind of hell connection. I want to get away from the hell aspect as *Spawn* goes on and on. Hopefully, Violator will be in all the video games and animation and movies. So, he becomes the equivalent of the Joker or Doc Ock.

Lucas: Developing a life on his own.

McFarlane: I want them to care about the bad guys. He's twisted and he'll kill. So, when he goes and challenges Spawn, there's a challenge there.

Lucas: Do you see Spawn living beyond your death?

McFarlane: I would like to say yes, but I don't know that it necessarily has to be Spawn. With all the things that I've got going behind closed doors, once you sell your first idea, the first thing they ask is, what's your second idea? Then they grab my second idea, then the third and the fourth. I don't know which one is really going to tickle the fancy of society, if any of them. You might find the third idea you sell is the one that, for whatever reason, happens to be at the right place at the right time and is the one that will outlive you. Would I like it to be Spawn? Sure I would. Because then I don't have to worry about going and creating a whole 'nother thing all over again and starting the whole process all over again. But I'm a creative guy. If the Spawn is just a tool to get maybe my third idea for that to the big hit, then that's what I'll do. I'll just have to hopefully know which direction to go to be able to take advantage of this. If anything that I do—I don't care if it's Spawn right now—lives beyond me, that my characters live beyond me, I hope that Spider-Man will live beyond Steve Ditko, that Ditko still has some control over this character. It comes down to, when I die, if I create a Potato Man, does the Todd McFarlane Potato Man estate have any control over that character? If that answer is yes, then I'll have accomplished what I wanted to.

Lucas: And what would you want them to say about you as a eulogy?

McFarlane: He was a fuck but he was fair about it.

The Last Todd McFarlane Interview . . .

GREG HYLAND / 1995

From *Hero Illustrated* 1, no. 21 (March 1995): 57–67. Reprinted by permission.

What do you get when you have a struggling young cartoonist interview possibly the biggest and most powerful man in comics? Hopefully you would get an interview where you'd laugh, you'd cry and maybe, just maybe, if you were lucky, where you might learn something. What did I learn from interviewing Todd McFarlane? I learned that to truly understand the horror that Todd endured being paid millions to draw for Marvel, you have to be Todd. To understand the problems of the superrich, you have to be super rich. I also heard about as much swearing as you'd hear in a Quentin Tarantino film.

KIDS LOVE "BOARD WITH A NAIL"

Hero Illustrated: There was more talk last year about the Spawn toys than the *Spawn* comic, don't you think?

Todd McFarlane: Yeah. You get to a certain point in our business where they've seen comics, y'know? I mean I still think that they like the comics and whatever else, but it's like, it's a new thing. I don't do too many things over and above the *Spawn* comic. And there was some skepticism whether I could deliver the toys. A lot of people thought we weren't going to pull it off, but we did it. And we've got the new toys being manufactured right now.

Hero: I've got the list of those. We've got Chapel and Badrock, and Angela, Commando Spawn and Malebolgia . . . which is, I guess, the first Satan action figure.

McFarlane: Yeah. We don't call him that in the advertising, though. "The Lord of the Darkness"; those are the kinds of toy terms that you use. You don't go into Toys "R" Us and go, "We've got this fifteen-inch hell guy who's actually Satan, Lucifer himself, and we was wonderin' if you could put it next to all your other nice, little toys." You hafta kinda give 'em something else.

Hero: Is there going to be a "Viking Spawn."

McFarlane: A "Viking Spawn?"

Hero: Well, there's apparently going to be a "Viking Batman" . . .

McFarlane: Oh, there is?! If I did one, it would be a bitchin' one. I'd make sure he had big horns and I'd make sure he'd kick your ass. When we're at the bottom of the line and we've done "Football Spawn" and "Baseball Spawn," now we gotta get to "Viking Spawn."

Hero: At the Heroes World speech you gave, you had an interesting reason why Spawn's figure is tall. He's bigger, than say, a Batman figure.

McFarlane: The Batman toys are like three inches, and a lot of the X-Men are five. My characters are five and a half, six inches tall. The Malebolgia is fifteen inches. F—k! Try and beat that! No matter how big their guys are, my guys are and will always look bigger. They've got their big, tall stalky guy, but in the Batman line, he could only be four inches at best. Even my little midgets are four inches tall. My guys always will be taller. There will be a perception that they are bigger, and they can kick the shit out of Batman. The Malebolgia, he'll be a hit, although he'll be hard to find. When you make a 15-inch doll who matches and plays with other fifteen inchers, it's no big deal. But when he's supposed to play with a five-incher, all of a sudden he's a giant!

Hero: You said the Malebolgia is going to be hard to find. You're going to produce less?

McFarlane: When you make a big guy like that, the molding time is longer than Angela, or something like that. With Malebolgia, I'm actually losing money. Most people don't make toys if they know they're gonna lose money on them.

Hero: You've said you're not making money on this line.

McFarlane: No. What I need to do is break even and survive and that will be enough of a f—kin' pain in their belly. "That son of a bitch! How does he do it?" Easy! I'll even give you the answer. I'm not makin' no f—kin money! If you were the boss of Mattel and you guys sat down and said, "Y'know, this year, we don't turn a profit," you turn out much better toys. Then you could say, "Oh and the ten million dollars that we were going to make, you put that back into the toys." There's only going to be one [Malebolgia] in every case. I'm tellin' ya, the stock boys will buy them all. It'll be gone, but because they know it exists, and it does exist. You're not going to be able to miss it when you see it. You'll think they mismarked it 'cause it's the same price as all the little dinky guys. People are going to be on the hunt for the Malebolgia. I'm sure on the secondary market he'll be a forty-, fifty-dollar figure in a heartbeat.

Hero: That's a real obscene market.

McFarlane: And there's nothing I can do about that. There's only one thing I can do about that, I could just overproduce to make sure that there is no secondary market. But if I overproduce, that's a death call, too. I can't have it sit on the shelf. I need it to disappear, but if it disappears, the secondary market will be able to gouge people. It's a life I can't control that much. I just have to do what's good for my business and hope other people will be a little bit more reasonable. I'm putting Malebolgia out there, at a loss, so that these people can steal it and put it out there for fifty bucks?

Hero: Spawn comes with a board with a nail through it. Why?

McFarlane: I go, "He needs something in his hand! What would he have in his hand?" He's in the alley, I go, "What would he have in his hand? What kind of weapon? Oh, a . . . board with a nail through it!" But the new Spawn that's coming out, he comes with f—king bazookas. Not the Commando Spawn. I got an updated version.

Hero: I'd rather have the board with the nail through it. I was impressed with the board with the nail. I don't think there have ever been toys with "Board with Nail."

McFarlane: People have been lining up for the board with the nail through it.

Hero: That's the reason I bought it.

McFarlane: I find that most of these figures look twice as cool when you put three guns on 'em. You get 'em all done and you go, "God, they're cool!" Then you go and add guns to them and you go, "Aw, that's wicked!" We didn't have one gun in the first six toys.

Hero: No, but you had a parking meter. Don't knock the board with a nail through it. If more Barbies came with a board with a nail through it, they'd do well.

McFarlane: People say, "Make a big Angela, because she's a real hot babe." I could do it. If she was successful at eleven inches, then . . .

Hero: It would be successful for the wrong reasons in the hands of the comic fans.

McFarlane: You have to understand the big boys would go, "Okay, Todd's got one Angela figure and it's doing pretty good. She's sexy. She's curvy. And we have a whole aisle of Barbie dolls." There'd be five thousand "Angel-Amazon-Warrior" outfits for her, and I'd be squashed like a f—kin' ripe tomato. I'd be out of business. I'm going, "Aw! I can't do it" because if it's successful, Barbie will beat me to the punch. But we'll have all our "S&M Angela" and "G-String Angela" . . .

Hero: The kids are looking forward to that. That and Satan.

Spawn action figure, December 1994, McFarlane Toys, Fair Use. The first Spawn figure produced by "Todd Toys," now McFarlane Toys, with the "board with nail" accessory.

IMAGE IS AS IMAGE DOES

Hero: I've got a quote here from Frank Miller from the Diamond show last year: "Todd McFarlane and his pals turned their back on guaranteed wealth, guaranteed fame. They risked all of that on something that had never been tried before—an imprint that represented a group of talent rather than a bankroll. And it was a gamble. When you take chances like that and you pull it off, later it doesn't seem like that. But I am sure Todd and Jim Lee and Rob Liefeld all had long nights, wondering if they'd made the biggest mistakes of their lives." We know how that all turned out. What do you think of what Frank is saying?

McFarlane: The only part I would disagree with is the long nights, because the change that I was making was so that I wouldn't be tossing and turning, and I was, up to that point. So to me, I didn't care if we made a lot of money or sold that many books, because I knew we'd sell enough. We had a reputation! There was a confidence factor. My confidence was probably the highest out of any of the guys, 'cause I'd go, "F—k! We can do this! We can walk away from this and survive." In hindsight, people could say, y'know, "They didn't take no chances and they knew they were going to do that." I'm tellin' ya, a couple of those guys at Image, we pulled them in kicking and screaming, and these are, like, the "Big Boys." We tried to get some guys, and they just wouldn't come.

Hero: But you knew the books were going to sell.

McFarlane: Right.

Hero: So there was very little risk.

McFarlane: No, I'm not disputing that there is risk! It depends on what your definition of "risk" is. The risk comes in when you take seven guys that you don't know: A) are they going to turn out books, B) going to clash, and C) we don't know how to do business. Basically, we didn't know what the f—k we were doing in terms of business and then we weren't really the best of pals. You go single, you know exactly what you're doing. You take partners on, you don't know where the dice are going to fall. The risk came in as to how seven ego-weenies are going to get along and set up shop and somehow not kill each other along the way.

Hero: Going to Malibu made it easy, too.

McFarlane: Initially, yeah. That's just because we needed a few months. Ultimately, three months into dealing with Malibu, we knew we were, like, gone. It was just soliciting your own comic books, and doing accounting isn't really that big of a deal. For the amount of revenue we were paying them it just didn't equate. For a couple of hours of work, here and there, every week, on each book, it didn't equate to what we were paying them.

Hero: Did you foresee that happening? Leaving Malibu?

McFarlane: Oh, yeah! Before we hired them, we knew! We just basically needed [time] where we could go and get the right people to set up shop and take it over for ourselves. Malibu did pretty good by us, because Malibu was pretty much a no-name company up until that point. We just made Scott Rosenberg a millionaire. I don't see him thanking us. If he thinks that he would've done it without us then he's fooling himself, because he was a no-name company. He came in there and took the biggest boys on the block, in terms of sales. After we left, he was able to keep some of that momentum by creating the Ultraverse or whatever else and eventually selling out to Marvel. If we hadn't spent a day in there, would he be acquired by Marvel Comic Books? I'd bet against it.

Hero: I feel that Image has become a big franchise system. Almost a "mini-Marvel," with all these spin-offs.

McFarlane: But you can't paint all of us with that brush though.

Hero: I can paint pretty much all of you! You've got a couple. There's a lot of *Youngblood* spin-offs. Jim Lee has a big section of books that all tie in to one another.

McFarlane: I think that there is a misperception. From the very beginning we said we never wanted to do anything beyond Marvel. We said, "We LOVE Spider-Man! We LOVE X-Men! We LOVE Hulk! We LOVE Captain America!" So we're going to go over here and create a new system that warrants that the creator gets more of his properties and more of the income and more input into the artistic input and some of the merchandising. But we still want to do Spider-Man and the X-Men and the Hulk. I didn't want to quit *Spider-Man* and go do something revolutionary. I want to do *Spider-Man*. I just couldn't do it under that system. So, I think that there is a bit of a misperception that just because we quit we have to go and redefine comics. We didn't want to redefine comics. We wanted to do superhero comics books.

Hero: Then how does Greg Capullo doing *Spawn* differ from you doing *Spider-Man*?

McFarlane: Good question, bud! When I worked on *Spider-Man*, they didn't report to me on what they did beyond the comic book. They didn't ask my input on anything. They didn't give a shit about what I did. They just wanted me to draw the book. Greg's involved in character design, costume design, the toys, some of the movie end of it, the plot line with what's going on. I try to incorporate anything Greg wants to do into the comic book— which . . . is the exact opposite of what happened to me at Marvel Comics. I value Greg Capullo's opinion on everything! The reason I quit is because they didn't give a shit about me, they didn't respect me. They sit there and go, "We're glad you're making us a boat load of money, but we don't give a f—k about you ultimately. As soon as another kid comes along who can run a little bit faster than you, you're gone!" That's why I quit Marvel Comic Books. But do I treat people differently? Do I have a different system than Marvel? Damn right, I do. That's where the difference comes.

Hero: You were worried that you would be replaced? That Marvel wouldn't have loyalty toward you?

McFarlane: Buddy, I come from a very simple stance. If they could f—k Jack Kirby, then they will f—k anybody. I am not bigger than Jack Kirby. I don't profess to be, and I will never think that. I'm tellin' ya, the day I broke into comic books, I knew my days were numbered at the big companies. I'd go, "Todd, you'd better protect your ass," even when I was a schmuck that nobody cared about. I have the same attitude I have had about comic books since day one. I have yet to hear the story where they go, "Y'know, you're a good, loyal guy. We will take care of you. We will make sure your family does well, and that you get a piece of this pie, and that if you get hit by a bus, we owe an obligation to you." I have not heard that yet, I guess they took care of Stan Lee, but he was only one half of that puzzle. It was a guy named Jack who was the other half of that puzzle, and somebody got left behind at the train station on that one.

Hero: I don't want to sound like I'm defending Marvel, but wouldn't you say that there is some sort of economic compensation?

McFarlane: For?

Hero: The fact that you are getting paid a lot of money. That's how Marvel takes care of you.

McFarlane: No. That's the same argument that drives me crazy about why people are pissed off at baseball players! I can honestly tell you that until you've been in that position, you can't understand it. That once you're getting f—ked at a job, they can't pile the money high enough for you to accept that job anymore. It don't matter how much money they give you. Now, when you don't like a job and they pile the money up really high, you'll put up with it a lot longer. You have to just throw your hands up and go, "Y'know, I'm bending over, and they're driving me real deep. And it don't matter how much money they put on the table, they're driving me deep. And I just don't like it anymore." That people are buying you with money is just a capitalist society f—kin' cop out! Obviously, you've never been dissatisfied with a job, then you would understand it doesn't matter about money. Then you and I have a philosophical difference. If you tell me, "Yeah, yeah, yeah, Todd, I had a job I didn't like, but if had a 50 percent raise, I would have stayed there," then you and I got a philosophical difference. You're a bought man. I could buy your ass tomorrow. You don't give a f—k what you're doing. You give a f—k about how much they're giving you to do it.

Hero: You said that you want everyone who's working for Marvel and DC to come work for Image.

McFarlane: I said basically everyone who's working for Marvel or DC could be potential people who could work at Image. [We] use Marvel and DC as a training ground. Now Marvel is beginning to pay better wages and giving these new megadeals to some of their people to try and keep them there. Because of Image comic books, all the companies—DC, Valiant, Malibu—gave better deals to their creative people. So there are people who have no inclination about leaving their company, who don't give a rat's ass about Image comics. They are now making more money because of Image comics whether they want to accept it or not.

Hero: I guess it boils down to the people who can take what you couldn't take at Marvel.

McFarlane: I'm not saying that if you take it you're less of a person. If anything, I'm saying that I've got a lot of faults myself. I'm not here to tell people not to work at Marvel or DC. I did it. Hallelujah to anybody who can do it. A guy like John Buscema who can do it for thirty-five years, bless that man, 'cause he's got something strong in him that I just don't have.

DOING MY OWN STYLE WILL GET ME TO
THE TOP OF THE HEAP

Hero: I have a quote here from you: "I don't want to draw like everybody else, just let me draw what I want to draw. Why don't you let ten people draw Spider-Man ten different ways? I don't see why that's a big problem? They [Marvel and DC] seem to have a big problem with that."

McFarlane: The thing is, when I was saying it, I could see them having a problem with someone wanting to change, let's say, the X-Men at that point, 'cause *X-Men* was the number-one-selling book. But when I came on *Spider-Man*, [the book] wasn't really selling worth a darn considering what a character it was. Neither were some of the other books, but they still wanted to keep doing what's not selling. Why don't you want to bring in some guys and go, "Guys, go crazy!" and let's see.

Hero: You have people at Marvel who are drawing imitations.

McFarlane: Right now I see Jim Lee and Scott Williams are probably the most imitated people in the business by far. We need the guy who breaks away from that. But it's what they were raised on. You gotta understand, the young twenty-two-year-old kids, that's who their heroes were and they are influenced by their work.

Hero: But there's something beyond influence and imitation.

McFarlane: They have to find their niche. They have to go, "Doing Jim Lee doesn't mean I'm going to get rich and famous. Doing my own style will get me to the top of the heap." Some of them are getting frustrated going, "Oh, I got on a 'Mutie' book now, and I draw just like Jim Lee and why am I not as big and popular as Jim Lee?" It's because Jim Lee has already been there. My mom could draw *X-Men* and make it sell right now. These young kids think that going to *X-Men* is going to make their career. That's not true. If that were true, then why has nobody made a career of *X-Men* so far?

Hero: The Kuberts?

McFarlane: Kuberts have done okay, but it's not like they've redefined comics. Why do you want to take the easy way out? To me taking the mutant books is the easy way out. It's like I go there and I A) do a "Mutie" book, B) it sells a lot, C) I make a lot of money, D) I get a big lineup at the conventions, and E) I'm on the *Wizard* "Top 10." That's the mentality of a lot of the young kids coming in right now.

Hero: But you have a guy like John Cleary on your *Boof* book, and his art really looks like your art. Where does he fit into all that?

McFarlane: He was just a kid who I met who was a good kid that just had the right attitude and turned out the book. You can't pick out John and say, "Look what you're doing, Todd, you're perpetuating what you just said." Well, I also did *Boof and the Bruise Crew* that Tim Harkins did that was completely different. I didn't factor in that John looked like me or did some imitations of me. You use John as a gauge, then the other book is an inconsistency to me. Did John happen to draw like me? Yeah, whatever. But if that was that big of a deal for me, the *Boof* book is over, why isn't John drawing another book for me so I can perpetuate that style over and over? I hired him to do some work, he did it.

Hero: He wasn't hired because of his style?

McFarlane: He wasn't hired because of his style. I just thought his style would suit Boof as a single character rather than the group book that has Tim Harkins. Plus, I wanted to give the books two different looks. So I had to find a style for each one of them. But that the guy happened to like my artwork? Well, whatever. It's probably why he was led toward me, because he liked me.

Hero: I feel that most of the Image books have that "inbred" look about them, like an animation studio, where people all have to draw like one another.

McFarlane: I'll agree. I've had the conversation with Rob and Jim, "God, how do you teach these guys to look like you?" and they go, "We don't!" It's just that they have studios right now. Maybe that's what you see as part of a problem. Everybody by each other, and because that kind of becomes like the "house style." They love Jim Lee's stuff. That's why they came to work for Jim Lee. Why would someone want to come work for me if they thought my stuff sucked, y'know? I'm not saying that's good! I'm saying it's just the way it is.

Hero: So that guy with the revolutionary style has to really struggle to get out there then?

McFarlane: He's not going to revolutionize anything, he's just going to be the next kind who we are going to think is "hot," 'cause he's not going to do Todd, he's not going to do Rob. I'm talking about a guy who comes on *Captain America* like you've never looked at *Captain America*. It doesn't mean it has to equate in sales, because it takes a long time in coming for people to recognize that something is happening.

Hero: You see a big difference between *Spider-Man* and *Spawn*. I read somewhere that you said *Spawn* in five years won't look like *Spawn* #1. Which way do you think you're heading?

McFarlane: Whichever way the audience wants it to go, whichever way I want it to go. I guess "tweaking" is more of what I do. When I was on *Spider-Man*, everybody expected that "look." But to keep my mind into it, after doing forty issues of *Spider-Man*, I was looking for a little change. I needed a character that [would] give me a bit of a change. Spawn was the character who allowed me to do a little of a change. Plus I could handpick my letterer and colorist, and those two tie into the overall look of the whole book. It kind of gave me a different look than the Spider-Man book. Where, when Jim Lee came on, he kept a lot of the same and you got a book that was just a slicker version of *X-Men*. But there's nothing wrong with that because everybody loved the X-Men. He chose one path, and I chose another. I ended up maybe looking like I changed my style.

Hero: I think things got a lot looser, a lot cartoonier.

McFarlane: Yeah, probably, because I'm having more fun with it. I don't mind the cartoon stuff. Some people have a problem with it. I was lucky enough to come in before Jim Lee. Jim Lee has been a curse to a lot of people. He actually showed people how to draw, you know what I mean? I kind of like had a "style" but it wasn't very authentic. Like, okay, Spider-Man's anatomy was kind of wonky and some of the people in the book they're kind of cartoony, and I could get away with that. But basically after Jim Lee came in, he spoiled it for anybody to do that funny stuff.

IF ONLY I CAN WRITE SOME DOPEY LITTLE STORY

Hero: That debate with Peter David didn't really go the way you wanted, did it?

McFarlane: Nope. I wasn't looking for a shit kicking.

Hero: That's obvious. I was in the audience early on, and when you started to take your clothes off, I realized this was going to be something kinda nutty.

McFarlane: That's what I was hoping for . . .

Hero: It didn't turn out that way at all.

McFarlane: They basically saw the kinds of things that I was going to do and they whispered in my ear that if I do it, then Peter walks. I was like, "F—k. Okay. Whatever." I didn't want to be the guy who had to say, "Uh, because of me, Peter David won't be here. You guys have been waiting for this, and now you can lynch me. Thank you." I saw an angry mob, and I saw they wanted a killing. At that point Image comics was the devil, and so I go, "They want a lynching? They want a mob?" I go, "Okay," so after I took off the clothes and they whisper in my ear, I basically clung to my passivist mode and I said, "Go! Go ahead, kick me, burn me, hang me, do whatever you want to do and feel better about it." And a lot of people did. The world was a far brighter place for a lot of people in the audience, there. Peter David gave Todd McFarlane and Image Comics a kick in the butt. It accomplished one thing. People saw Peter David in a different light. They already knew I was a kook and whatever else, so . . . Peter had the respect of a lot of people, and he lost some of that at that debate. If I accomplished one thing, inadvertently, it was to show Peter David takes his stuff too seriously and he can be pretty mean-spirited.

Hero: One thing he did do was give you a list of tips on writing. At the time you said you'd look into some of that. Did you look into any of that?

McFarlane: Uh . . . I don't remember what any of the tips were.

Hero: Obviously you didn't look into it too much.

McFarlane: It doesn't mean I didn't do it. I do a lot of stuff without making formal efforts to do it. But I forgot what it was he wanted me to do. Put on better writers or something? I did that. Read some more books. I did that. Put an editor on the book. I did that.

Hero: Was that before or after you had all the guest writers?

McFarlane: It was after.

Hero: Why did you decide on those four? Alan Moore, Neil Gaiman, Frank Miller, and especially Dave Sim, who was an unpredictable choice.

McFarlane: If you're going to get people to write your book, why not pick the best? To me it was fairly obvious. In my mind, those are good guys. I'm in control of my book so I can pick whoever I want. So why not start at the top and let them say, "No" before you go to the bottom. I was fortunate enough that they all said, "yeah." Why Dave Sim? I like him because he's Canadian and a shit-disturber. It was not much deeper than that. Let's not forget that Dave Sim is a hell of a writer too. His books are brilliant.

Hero: You read *Cerebus*? Were you reading a lot of what those four writers were going?

McFarlane: Not really. It's more just a feel than anything. Could I say that I follow all their careers? Nah, not really. But I know of them, and I know of their skill level.

Hero: So in a way, you only got them for their reputation.

McFarlane: Right.

Hero: You've worked with Frank Miller twice. On *Spawn/Batman*, what was your work relationship like? Did he write the script? It didn't read like a script to me.

McFarlane: Yeah, I think we did it Marvel Style.

Hero: Which is you drew it then he . . . *tried* . . . to fit the dialogue.

McFarlane: Right. I think that's how we did it. We just did it Marvel Style. In terms of relationship. I guess it depends on what you want out of the book. We accomplished what we wanted out of the book, which was to do some simplistic, little, trash-talk fight story. I think there is a misconception that people wanted Frank to write some deep and meaningful, philosophical issue. He never meant to do that. He said, "Todd, I'll only do this if I can write some dopey little story." "Oh yeah. Cool. That sounds good to me!" 'Cause he was getting tired of being the guy who had to write the Gettysburg Address every time he went on a book, like Alan Moore or someone like that. Frank accomplished exactly what he set out to do, which was to do a book that was a fun read for an eight-year-old kid, and if the twenty-year-old didn't like it, then so be it.

Hero: What sort of input did you have on the DC version?

McFarlane: None.

Hero: None? What did you think of it?

McFarlane: It was okay. Not my choice of story or art. Did I like mine better? Yeah, sure I did. Just as long as the costume was right, I okayed everything. Why would I want to give them any help? Why would I want to make their book better? No way! I was the competition, bud! If mine is the better project, why would I want to help them? When they sent me something, I LOVED IT!

SPAWN #19 AND #20: I DROVE 'EM NUTS ON THAT!

Hero: What was the reasoning behind the *Spawn* #19 and #20 deal, besides the reason in the comics that "Todd can't count?" That really drove stores nuts.

McFarlane: Did it? . . . Yeah, it did!

Hero: Did you get feedback on that?

McFarlane: Oh, yeah. Yeah, I drove 'em nuts on that, but I can honestly tell you that there are a lot of guys running stores that drove me f—kin' nuts as well. The reason behind it, in terms of a business one, is that they decided to change the window of returnability from ninety to thirty days, bang! Those two books were caught in that, so I just go, "I'm not going to give those guys the satisfaction. Guys, this is my book. And I don't want anybody telling me how to write and draw my book. And I don't want you to tell me what I can do with my book. If I want to put my book in black-and-white, color, put it upside down, put a #20 on the book, put a #97 on the book, you're not going to tell me what to do." So, it got to the point where it was going to be returnable. Now let's think about this for a second, all the f—kin' retailers that are out there that are still in f—kin' business. Luckily, most of the guys I'm pissed at have gone bankrupt! It is that they have the number one book in the country, or number two; whatever, it was right up there at the f—kin' top, and they're bitching about the number one and number two book that is putting the number one and number two amount of money in their pocketbook. And they're sitting there, trying to figure out how to return the best-selling comic book. That makes no sense to me. Figure out ways to return shit stuff that you can't sell! Why would you return the stuff you *can* sell? You've got two choices, either don't order the books or take them in the order I am giving them to you. The choice is yours. I'm not forcing you to take these two books. If I put out issue #19 and #20, because it's going to take me X-amount of days to finish it, because we just got dumped into thirty-day returnability, #21 is going to be returnable, #22 is going to be returnable, #23, #24, #25, #26. They are all going to be returnable, unless I stop soliciting for five months. Why would you want to force me from producing the number one or number two book in the country? That's idiotic! I made a mistake. Instead of having ten returnable books of *Spawn*, I found a way to have two returnable books, and I would resolicit the other two books. Like I promised, and I did, four months later I gave them to you biweekly. Like I promised, boom, boom, you got them, beauty, everything's good. And the distributors, too: I want to let them know [they] don't control my book. So, ultimately, you guys can say, "We're not going to carry your book, we're not going to sell it, we're not going to do whatever." Fine. That's your prerogative. But you don't have the right to tell me what to do with my book because if you do that, then I got equal right, equal time, to tell you how to run your shops, and how to run your f—kin' distribution. I'll bet if I spent more than five minutes in one of those areas, I'd find twenty different ways that I could improve the system. If it hurts the kids, then that's the point that kills me more than anything else. I made plenty of concessions over the years just to appease certain people in the industry to keep the kids happy. Unfortunately, the consumer got caught in this.

Hero: You've made some interesting threats about starting your own distributor.

McFarlane: Yup! I started my own company! So what the f—k would be the problem in shipping my own comic books?

Hero: Do you see that happening?

McFarlane: Not today. But I don't know who's going to get me mad tomorrow.

Hero: But with Marvel buying Heroes World . . .

McFarlane: Did they do us a favor! If anything were to happen, it makes the other distributors more friendly to us. There's the potential you gotta read between the lines, the potential that they may not be getting Marvel comic books one day. So what do you do? Either A) go out of business, or B) get real friendly with the competition. And we happen to be one of the competition.

Hero: Do you think Marvel will go exclusive?

McFarlane: Yeah. That'll happen. Whether they tell you it won't happen, it'll happen.

Hero: Exclusive distribution for Image?

McFarlane: We'll move when Marvel moves. Right now, Marvel wants to maintain the status quo, so there's no reason to panic. I'm in no panic mode. Everyone else seems to be in a bit of a panic. Marvel's not doing anything different right now. Will they? Yeah, they will! I'd bet my life on it! But are they doing it today? Let's not worry about it today.

Hero: What do you think of what Marvel has been doing? With Malibu and Heroes World and all the really strange stuff they have been doing in the past twelve months?

McFarlane: I think what they are doing is completely predictable. They went public. They became "Corporate America." They got this big machine that's moving. And then the public stock market, the only thing you can do to keep your sales up and your profit margin up, once something slows down to the left, you gotta gobble to the right. Once that slows down you gobble to the left again and to the north and south. So they are doing exactly what a big business, privately owned company that's gone public has done ten times over. They've got their own distribution system, I'm going, "Why'd it take them so long?" That doesn't surprise me in the least.

Hero: What do you think of their books?

McFarlane: I'm not that impressed by them. But again, I'm sure the same can be said of the Image stuff. To each his own. Is the quality there like it used to be? No, not really. That's one of the reasons why they aren't selling as many books, amongst other reasons.

I'VE BEEN AN ASSHOLE FOREVER

Hero: It goes without saying that you are one of the most outspoken people in comics. Is that intentional, or is it just the way it turned out? People want to hear, or people just end up hearing what you have to say?

McFarlane: Anybody who tries to mess with the system is branded a traitor. So I think there are a lot of people who have the same opinions as I do, but they don't have the power to say it or enough people to pay attention. But there's enough people who think like I do. Do I like to have to fight every day of my life on these things? Nah, not really. I'm just a believer in controlling your own destiny, and if that means you've got to f—k the system, then f—k . . . I'll f—k the system! Again, it's not just comic books, because they're like, "Todd! [You've been] a psycho for the last three years!" I mean, I get that, "He's turned into such an asshole." You want to use that as a definition, then I've been an asshole forever. I can show you report cards and stuff that literally said, "The kid is hyperactive!" What I do in my life is just a natural progression of how I've dealt with things for a lot of years. I just took that into toys. They said I couldn't do my own toys, f—k you! I'll show them I can do my own toys.

Hero: So if someone tells you you can't do something, you're going to do it and do it twice as hard. So there is no concentrated effort? You get your fair share of negative press . . .

McFarlane: Yeah, but that's okay. This isn't about getting negative press. I'd be doing exactly what I'm doing if everyone loved me or everyone hated me. I'm not doing it for the press of it, I'm doing it because I believe in what it is that I'm doing. That Peter David or John Byrne likes me or doesn't like me

I don't give a f—k. I get a lot of kids who say a lot of nice stuff, and God bless them. And the people who hate it? Well, whatever. I don't expect everyone to like me. Then they'd have to change my name to "God" and not Todd.

Now, we at Hero don't like beating a dead horse any more than the next magazine (unless, of course, the horse is the famous Mr. Dead), but Todd and Greg brought up this whole Philadelphia debate thing for one more go-round, and since we've now heard Todd's final word on the subject (or so we hope), we thought it only fair to get a final response from the other party involved. Ladies and gentlemen, Mr. Peter David:

> It is nothing short of amazing to me that a year and a half after the ill-advised ComicFest debate, Hero is still obsessing about it. What does not surprise me at all, however, is that Todd still has no grasp of the simplest concept of "truth."
>
> The truth is that when Todd fast-talked George Pérez into moderating the debate, George (who takes debating very seriously) was concerned Todd would try and turn it into a circus. Todd swore to him that such was not the case; that Todd was out to engage in a serious and thoughtful exchange of ideas.
>
> The truth is that, on the day of the debate, George became aware of Todd's plans, including slide shows, music, cheerleaders, and costumed characters. George made it clear to Todd that he was furious that Todd had lied to him. Todd told George he intended to proceed with his circus act. George said angrily that he was going to inform me of this, and if I objected, he'd call off the debate.
>
> The truth is I shrugged and said, "If I'm not for free expression, who will be? Todd can say or do whatever he wants during his time. I'm here to talk seriously about issues, as Todd claimed he wanted to do. If he wants to screw around instead, I don't care."
>
> The truth is that Todd challenged and insulted my integrity, my veracity and my character, and then made no effort to back up or prove his case, as if such calumnies were trivial. He initiated and organized the debate with one simple goal: to try and lampoon and humiliate me. Nothing else. When it came time to try and support his lies, he was unable to put up and, going on two years later, he has yet to shut up. A successful multimedia millionaire who still can't refrain from dumping on one lone freelance writer who he says was "mean" to him.
>
> Todd said if anyone could cite blatant falsehoods of his, he would give a sizeable sum to the Comic Book Legal Defense Fund. I suggest he make out the check immediately. The good news, though, is Todd needs no writing tips from me. Clearly, he's mastered fiction. Now if he could just keep it out of interviews . . .

The Man Who Would Kill Image:
Todd McFarlane Meets Hart Fisher

HART D. FISHER / 1995

From *Hero Illustrated* 1, no. 21 (March 1995): 60–64. Reprinted by permission.

On paper, it seemed like a natural fit: one of the most prominent men at Image talking with the man who produced last year's controversial Kill Image. Clash of the titans or battle of the psychos? You be the judge.

Hart D. Fisher: How'd you first get introduced to the *Kill Image* comic?

Todd McFarlane: Maybe San Diego last year? I said, "Oh, look. I've got my mug on the cover of another magazine." I looked at it and went, "Oh, cool he only blew my hand off. He likes me." I'm not the distributor, so I'm not calling any shots. I gotta be man enough to stand up and take a few shots. Sometimes it makes people feel good.

Fisher: You're getting your product out on time now. Last year at this time everyone was pissed, and I did the *Kill Image* book. Absolutely perfect timing.

McFarlane: That's right. You got in there. I was gonna actually write you a letter and go, "You f—ked up Hart, because you blew off my right hand, and I'm left-handed, you didn't do dick to me." You f—ked up. You killed everybody else but ol' Toddy was still ready and raring with pen in hand goin' full speed for the next issue. I haven't let the snake outta the bag here but I could really wreck your credibility.

Fisher: It'd be pretty easy.

McFarlane: I've got you over a barrel, I just want you to know that.

Fisher: At least you're not worried I'm going to kill you like Rob was.

McFarlane: Rob and my wife.

Fisher: Oh, yeah?

McFarlane: "Todd, this is disturbing." Ah, c'mon, we're comic book people, we're harmless.

Fisher: It's a gag.

McFarlane: Oh, yeah. Football players do weird stuff. We're just crazy. We need to put it on paper, once it's on paper we're normal people. But then again, you don't want people to really know that because it wrecks the whole mystique. A normal guy, aww, that's not fun. You want to think some psychotic is drawing this stuff. "This guy is f—ked up, I hate what's happening to society from this stuff."

Fisher: Do you catch a lot of flak for the violence in *Spawn*?

McFarlane: Yeah, you know.

Fisher: Does it bug you?

McFarlane: F—k, I can't allow people to tell me what to put in my book. Never have, never will. I'm sure you do the same thing. You don't like the product, go buy someone else's book. Just 'cause I'm putting out a product that disturbs doesn't mean you have to buy it. Go spend your money on something you do like.

Fisher: I think the only thing someone could freak about is that it's a violent book marketed to kids.

McFarlane: There is some legitimacy there, but then we'd be getting into a conversation that could go on forever. Just because little Johnny can't take it doesn't mean there aren't a lot of other Johnnies that could. I've gone to plenty of conventions, and I've got the kids with their moms and their dads. I even go, "Do you know what's in these comic books?" They go, "Oh, yeah, just good, clean fun." "But they are violent." "Ahhh, so what." So I'm sure it offends some people's sensibilities, but I just have to ask would this have bugged me when I was twelve years old? Nahhh, I woulda thought this was cool. That's all it is. If Mom doesn't think it's cool that's out of my control. I can control my sensibility. I draw other lines. I don't put the word "f—k" in there.

Fisher: That word is all over my books.

McFarlane: You just make your own personal judgments and go to bed at night.

Fisher: What kind of fans you got? Any crazies?

McFarlane: Yeah, my fans are probably a lot crazier than the average Image fan. But I think my book has a little bit of an edge to it so it appeals to an older crowd. A little bit weirder.

Fisher: I had one guy send me photos of a dead guy.

McFarlane: [*Laughs*] I don't get that cool stuff. I get a sweater.

Fisher: What do you think about Spawn?

McFarlane: The book's doin' okay. I'm puttin' a smile on it.

Fisher: How do you feel about it? Do you think it's battin' a thousand? Are there things you want to change? I mean, you're the creator so you're probably your own worst critic.

McFarlane: It's a book. I think I'll get a better feel for it when I'm up to issue #45 of it. Then I'll know this works, this doesn't work, this is cool. Everything is still in a growth pattern, you know. I'm just pouring water on it seeing exactly what is or isn't sprouting. Then I'll go, "Okay, this is the direction to go." You'll never turn out that perfect comic book.

Fisher: I like a lot of the artwork in *Spawn*, but I find that since it's not written for me as an adult, it doesn't appeal to me.

McFarlane: And that's okay, because I'm not appealing to you. Right. So it's like if Hart Fisher goes on a rampage, "*Spawn* sucks, blah, blah." Well, okay, you're welcome to your opinions, but the book isn't aimed for you. So you might as well write an article about how bicycles aren't good for you either.

Fisher: What kind of movies do you like to go see?

McFarlane: Movies?

Fisher: Yeah, what was the last movie you paid to go see?

McFarlane: I'm, like, the bad guy who waits for everything to come out on video. I like reality doses, or as much reality as you can get out of Hollywood.

Fisher: Movies like *Born on the Fourth of July*?

McFarlane: Right. *JFK*. Cool movie.

Fisher: That was a good movie.

McFarlane: I'm not into *Star Trek* or *Star Wars* or *Terminator*. I draw that stuff. I'm more into *The Color Purple* or *When Harry Met Sally*. Something that could technically be true.

Fisher: What about westerns?

McFarlane: Yeah. Something that could've happened, that's not too Hollywood. I want a dose of reality after drawing fantasy all day.

Fisher: What about tunes? Do you listen to music when you write or draw?

McFarlane: Ahhh, not much. I'm pretty mellow. I like mellow music.

Fisher: You gotta come by the tuneage somewhere. You use the radio or what?

McFarlane: No, I got some CDs here.

Fisher: Cough it up Todd, gimme the goods.

McFarlane: I'm trying to think. I got Jim Morrison's *Greatest Hits*, Tracy Chapman. I like stuff that I can listen to and I can still have a discussion on the phone.

Spawn #7, p. 16, January 1993, Image Comics, Fair Use. Not only is the page an example of McFarlane's use of violence in *Spawn*, but a direct reference to the infamous *Spider-Man* panel that depicts the blinding of Juggernaut, leading to McFarlane's departure from Marvel after a confrontation with the Marvel editorial team over the Comics Code.

Fisher: Like Enya?

McFarlane: [*Laughs*] No, not that mellow.

Fisher: *I* just picture you listening to Yanni. [*Laughing*]

McFarlane: Nahhh.

Fisher: So we got the Doors here, we got Tracy Chapman. What else we got here?

McFarlane: What else we got? I'm pretty mellow, top forty. Although I haven't listened to that for so long that when my wife tells me what's hot, I go, "No way!" What happened to Queen? Where's Queen gone? I'm like one of those guys living in the past. I sound like my dad. That music's not as cool as the stuff I listened to.

Fisher: You gonna go see the Eagles? You know they're on tour now.

McFarlane: I know they're touring . . .

Fisher: And we know you've got plenty of money for tickets.

McFarlane: Rob saw them and said they were awesome. Yeah, I should. But I went and saw Barbra Streisand.

Fisher: Have you caught a lot of flak on *Violator*?

McFarlane: Yeah, some. I ignore it. I ignore flak. God bless the retailers, but they do the exact same thing every single time. It's out for two weeks then they forget about it. As long as you don't respond to 'em then they ignore it and they go away and all of the sudden they're arguing about somebody else's book. Somebody else's book, interview, Marvel Mart. All you gotta do is wave another shiny object in front of 'em.

Fisher: We've done an O. J. book, *Doin' Time with O. J.*

McFarlane: Whatever. Hart Fisher can yell and scream all he wants, do all he wants as long as he keeps in mind, that if you want to go out there and *really* f—k with them, I mean really f—k with them, unfortunately you've gotta be somewhat more commercial 'cause then they go, "Hart Fisher who also sells twelve zillion cards a year . . ." then all of a sudden there's a story to write. Up until then your opinion means nothing unless you actually damage them financially. That's the only time they want the story.

We can get away with crap. We're the psychos that actually have sales. It's that old commerciality in the end coming back. Until you're sellin' a zillion copies then it's like, "Oh my God, we've gotta listen to Hart Fisher, oh God no." Then it's the same thing with us. They're getting bleeding ulcers, because we don't care how things were done for the last twenty years. We've gotta fight the fight, whether the independent guys believe it or not. We fight the fight and I personally fight some of the fight because you guys aren't gonna get away with it because you don't have a voice. You need us on some level.

You don't have to like us, you don't have to like our books, you don't have to like anything about us, but you need us on some level to be the guys on the firing line with some part in it.

Fisher: So you think it's cool about Frank Miller jumping on the Comic Book Legal Defense Fund?

McFarlane: Yeah, rock 'n' roll. I'd like to see all of us independent guys under one banner. Not Image. We'd call it Creative Community Incorporated, because you gotta say incorporated 'cause then it's like official. Then we just go up to Diamond and Capital and go, "By the way, Marvel and DC make up 50 percent of your market and we make up the rest, now here's our demands." I'd love to go in there with all the small independent guys, we'd have a little bit of a voice and go bust some chops.

The Man Who Wouldn't Give In . . . :
A *Combo* Interview With Todd McFarlane

BUDDY SCALERA / 1995

From *Combo Magazine* 1, no. 1 (February 1995): 38–42. Reprinted by permission of Buddy Scalera, Comic Book School.

Todd McFarlane is widely regarded as one of the most powerful individuals in the comics industry. He and his Image cofounders made publishing history with their very public departure from Marvel in 1992. His first Image venture, *Spawn*, is a consistent favorite among comic fans.

Todd talked with *Combo* recently about his start in comics, his future plans for Spawn and what he will say on his death bed.

Combo Magazine: Where were you born and raised?

Todd McFarlane: I was born in Calgary, Alberta, Canada, on March 16, 1961. I grew up in Southern California and in the San Jose, California, area for the most part before we moved back to Calgary when I was about fourteen.

CM: How did you get your start in comics?

TM: Same as everybody else. Just flogged the mailboxes with my samples and sent it off to the editors and went to conventions and bugged people. After bugging the crap out of them for about a year-and-a-half, they finally acquiesced and said, "Okay, kid. You stop bugging us and we'll give you a job." Just hard work and a lot of determination and not taking "no" for an answer.

CM: What was your first published work?

TM: The first published work was . . . actually, they both came out the same day. You remember these things. It was mid-February of 1985 and it was an issue of *Infinity, Inc.* #14, which had been done months after the other book that also came out that week, which was Steve Englehart's *Coyote* from Marvel Epic.

CM: What would you have done if you hadn't done comics?

TM: I've got a degree in graphic arts. My dad's in the printing trades business. I was planning on following my dad's footsteps in the printing business. That was one of the reasons why when we made the break from Marvel to Image, I knew that we could pull it off. The one thing they didn't think we had was technological insights and I had grown up around it.

CM: What were your influences inside and outside of comics?

TM: In terms of the comic books, I got into them kind of late, so it was who was hot at the time like John Byrne and George Pérez and a little bit later Frank Miller. Jack Kirby's a big influence, but he's an influence not so much in drawing style, but in terms of the energy that he brought to his pages. I tried to duplicate some of that stuff when I was on the *Hulk* and *Spider-Man*.

CM: When kids come up to you and say they want to draw comics, what do you tell them?

TM: I say to them the thing I used to hate when [the editors] said it to me. Continue to draw. You can't get any better unless you're doing it. Some kids just aren't ready. I've some kids that look like they're on the verge, but they never apply themselves and they don't get any better. Then you get another kid that can't draw his way out of a paper bag, but he keeps drawing and six months, eight months, a year goes by, and you wouldn't even recognize that it was the same kid.

CM: Was there ever a point when you were a kid where you almost gave up?

TM: Nope. I'm the guy who fights against the "no." I was going to give it only so much time and I was going to self-publish.

CM: We have *Spawn* and the *Violator*. What are some of the other things that you have up your sleeve?

TM: We've got the *Angela* miniseries, which is a spin-off of a character that Neil Gaiman and I cocreated. Most of the stuff that occupies my time isn't really comic book related. I started the new toy company [Todd Toys, Inc.] and that takes up a lot of my time. I do a lot of stuff in Hollywood. Since I own the rights to it, I'm the one who's controlling all of the merchandising stuff. I've got plans to start a textile company. My goal is to take these things that I've created in comic books and see if I can't bring them out to the world and say, "Look at what we do in comic books. It's neat stuff. Don't look at us as being little geeks."

CM: What's the scoop on the *Spawn* video game?

TM: We're doing a Super Nintendo version, a Sega Genesis version, a Sega CD, PC CD-ROM and Sony PSX version. According to my contract, that stuff has to hit by the summer of 1995. Sony Imagesoft's been working on it for a long time.

CM: What can fans of *Spawn* expect to see in the comic in 1995?

TM: For 1995, Greg Capullo is going to come onto the book and help me on some of the artwork so that we can keep the pace of the book a lot better than I've been doing the last couple of years. He'll take a big burden away from me. We'll tag team and try to become the "team supreme." I'm going to try to move Spawn into a direction where he's going to get back to the reason of why he's on Earth, which is trying to hunt down his wife. Then he's going to try and come to grips with: If he can't have his wife, what's the reason for him to go on and what's his purpose in the whole scheme of life, so to speak. At the same time, I'll bring a couple of new characters into the book that will eventually spin off into their own toys. If everything goes okay there'll be an animated *Spawn* on TV, too.

CM: What sort of relationship do you maintain with the other Image creators?

TM: Oh, I love 'em! We talk all the time. I'm going to be making their toys. Unfortunately, the downside of us being ambitious punks is that we're all busy, so we don't get to see each other as much as we like. We have our meetings and our last meeting actually was at my house, where everybody came up to my house and we hung out for a few days and did the big slumber party and stuff.

CM: How come we haven't seen any major Image crossovers yet?

TM: Part of it is because of scheduling. We're not the best in the world at that. I really haven't defined what Spawn is to a lot of people so I'm not really concerned with Spawn meeting up with *WildC.A.T.s* or something until I get to that point.

CM: Any intentions of doing other intercompany crossovers like *Spawn/Batman*?

TM: The obvious one would be Spawn/Spider-Man. He'd be the only one that I'd go, "Yeah, that makes sense." He'd be kind of a cool guy to do, but for right now it's tough enough to just get the regular book out there. Unfortunately, when I did *Spawn/Batman*, I had to leave the regular book and I don't like doing that that often.

CM: What was the strangest untrue rumor that you've ever heard about yourself?

TM: That I've been dead. Some of them have been pretty good, "I heard it on CNN!" First off, I'm not dead and even if I was I doubt CNN would care.

CM: Let's play fill in the blanks: If I had to color both love and hate, the colors I'd choose would be . . .

TM: Love I'd color red just like a nice big heart. And hate . . . when you get pissed off your blood boils, so it's also a red color. It's just a real intense red with lots of veins popping out of it. They both come from the same place ultimately.

Spawn #9, p. 6, March 1993, Image Comics, Fair Use. Angela, cocreated by McFarlane and Gaiman, would be the subject of a legal dispute where Gaiman would win the lawsuit and settle with McFarlane for full rights to the character. Gaiman would then sell the rights to Marvel, where the character is now the long-lost sister to Marvel's Thor.

CM: If I could meet any person living or dead, it would be . . .

TM: I'm intrigued by people like Martin Luther King and people who tried to break away like Jackie Robinson, who had the weight of a country and the weight of a race on his shoulder and somehow managed to survive. To me those guys are amazing people. Basically they risked their life and their livelihood and their happiness just to make their point and to try and help others.

CM: If I were standing on a desert island and I could have with me three of my current possessions and one other person, family members excluded, I would choose . . .

TM: Hmm. What do I need? I don't need much. I'm pretty simple. I'd probably take a soft bed, an electric refrigerator so we could keep the food cold, and probably my ball glove so I could play. And the person I'd want to have out there, you're telling me to exclude my family, but ultimately I can't really see myself without my family.

CM: In the end, with my last dying breath, my words shall be . . .

TM: That I never surrendered. That I was my own man. If that comes across as being egotistical at least I can go to my grave knowing that I wasn't bought and that I didn't have to sit there and have people tell me what to do. So I would just put, "I'm free. I'm free."

Dossier: Jeffrey Goldsmith Interviews Todd McFarlane

JEFFREY GOLDSMITH / 1997

From *Heavy Metal* 21, no. 3 (1997): 10–11. Reprinted by permission of Jeffrey Goldsmith, a writer living in San Francisco.

Todd McFarlane created Spawn, *a comic that sold one hundred million copies. Now he's animated on HBO at midnight, and in a forty-million-dollar movie set for August.*

Jeffrey Goldsmith: Is Spawn good or evil?

Todd McFarlane: That's the intrigue about him, the capability, just like each one of us, to do either. It's just a matter of which button gets pushed. He isn't Clark Kent, boy scout. Somebody pushes him, he pushes back. Somebody kicks him, he kicks back. Somebody shoots at him, fuck, he shoots back. It's the reason we like Rambo and stuff like that. Because if somebody touches my wife, I'll fucking take their head off. So, he's got the same mentality as I do; you leave my family alone.

JG: Do you believe in life after death?

TM: Not really. Then again, Spawn didn't believe in the afterlife, but he finds out that there's something there.

JG: Do you suspect there's something there?

TM: I don't. I think there's infinity before us, sixty years of life, and infinity afterwards. So, given there's infinity all around us, then what is the precious time? The time we have on Earth. So, this is the time you're going to kick yourself for the rest of your life if you fuck up. If there is an afterlife and we judge ourselves then, I'm hoping Hitler tortures himself for the next twelve millennium going, "Fuck, I should have been a little bit nicer."

JG: Funny you mention Hitler. Elvis is in hell in an early issue of *Spawn*. Are you going to draw Hitler in hell?

TM: I don't know where Hitler is, but I'll get around to him probably. I've set up [the story] in my mind, like a slow, boring chess game, a long time between draft picks. Which is why again the Spawns only appear every three or four hundred years.

JG: Huh? I know there's a medieval Spawn. So, we're going to see Spawns in the future and Spawns of distant past?

TM: Right, it's the curse. We have versions of these guys. Some are futuristic and some are in the past, the curse just keeps coming back. It takes that long to find the guy that is the right draft pick. I'm not religious, it's not about good and evil, it's about the capacity for both. It's about the wiring. If you think about each of us being a computer, then you have to have the right wiring. And if you got the computer with the right wiring, then it's just a matter of pushing the right buttons to get what you want out of it. It takes that long before you actually go, "Here's the guy." And Al Simmons [Spawn's name when he was human] is one of them. If I push the right button, this guy will have the capability to be one of the greatest fucking generals of hell's entire kingdom.

JG: I see, and the Clown's wiring?

TM: The Clown is a local from hell. The duty of the Violator, which is the Clown's true form, is that . . . and he looks like the Malebolgia because, if God created man in his image, then why wouldn't the Malebolgia create his guys in his image?

JG: The Malebolgia being the Devil's henchman?

TM: Yes, there's a different Devil at each level.

JG: Leviathan being the Uber Devil?

TM: Exactly. If you think Malebolgia is tough, Malebolgia is like a two-year-old compared to what Satan is . . .

JG: The Clown, why does he use his own initiative?

TM: His job is not to kill Spawn, he's supposed to watch him, but his agenda is to keep proving throughout time that humans are not the people that should lead the army.

JG: The Clown wants Spawn's job?

TM: Essentially, but he can't just kill him because then he's in trouble. So his job is to just keep proving that these guys aren't as worthy as he is. But he has to be somewhat clever about the whole gig.

JG: How do you feel that your mythology—if I may call it that—how do you feel that it's going to end up on a big screen?

TM: How do I feel? Well, you and I can talk for an hour about the mythology, but given that you've got a two-hour movie that needs a beginning, a middle, and an end and is essentially the coming of the curse of the Spawn, then you just take a small piece of it. You don't get into God's side, you don't get into Armageddon. You just get this guy, a piece of this huge puzzle. Although, what I think makes him interesting to people is that, though he's caught in this biblical game, all he's concerned about are personal things like, "I want to go see my wife, where are my friends, where are my pets?" That's what he's concerned about. Now, he's standing to the left and the biggest goal is standing to the right, and heaven and hell and everybody else throws these gauntlets in between. That's where it looks like revenge. But it's not really revenge, it's if you want to see your wife, then you got to get through these trees, and if you have to happen to fucking kill them, then, given that he's a trained assassin and he has that wiring in him, then he's like "Oh, OK. So, there's my wife. Can you please get out of the way? No? OK, there. Now you're out of the way."

JG: Is getting to his wife a subplot or . . . ?

TM: No, essentially that's it. But again, he's shot five years into the future to get back to his wife. Everything is out of whack. He made the deal, which all of us would make in a heartbeat. "I want to see my wife." That's all he asked for. Given that Devils are tricksters, they went, "Yeah, OK, fine. Here."

JG: But?

TM: "BUT I forgot to tell you, since you didn't ask, that you're burnt. [Literally, charred.] You look exactly what you looked like the moment you died. Five years in the future, your wife has remarried, to your best friend, so it's not even like she's married to the bad guy. And you were impotent. You couldn't even give her kids. Now she's got a kid. You knew that was important to her. And so basically, there she is. You can go say hi to her, but you know what? You're fucked."

JG: You set up a real damned situation.

TM: Well, here's a man that has all this power and he's back for a reason, his wife, and that reason has been taken from him. So the answer is, can he find any purpose in going on? That becomes the inner quest, although he's not thinking in those terms. Can he come to grips with what he is? And what he is, is not Al Simmons. He's not going to have his wife. He has these powers, but what is he going to do with them? The thing is, most Spawns just go, "Fuck, accept the power and do evil." What if Genghis Khan got the power? Fuck he'd love it!

JG: Spawn would conquer China, just like Genghis Khan really did.

TM: They all come around to evil. It's just that he's going to kick and scream. So the question we bring up in the movie and the animation and the comic book is, is he the one?

JG: Is he the one to bust out of the cycle?

TM: Right. Can he break the chain? I don't know. I haven't written the ending yet, but I know what the ending is in my mind.

JG: You never know until you get there. I want to ask you something specific about the HBO animation. A friend told me you wanted to make sure there was butter on every kernel of popped corn in a scene. True?

TM: I think you're getting a distorted version. There was popcorn, and it had a bad shadow. It's like that's not a shadow that goes on popcorn. Am I anal? Yeah.

JG: It's good to be, though.

TM: It's a fine line because they tell people, "God, can't that Todd be a bit nicer?" I don't think I'm harsh. I'm just the guy that goes, "I think you guys can run twenty-five miles an hour." And they're saying, "Fifteen is ok because Saturday morning cartoons are only running at eight." I don't give a shit. We can run twenty-five. I'm not comparing the show to anybody else's drivel. It's like saying you get the best seat on the *Titanic*.

JG: The movie comes out in August, the animation is on HBO now, which interests you more?

TM: It's not a fair question, because they're dramatically different. The animation is more like my toy company. You come up with designs and the best blue prints you can, you ship it overseas and they manufacture it. You can do retakes but that stuff is limited. When you're making a movie, it's three dimensional and you're right there. A guy can say, "Pass the butter, Charlie." And you go, "Can we change the lighting?" Know what I mean?

JG: Were you there on the set?

TM: Sure. Not every day, but I was there. I got a cameo.

JG: What's your cameo?

TM: I'm a bum. I wanted to meet my Spawny boy. I get to hand him a gun.

JG: In the alley?

TM: Yeah. The thing is, there's more instant correction in movie making. The plus side of animation is that the only thing you're limited by, which is why I'm always kicking, is your imagination. On a movie they go, "OK, you got a $40 million budget, that's it." In animation, there is no budget. It's like, "Let's blow up Tokyo. Cool. Let's blow up Beijing. Cool, man." It doesn't cost you any more to blow it up than not.

JG: Special effects?

TM: In a movie, that's very costly. In fact, that's where the bulk of our cost went. How do you make the Clown into the Violator and make him move around? The answer is, 90 percent of the Violator is computer. The guy who created the T-Rex for *Jurassic*, he's a friend of mine, he's been up for an Academy Award, he's doing the Violator.

JG: "Spazz" Williams.

TM: Right, Steve "Spazz" Williams. And Mark Dippé, another computer whiz, directed the movie. So, we're in good shape on that end.

JG: What comes after Spawn?

TM: Do I have second and third ideas? Yep. The game in Hollywood is to sell your second and third ideas now so you can hedge your bets. So, if *Spawn*'s a failure, then you go, "Well I'm not dead because I've got the second and third idea." If those take off, Hollywood being what-have-you-done-for-me-lately, you're back in the game. But I'm either just stupid or cocky enough to just go, "It's going to work. Why should I give you my second idea for half the price and half the power and half the control when, if *Spawn* works, you're going to basically give me everything I want on the second idea anyway?" I'm a betting man and I bet my second idea is going to have just as much value as Spawn. Ideas are fairly precious to me. They're my creative children and I just don't feel like giving them up for adoption so that I can make a buck. I've got plenty of money in my bank.

JG: If the *Spawn* movie is a success, will we see a second idea in 1999?

TM: Not necessarily. If *Spawn* is a huge success, I know what I'm doing for the next three to five years. The *Spawn* sequel, three more years of Spawn on HBO, the toy company, the comic book. I'm out to create my Mickey Mouse.

JG: Very edgy Mickey.

TM: In my mind, the best I can hope is for Spawn to be half a household name. Half isn't going to get it. Mom is not. Five-year-old Jimmy and most of the girls aren't going to get it. But the guy upstairs playing his rock 'n' roll music and Dad who fucking sits and goes, "I can't endorse it in front of Mom, but right on." They'll get it. If it works, it will be a huge cult thing that's still cool. The only way to get it bigger is to start pandering him, which is why I have control. I know Hollywood people, to make a few extra bucks, they'd want to make him cute. And I'd go, fuck this. This is a guy from the pit of hell who's going through personal torment. You have to keep the edge. There's a reason the HBO show is on at midnight. It's going to offend a few people because they're not used to seeing little cartoon characters say, "Fuck you, asshole."

Hellbent for Action

JIM RICCIOLI / 1997

From *Collecting Toys* 5, no. 5 (October 1997): 50–57. Reprinted by permission of Martha Lundin, © Collecting Toys, October 1997, Kalmbach Media Co.

KISS-ed by success, Todd McFarlane has spawned a toy company and comic creations to higher heights.

Like many successful businesspeople, Todd McFarlane has often drawn on his instincts and own sense of perfectionism. But, here in his Arizona home, something is decisively different than the rest of corporate America.

Perhaps it's just that so few toy magnates can be found wearing a personalized baseball T-shirt while sitting beside an ink-stained drawing board in a cluttered production office—and look perfectly natural in that setting. This, for the most part, is Todd McFarlane and, by extension, McFarlane Toys.

Amid the foothills outside Phoenix, McFarlane's home and office serves as the creative base for his enterprises, which have blossomed in what many would have considered the most unlikely environments. Like the irrigated lawns that provide greenery in the desert terrain of central Arizona, McFarlane's company has stood out and grown in a world dominated by Mattel and Hasbro and in a category that includes action-figure icon Toy Biz.

McFarlane Toys was spawned from its founder's sense of perfection. Plainly put, when Todd felt it was time to create a three-dimensional image of his highly successful *Spawn* comic book series, he simply didn't trust the rest of the toy universe to do the job. So, much like he would have reached for his pencil to sketch a comic creation, he reached into his assets to create a new toy company. Instinctively, he knew it made sense.

And what could have once been perceived as an exercise in self-indulgence has turned into a success story. Today, four years after its fast start, McFarlane Toys (originally Todd Toys) is among the most widely recognized action figure companies in the world. With a second office close to home in Tempe, a design office in New Jersey, and a corporate center in Michigan that combined employ around sixty people, the action figure company has expanded to product lines that include such icons as the rock group KISS and numerous comic characters beyond McFarlane's personal creations.

Not that his trademark character, Spawn has been forgotten. An HBO animated series that debuted in May and a New Line Cinema motion picture released August 1 have focused even more collectors on Todd's rising star.

With the *Spawn* movie's imminent release, it seemed like a good time to take a closer look at this story of success. We sat down with Todd McFarlane in his home office to see the artist and toymaker at work.

STAND-UP COMICS

Collecting Toys: Your background is amazing, given that most comic book artists don't end up as widely recognized toy makers. Tell us a little about your background and how it led up to *Spawn*.

Todd McFarlane: Comic books really aren't any different than any other business: They start you off in the mail room, right? The equivalents of the "mail room" or the "penthouse" in comic books are what characters you draw. You know you've made it to the penthouse when you're doing Superman and Batman and those kinds of characters that your mom would know. I started with Marvel in 1984, and also worked for DC. In about my third or fourth year, I ended up getting *The Incredible Hulk* at Marvel. Then I did a couple of *Batman* issues for DC while I was busy with the Hulk. The next gig I got was *Amazing Spider-Man*—not just penciling the artwork, but inking it as well. From there, I went to the new book called *Spider-Man* where I ended up doing the writing, penciling, and inking. I stayed on that book until I left Marvel Comics in 1991, and a bunch of us started Image Comics, which has published *Spawn* since June of 1992.

From there, I've been learning. The business side is the side that really is the toughest thing to balance. Before, we were just artists, but then we became businessmen, because we own our trademarks and copyrights. I'm one of those few guys out there who actually lives on both sides of the fence. I like to have the creative hat on as long as possible, though.

FIGURING IT OUT

CT: What is it about you that said, "Hey, I should make my own action figures," and then prompted you to form a company to do it?

TM: The same thing that basically drove me to do the comic books and everything else that I do—I wanted it to be done in a certain way. I guess that I don't trust that other people would take care of your stuff as much as you would. Given that these characters were my little children, I didn't feel that anyone would raise them properly.

All that I've ever wanted is to have the final say on the product. While there are companies that agree to that, others are basically so bloated and convoluted that you're just an annoying gnat to them. Those are the guys that really get the hair up on my back.

I knew that the only thing that really stops people from manufacturing anything on the planet is money. I figured I could pay the bills to manufacture toys, find sculptors, and send them over to China. Most people would find that when you actually try to duplicate what corporate America does, it's not really rocket science. Because there's a thousand workers at a company, it just seems more overwhelming, but the basic process isn't really that big of a deal. The people at a toy company aren't usually doing any of the actual physical labor in manufacturing.

In terms of toys, I thought I had a bit of an advantage because toy companies deal with teams and executives giving final approval on their stuff, which to me seems asinine. I always found it kind of odd that these companies wouldn't have creative executive guys signing off on this stuff. Now that I know their process, I believe they'll never consistently make better toys than I can because the guys who actually have final approval don't know how to sculpt or draw. I'm sure there's the odd exception, and I know I'm painting them with a broad brush, but I believe that to be fairly accurate.

DOLLARS AND SENSE

CT: Obviously, we've seen a huge collector market emerge for well-sculpted figures, which includes the *Spawn* line. What are your thoughts about how the action figure market has evolved toward detailed figures? Is there room for improvement?

TM: I've had this discussion about some of the sports figure companies. Some collectors are very loyal to Kenner with Starting Lineup. I think that's good that they're loyal. But there's the side to me that says because you're so loyal, you're not giving a chance for anyone else to do those figures. You're encouraging mediocrity.

I'm a sports fanatic, and you know what, I'd rather puke on those toys before I'd buy them. I understand it's a business that needs to keep costs down. But that doesn't excuse why you don't show body language or wrinkles in the uniforms. It doesn't excuse the fact that when you make a figure of a shortstop, God forbid that you'd actually get a photograph of a real player bending over for a ball. At least make them look like shortstops instead of something to me that's so friggin' juvenile. You're basically cheating the public. They could be doing a better product, but they're not.

Everything I do with my figures, there's a reason behind it. Ultimately, some other companies are not going to be able to do what I do because they're going to sit there and say, "Gosh, to do that, it costs money." In Frankenstein's operating table, we washed colors into the pieces so that you see the wood's grooves. It's easier for manufacturers to say, "Eh, let's just make it brown." But you've got to pay attention to texture, feel, and content.

If the answer is always the bottom line, that's where you get in trouble, and it starts at the top. Executives might say, "OK, we want to do X-Men toys"—and I'm just picking an example that's not necessarily based on any facts, but it's pretty damn close, I bet. They'd say, "Well, how much do we want to make?" "Well, we want to make two million bucks." "OK, how do we make that?" "Well, we gotta sell two million units. That means we have to make a clear dollar profit." "Well, what's our overhead?" "Our overhead is $4." And when the conversation is finally done, they decide that to make $2 million, the creative people have 76 cents per unit to make two million figures. They then go to the creative people, and say "Here, we want you to make the coolest, best thing, but, oh, by the way, you've only got 76 cents to work with." They've already stifled them.

Make the product, and then from the product's costs, price it. If it's a good product, people will pay the extra buck or two. Obviously, you want to be competitive, but price really isn't an object if you have a good product. You can't sit there and say, "We can't go to $9.99 from $7.99 because they won't buy it." What they won't buy is a product that they don't think is worth the price.

EVOLUTIONARY IDEAS

CT: Are you among the reasons that better action figures seem to be emerging today?

TM: I'm among the reasons in that I'm just another guy to add to the competition. Competition allows, at some level, for the cream to rise to the top. I just think that the more things that you show to the public and the more options they have, the more you are forcing other manufacturers to think.

Let me put it to you this way: If I had come in and I was a complete failure, I don't think they'd be doing some of the little extra work that they're doing right now. Only by the success of others does it force people to improve.

Now, the vast majority of my toys are being sold to collectors, per se—although I'm hoping that the *Spawn* movie and television stuff changes that a bit. What other toymakers are doing is selling 90 percent to the public and 10 percent to the collector, so even if I strike gold, they don't even have to pay attention to me because that's not their market. Just like I don't have to pay attention to them doing cute, fuzzy toys.

I don't even know if large toy manufacturers see the collector market as a viable option that increases their market shares that much. I just think they have so many divisions that it's like corporate America: You see a cow, you milk it. If they can get two million bucks out of the collectors' market, they'll take two million bucks. I'm cynical, but I just think it's really about that deep.

MONEY CAN'T BUY ME LOVE

CT: Given that toy manufacturing is a profession dealing with overseas plants, cost analysis, market research, and any number of bean-counter issues, how has this process changed your views over the years about what toymaking is all about?

TM: As I see the process, I think they are working backward—again, I think you let the product dictate the price—and I can now look at a toy and almost see where they started cutting corners to save themselves a dime. I think toy executives are far more proud of the fact that they can say, "Hey, I made $2.4 million in profit instead of $2 million." That's going to get them a raise in the company more than the idea that "This is an awesome toy, and volume-wise, we're gonna sell a lot."

I think success is the by-product of a lot of hard work. That whatever luck is mixed in there, you can create your own luck by hard work. I believe there is a correlation between the two. Most people who basically aren't very hungry aren't very lucky—unless you win the lottery.

A MOVIE STAR

CT: Let's talk about your transition to the movies, starting as executive producer of *Spawn: The Movie*.

TM: The director Mark Dippé, producer Clint Goldman, and special effects whiz Steve Williams, who all came out of the ILM [Industrial Light and Magic] house, were all friends of mine prior to this deal.

In the preproduction stages, I was involved a lot in terms of designing, story elements, script writing, and all those kinds of things before the cameras start rolling.

Once you roll the cameras, actually making a movie is a slow, arduous process—kind of like comic books, which you read in fifteen minutes, but takes thirty days to do. It can be boring in that you wait a long time for a scene to get shot. Once the process started, I wasn't out on the set that much. I still had the special effects producer and director calling me up and saying "Todd, what do you think of this or that?" I still went out to the set every now and then, but I felt that my value was to get the message out so that when the movie was done, we'd have a big enough crowd already aware of it.

When we were in postproduction, I was back and involved in it a lot more—how are we going to edit it, what's important, how do we move the scenes around, what kind of music should we use, and all those other final things. There are so many special effects: the creature, the cape movements, the morphing—all the things that the kids are going to remember.

ONE TRICKY PONY

CT: As time has worn on, it seems like McFarlane Toys has become less dependent on the traditional superhero or supervillain comic characters. I'm thinking of your new lines, like the monster series. Has this been diversification or just something you decided you wanted to try?

TM: I believe you need to diversify in anything you do so that you don't become a one-trick pony.

It's still just an experiment on some level—the whole company is. We don't do any test marketing. I just let my guys do it on intuition and gut feel.

For the most part, those are pretty good guiding forces in anything you do in life anyway. Do we need to sell in places that aren't Toys "R" Us? Yeah. Do we need to sell monsters to places that are going to have big Halloween setups? Uh-huh. So we are diversifying within our marketing tactics, too.

Spawn is still leading the company. Given the fact that we have Spawn as a cash cow, I think we can diversify within him. We're trying to play with themes, such as the one we have coming out at Christmas, Manga Spawn. I'm trying to create a shelf life for Spawn. If we get a movie sequel that would come out in two or three years, in between you would have the animation, toys, and electronics to remind you about this product. It becomes, to a smaller degree, what has happened with *Batman*.

KISS IT HELLO

CT: Let's talk about KISS. You had to be a fan, but how did this lead to the incredibly accurate figures of the 1970s rock band? It certainly seems like a major offshoot for McFarlane Toys.

TM: For our company, I'd say yeah, it's people going off in a direction that really is unproven territory for us and, to some extent, for a lot of other toy manufacturers.

I'm not a KISS fan in the truest sense. I had a brother a year younger and another year older who were big KISS fans, so KISS was in the house. Just by osmosis, I was a KISS fan. The appreciation I have for KISS is based in their longevity. I'm in year five with *Spawn*, and it's very hard for me to fathom that *Spawn* is still going to be a big deal twenty years from now, or bigger than it is right now.

I wouldn't say my KISS figures are completely accurate because we are trying to bring in a sense of melodrama, so we tweaked them. We were going for more of a comic book feel with the characters, but not losing sight that they must still be instantly recognizable. It's still Gene, Paul, Ace, and Peter.

The real guys just look like toys when you see them. In fact, they look like McFarlane Toys to me. They've got so much stuff on them that other companies wouldn't pay attention to. I made sure that I painted everything accurately, that I have chains on the boots, and that we make the hair as close to the real thing as possible. I just felt that, on some level, if somebody was going to do KISS figures, then we probably would make the best toy. I'm not saying we'd sell the most, because we don't have the marketing clout that the other big companies have, but since we are selling to collectors, I think collectors will appreciate that we at least made a gallant effort our first time up.

KID STUFF

CT: So, where do you go from there? Licensed products for other companies, maybe?

TM: Yeah, potentially. But the thing is that it has to be stuff that fits the McFarlane Toys attitude. There are other licenses out there that we could do, and people have approached us. But we don't want to do it just for the sake of doing it and making money. I'd rather do something that I'd actually want to have if I was a kid. When I was a kid, I'd want Dracula with a stake so you could jab it in the heart. I'd take that toy every time.

We're going to try to expand this whole manga field, and I think we'll be able to present these really wicked new toys that are going to have the Spawn name in some way attached to them, and that really have the sense of a Japanese feel to them, as well.

Virtuoso: Todd McFarlane

JASON SANTA MARIA / 1999

From *Fright X* 1, no. 11 (September 1999): 28–33. Reprinted by permission of David Paul Wyatt Perko, creative director.

Fright X: Inside and outside of comics, who and what are your biggest influences and achievements?

Todd McFarlane: When I first broke into the business, my influences were the current artists. But as you get further into the game, you start to expand your history of the medium. So, when I first got into comics and started collecting in the midseventies, John Byrne, Frank Miller, and George Pérez were like the hip guys. Some of the old guys you just kind of thumbed your nose up at, but as time went by, I started to appreciate their work for what it was. Overall, Jack Kirby is probably the biggest influence on my work. It's one of those things where people say, "You don't draw like Jack Kirby," but that's not what I got out of him. What I got out of Jack Kirby and his artwork was a sense of dynamics and energy so that when you read one of his comic books you went, "Fuck, that was cool, man!" It wasn't about squiggles on people's knees—It was about energy.

FX: As legend has it, when you were trying to break into comics, you received over 700 rejection letters before getting a break . . .

TM: Actually, I sent out over 700 submissions. I got back about 350 rejection letters—the other 350 never replied.

FX: Does that make you more apathetic or sympathetic when looking at work from a new artist?

TM: Well, it makes it tough when the young guys come and say they sent out like two samples, haven't gotten anything back and are thinking of going into sheet metal welding or something. I just sit back and say, "Fuck, that's as strong as your spine is?" If you're an artist, you are getting into a field where people are going to be critiquing your work and you have to develop a thick skin after a while. Not everyone is going to like your stuff and if you can't take it from the get-go, then you're sort of barking up the wrong tree.

FX: Do you think you'll ever get back to drawing comics full time?

TM: I don't think so. I think that it was something that I did and loved, but as I get older and we continue to expand, I realize that the outgrowth of comics was to tell stories. Now I just tell the stories in different mediums—some in music, or TV and movies. To do comics full time—writing, penciling, and inking—was an incredible task. I would have to find a way to do that, run my six companies and do my other fifteen jobs that I do every day. So as of right now, I'm not capable of doing it. When finding venues to show your work, comics right now are still a limited field in terms of the amount of people that see your stuff. I'm far more aggressive—I want to know where the millions and millions of people are.

FX: Why do you think *Spawn* is still popular as ever?

TM: I think I've been fairly shrewd in not milking *Spawn* for everything he's worth and not just pimping him out from the very get go. Six or seven years later, the price of the *Spawn* comic book is still the same as it was in 1992. The cost of the comic is the same even though the cost to print the comic has gone way up and my print run has gone way down. The only person to really suffer was me and I was willing to take it on the chin. I didn't want to be like Superman or *Batman*, put out nine versions of the same book and have a new poster or trading card set out every week. I resisted all those things and that's why there is still a hunger for the character on a commercial level—because I haven't overfed it. In terms of the character's appeal, he's a dark hero that has his rough edges. Some people are turned off by that because they see him as evil, ugly, and violent—but it is also the same thing that I think draws people to it. He is rough around the edges, he is imperfect and he is flawed. You just get sick of perfection after a while and I think that he is the farthest thing from that.

FX: What is your relationship with Greg Capullo like?

TM: Great! Greg is awesome. As the company grew, I had to make a reality check and realize that I couldn't continue doing the book. It got to the point where I wasn't focused enough on the job and I would have cheated the public. I needed someone who could sit down and work all day on a page. All I could afford was to quickly get a page done so that I could go do nine other things. He's a good, hardworking, honest guy, which is hard to find in our business. He has also improved dramatically from his first issue to where he is at today. I also think that the book is better for his presence, because I know that, over the years, I wouldn't have been able to develop and improve the look of the comic as much as he has.

FX: What about your relationships with the other original Image cofounders?

TM: Whilce Portacio sort of bailed out in the beginning because he didn't want in on the business side of things. Jim Lee just recently sold out to DC. I like him but I'm sure there will come a time when I'll have to say, "You're standing on the other side and that's the direction my gun is aimed at." For right now, we're still friends. The other guys like Jim Valentino, Erik Larsen, and Mark Silvestri—we all still get along. As for Rob Liefeld, we went from being as close as you can be, to literally becoming enemies.

FX: Was his dismissal from Image tough on you?

TM: Not really, because at that point you're enemies. Are you remorseful that you killed your enemy? No.

FX: What do you think of the general state of the comic book industry today?

TM: I think that it continues to deteriorate and we are really doing nothing to stop it. I don't know where it's going. I think that comic companies are making money, but it's not on new comics, it's on things like toys and other things like that. The actual hard sales are down.

FX: Tell me about the *Sam and Twitch* comic you're working on with Brian Michael Bendis (also interviewed in this issue of *Fright X*) from *Jinx*.

TM: As I get older, I like to take these indulgences. I'm not nearly as enamored by superhero comics. What interests me more are these sorts of real stories that could take place. They are still fantasy, but it's fantasy in a world where it could happen. The *Sam and Twitch* series will be in that vein. Brian Michael Bendis, who did the *Jinx* series and *Goldfish*, that's the type of world that he lives in. It's like a true crime stories thing, which is actually just an outreach of the things that you see on page one of your newspaper.

FX: Do you still have a chance to read a lot of comics?

TM: Not as much as I would like. By the time the day is over and I get home, I have kids and a wife and I just want to read about something like sports.

FX: You were nominated for an award for the Pearl Jam video "Do the Evolution." How did the video come about? Who approached who?

TM: The way that I heard it was that the record company was trying to get them to do a video to promote their new album at the time, *Yield*. They hadn't made a video in years. The band said that they would make a video but they didn't want to star in it. The lead singer, Eddie Vedder, came home one day and saw the *Spawn* series on HBO and thought that it was cool. So, they said, "Hey, let's call this guy and make the video animated so we don't have to star in it." We just kind of got on the phone and worked out the movements of the video.

Spawn #300, p. 36, September 2019, Image Comics, Fair Use. McFarlane wouldn't draw another *Spawn* interior page for another twenty-five years after stepping away from penciling duties after *Spawn* #25. Despite the now digital artwork, McFarlane's lines are instantly recognizable, if not a little more refined than in the early issues of *Spawn*.

FX: What are the plans for the *Spawn* movie sequel?

TM: We are working on the screen play right now. Hopefully we'll get New Line Cinema to approve it and then we can start filming by Christmas, with the movie maybe ready to go by the spring of 2000.

FX: Are you using the same actors?

TM: I don't think so. It is completely different in terms of intent. The first movie was PG-13 and this one will be an R-rated suspense-thriller. I'm throwing all of the special effects out the door. This one will focus more on *Spawn* the character and the characters around him. Before that comes out, we have the new season of *Spawn* on HBO coming out at the end of May and hopefully that will carry some *Spawn* momentum.

FX: Are there any plans for a fully animated *Spawn* movie?

TM: We've talked about one, but not here in America. In terms of another story, I wouldn't mind trying my hand at an animated movie that is more adult oriented. Maybe something like the stuff they do in Japan, like anime, that stuff is just incredible. We never really gripped that level of detail here in America.

FX: Looking back from 1992 when you left Marvel Comics, has everything turned out the way that you wanted it?

TM: When I left Marvel, I just wanted to create enough success that I could still maintain my personal freedom. So, in those terms, I still have my freedom and I'm content.

FX: What is an average day in your life like?

TM: There is no average day. You put out the fires as they come. It's the difference between what I did five years ago—I would come to the office and make ten decisions a day, and now I come to the office and make a hundred and ten decisions a day. The density of each day is a lot thicker. I don't have the time to gallivant around and have social conversations with people. I have to be all about business and just get the stuff done.

FX: What kind of breakfast gets your day started—Canadian bacon or American bacon?

TM: No, I'm pretty simple. Today I had some Cap N' Crunch, some peanut butter and jelly, and I was ready to go.

FX: What sets McFarlane toys apart from other toy lines?

TM: I think that we actually make better products. People are seeing that for the same amount of plastic, you can get something that looks decent with a nice paint job and detail. I don't see why it's so surprising that we come out with these great toys that have so much detail. That should have been happening ten years ago. It's odd that some young punk like myself, who comes out of the woodwork compared to these supposed "masters" who have billions of dollars, shows everyone how to do this. They just have more people and more money—they don't have any more common sense or creativity than us. I think that their creativity is hindered by the management groups. By the time they have their twenty memos and their market research, the creative guy can only move two inches in either direction. I let my creative people move as far as they want—as long as it fuckin' looks good.

FX: Where do all the ideas for the figures come from? Are they exclusively yours?

TM: Right now I have a good band of guys that can read my mind very well. I used to be more influential, but I've given the creative people so much room over the years that they are to the point that they think, "Will this pass Todd's criteria?" before they even do anything. So by the time something gets to me I say, "Wow, that's just what I was thinking of!" or it's even better than that.

FX: What is your relationship with Gene Simmons from KISS like?

TM: He's a great guy. He's one of the only guys that has faith in my company unconditionally. He drives the guys here crazy because he's a bit wacky, but once you get past his tough guy exterior and nobody is looking, we can just be ourselves—which is just a bunch of kids playing with toys.

FX: Did you ever see him cry?

TM: No, no. . . . We're not that sensitive.

FX: What are you working on with Ozzy Osbourne right now?

TM: Well, we might be doing the cover to his next album and we just came out with his action figure. We are also doing this sort of unofficial autobiography magazine of him, which kind of takes all the things we know to be true about Ozzy and just throws a slant on them.

FX: How did the Korn video come about? Was it under the same circumstances as the Pearl Jam video?

TM: No, that was a bit different. The cover that Greg Capullo and I did for their last album got a lot of attention and they were also very pleased with it. They decided they were going to do a video, so we stepped over and said, "Well . . . we do videos." So, they gave it to us and it turned out to be this sort of really cool half animated, half live-action music video.

FX: If the United States and Canada ever got into a war, would both countries still be able to buy *Spawn*?

TM: That's a tough one . . .

FX: What side would you fight on?

TM: Oh no . . . I'm a pacifist. No, I would die for my honor. I guess that it would depend on what the argument was over . . .

FX: What about a baseball?

TM: I don't know. I'm a Canadian through and through.

FX: Well, that's it, thanks for your time.

TM: Sure, anytime.

The Writin' Side of Me: The Todd McFarlane Interview

DANNY FINGEROTH / 2007

From *Write Now!* 1, no. 16 (Summer 2007): 3–22. Reprinted by permission. © 2007 Danny Fingeroth.

Todd McFarlane's comic book career spans more than twenty years and dozens of popular characters. As artist, his work has graced the pages of *The Amazing Spider-Man* (where he cocreated Venom), *The Incredible Hulk*, and *Detective Comics*. His professional writing career kicked off with the launch of one of the bestselling series of all time, *Spider-Man*. After years as one of the industry's top creators, Todd joined several other popular comic book artists to form Image Comics. There, he launched his own creator-owned series *Spawn*, which soon caught the attention of Hollywood and was the inspiration for a live-action movie and an animated series. In addition to his comic book work, Todd also heads up his own toy and collectible company, McFarlane toys. A busy man of many interests (including part-ownership of the Edmonton Oilers NHL hockey team), Todd was able to give us some time to speak about the subject of *Write Now*: writing for comics and related media.

Danny Fingeroth: Did you write as a kid at all, or in school, Todd? Was that anything you were interested in then?

Todd McFarlane: I was pretty good at sort of short story stuff, but I think that was just a byproduct of my wild imagination as a whole.

DF: What kind of short stories? What would they be about?

TM: The teacher would assign us to do a factual composition about, say World War II, I couldn't do something like that. But if they said, "Go home and come up with a made-up story and bring it in," and you could add fantasy stuff and big, dramatic melodrama to it—the equivalent of the Jack-in-the-Beanstalk stories—then I could put in a flying elephant, and purple dinosaurs a thousand feet tall, and I could do it easily.

DF: This was in elementary school?

TM: Oh, yeah. You know, the "creative writing" classes.

DF: What about in high school or college? Did you do any writing then?

TM: Not nearly as much. The writing there was more serious so a lot of it was more historical reports and dissertations in some of the classes. And you had less of a chance, or at least in the classes that I was taking, to just have fun with writing like I did when I was in high school or younger.

DF: I've read that you didn't really read comics until high school. How'd you avoid them?

TM: Umm . . . I played a lot of sports. You know, when we went on road trips, Mom and Dad would stop at the 7-Eleven and buy a couple of Slurpees and a couple of comics and throw them in the back to me and my two brothers, so it's not that I was devoid of comics. I'd read a handful, so I was aware of what comic books were. I never bothered collecting them, though. But at the age of about nine, I started collecting baseball cards and football cards, so I was collecting, it just was in a different place. Later, all of a sudden I went, "Hey, you know what? Let me check out these comic books that I keep sort of walking by."

DF: You must have been drawing as a kid.

TM: Oh, yeah. I was the proverbial "best-artist-in-the-class" kid from day one. It really goes back to the first Major League Baseball game I went to in the Anaheim area in California which I got to attend because, as a kid in kindergarten, I won an art contest. I drew a pitcher throwing a ball, and it got hung up in the stadium. My dad said, "I'll take you to the ball game and you can see your artwork and you can watch the game." So we went. Maybe around then I would have started collecting comic books or done something different, but Dad took me to a ball game that day, and I got to see art, and at the same time became mesmerized by sports. And that was after watching sports on a black-and-white TV my whole life, then walking into a stadium. That was a big moment for a kid back then. In person, you see the bright green grass, and the reds were fire truck red, and it was like walking into the Land of Oz. You went from the black-and-white into the color. You just went, "Wow."

DF: With your love of sports combined with your artistic talent, you could have gone on to paint sports portraits or do sports magazine illustration.

What was it about comics that made you at some point realize that the story-telling in them appealed to you?

TM: This is weird, Danny. I remember the day of consciously going into a store to buy my first handful of comic books. I mean, I close my eyes and recreate it. I remember the books that I bought. They were on a spinner-rack. What I don't remember is, "Why now?" I mean, why, at the age of sixteen? I'd been walking by comic books all my life. The closest I can give you is that I had been that incessant doodler for so long, but I didn't have any focus for my art, and maybe I was just getting older, going, "Somewhere along the line I'm going to have to figure out what to do with this." And so what happened very quickly was that when I bought those comics and fell in love with them and became a fanatic of comics, that I went, "Aha! Now I know what to do with this doodling. Train myself to draw American superhero comics." Because I had, like, fifty styles back then, and all of them were raw, at best. And so I thought, "Focus on this one task called "superhero comics," see if you can teach yourself this, because it's kind of cool." And from there on, from the time I started collecting, I stopped drawing just willy-nilly doodled stuff and *MAD* magazine–type stuff, and I just went, "Everything's now going to be superheroic stuff."

DF: Was there any friend or relative who said, "Hey, you should check these comic book things out," or did it just sort of dawn on you?

TM: Like I said, I'd walked by that store five hundred times. And I just thought—because comic books were only thirty, thirty-five cents back then, and I had a couple of bucks in my pocket—"I'm going to go buy five comic books." Why then? I don't know. And those five soon turned into 35,000.

DF: Now, you said somewhere that you got over seven hundred rejection letters? I remember seeing them at that exhibit at the MoCCA [Manhattan's Museum of Comic and Cartoon Art] last year.

TM: I sent off about seven hundred samples, and about half of them came back rejects, so about three hundred fifty out of the seven hundred were officially rejected. The other ones just filed it in the garbage and didn't even bother to send a rejection letter.

DF: What kept you going through that?

TM: A lot of the same things that keep me going now: stubbornness and immaturity—the two things I'd rather not teach the youth of America. You know, I give seminars and discuss, how do you succeed? I hate to say it, but it's about characteristics I'd rather not even give my own boy, let alone you good people reading this. But you've just got to get myopic and stubborn. Those aren't really the best traits to have. But that was it. I was blinded by my own talent to think that I was better than I was.

DF: Well, that's often what it takes to get through the rough spots. When you sent in the art, was it drawing stories you had written, too, or you would take other people's stories and interpret them your own way?

TM: At first it was just pin-up shots. But then, the people who were responding, said, "Hey, you've got to give us page-by-page story stuff." So there were two ways of doing that. You could either, go and look at a comic book and then do your own reimagining of an existing comic. I did that from time to time, and, as I've told kids, it's a good way to do it, but make sure you don't take the Byrne-Claremont X-Men at the peak, or whatever's a top ten book and try to do better than that. Go get a book that's floundering, and reimagine *that* book, because you've got a much better chance of inspiring somebody to hire you with that than trying to draw like Neal Adams or write like Chris Claremont. But I also did, at that time, create my own characters. So in high school I created this character amongst many, called Spawn, and I actually did like a twenty-five-, thirty-page comic book of that, and that was part of some of my samples when I was sixteen. And then they just went dormant until I pulled them out in the early nineties.

DF: Sort of like Erik Larsen with the Savage Dragon.

TM: That's it, yeah. Along those lines.

DF: So you would do some of your own stories and some adaptations of other people's stories, it sounds like.

TM: When I was reimagining someone else's stuff, like if I were looking at a badly drawn *Captain America* story, then I would use that story, but draw it my own way. If it was *my* character, the true writing came then. I wasn't trying to rewrite *Captain America*. They've got a writer for that book. I was never, at that point, trying to take over a writer's spot. I was trying to take over an *artist's* spot. But when I did my own comic, then there was no writer, so I had to be the letterer, writer, penciler, inker, all that stuff.

DF: And would the character always be Spawn, or did you have other characters, as well?

TM: I had some other ones. I had a group called "Blood, Sweat, and Tears," and then I had this other one called the "Bruise Crew."

DF: So people may think, "Oh, Todd just suddenly started writing one day, with *Spider-Man* #1," but actually you had writing experience.

TM: I was writing, but not nearly at the prolific pace that I was drawing. I was probably doing five pages of artwork for every one page I was writing, where a true writer writes all the time. But at that point, my first drive was to do artwork.

DF: I imagine you weren't doing much writing once you actually broke into Marvel and DC as an artist.

TM: When I first broke in, it was strictly as a penciler.

DF: In your early propenciling career, did you work collaboratively with any of your writers, or did you just take a script or a plot and draw it? Did you ever do any coplotting?

TM: I never really did that. You know, on some level it was more out of respect for them, for the writers. I was working with guys, early on, like Roy Thomas, and then later with David Michelinie, and a little bit with Larry Hama. And Peter David came on, although I don't think he'd been in the business that long then. But I just went, "These guys have been here before I was." So my input with them early on was more of me asking, "Could you do a story with this character in it? Because it would be cool to draw that guy," instead of my telling them, "Here's how the story should unfold." They had their own visions themselves.

DF: Would you talk to them directly, or go through the editor?

TM: I was usually on the phone to the writer. Because if I had questions about stuff, then they would explain it, and I'd go, "Oh, I see." Or, "Can I condense this fight scene down because it seems like the plot is a little dense. Is there any way I can do this?" Or, "It seems a little sparse. What if we added this and this and this? How does that sound?" But it wasn't, "Let's sit down and plan out the next six months, and let's get Todd on the line."

DF: Did you work mostly from plots, or did you ever work full-script?

TM: Early on it was all plot. And, again, even in my advanced stage, I'm pro-plot from an artist's point of view. Just give me the *framework*, and let me pace it. Let me *direct* it, if you will. You be the screenwriter, let me direct it, and then after I direct it, I'll give it back to you, and then you are brilliant enough that you should be able to get your ideas across with words that fit my pictures. I've worked full-script, but the writer's style of pacing and story-telling, is usually different than mine. So even when I was drawing stuff over, let's say, Alan Moore, who's brilliant, I still would have paced it differently. And this is the thing that's interesting. All of them have been gracious enough to say, "Do whatever you want." But the problem is that you're still aware that you're physically changing something that is meant to be a certain way, and it almost felt to me like it was insulting to change their pacing. It's much like when I was inking over Jack Kirby and I had to erase the pencils. It's like blasphemy. So I always preferred, "Just give me a plot." Usually, a plot for me at that point was about four-and-a-half typed pages. Then I broke each page into five segments, so that by the time I got to the fourth plot page, I was on page twenty of the story, and then the last half-page of plot was pages twenty-one and twenty-two of the comic [the last two pages]. So I sort of had a methodology. Then I would actually mark off, in my mind, at the page breaks.

DF: That makes sense. But you said that you've also worked from full scripts?

TM: Yeah, I have. But like I said, I find it restraining. I find it the same as working as an inker working on very tight pencils. There's no room to inject your own personality. I mean, as an inker, of course I can change anything, no matter how tight the pencils are, but the reader is *aware* of the change. I like to work on rough pencils when I'm inking, and I like a plot outline when I'm doing the pencil artwork on a story.

DF: When you write for another artist, it sounds like you do a plot for them, for the most part.

TM: Oh, yeah, it's very loose. For a long time, when it was Greg Capullo and me on *Spawn*, I either just sent him a very short plot, or what I usually did was, talk to him on the phone, and he would record it, and I just paced him through it. It was all pacing. I knew what I wanted him to do, and I'd say, "Okay, here're the page breaks. Page one, we start with Spawn in the alley. I'd like to start with an extreme closeup, eventually pull the camera back, and then what we need to see is him standing there, and then there's two football helmets next to him," or whatever I needed, and that's the end of page one. So, and then when you got to the fights, for the most part it would be, "Okay, now Spawn's fighting the bad guy. I need three pages of that. I'll let you choreograph it any way you want, but here's the two things that I do need in your three pages. I need this, and I need this, and as long as you can get those two pieces in those three pages, do whatever you want with the choreography of the fight," because everybody has their own style for that. "And knock yourself out artistically, as long as I've got my story information there, because if those two things happen, then I can continue my story, because a plot point is moving forward, and I need those two visuals to hook everything together."

DF: What's your working process when you write and draw a story yourself?

TM: I usually have a page, and I number it from one to twenty-two, and then I put the story together in my head just when I'm at ease. And then, now that I've got it very basically broken down and I've sort of put it all together in my head, then I would write five or six words describing each page, just to keep it going, so I had a "cheat sheet," if you will. And then, from those twenty-two pages, I would then do my rough of each comics page. So now I knew, "Okay, page one, we're at Sam and Twitch's office. We're at the precinct.

I have Sam and Twitch at the precinct." And if there's anything specific I need, I give myself a little note about it, just like I would give to Greg verbally. Not anything as detailed as, say, "This is where, at the end, Sam walks out and slams the door. Why? Because they had a disagreement over whether they should report Spawn to the authorities," or something. I'd just give myself a couple words to go, "Okay, I know what's going on at this point in the story."

DF: When do you put the dialogue in?

TM: Well, it's interesting, because there are different ways of doing comic books. I wasn't a fan of paste-on lettering, which is, I know, a byproduct of deadlines, for a couple of reasons. One, later on, the glue dries up and the lettering falls off of the art. Two, the lettering yellows, it doesn't look so good. So what I would end up doing when we went over to Image, and I did the same thing even on *Spider-Man*, is that I would "blob out" the pages, that is do very, very rough layouts that pretty much only I could understand. The figures were literally blobs. There were times when I was doing *Spider-Man*, and I believe Rick Parker was the letterer, that I literally had to draw arrows and write, "This blob is Peter, and this blob is Mary Jane, so here's the balloon placement." After the lettering was on the art boards, then I would do a lot of the artwork in the inking stages. But when I did *Spawn*, when I dialogued it, I would actually first dialogue it very roughly on a small piece of paper, and then I would actually go in there and rewrite it on the actual page and do all the big, wildly dramatic lettering. Tom Orzechowski was the letterer. I liked bouncy lettering done right, at least my view of "done right."

DF: That's the whole point of having your own book.

TM: That's true. Because I always felt, Danny, that a comic book was the sum of all its parts, that it wasn't about this and that, that it all had to work together. So to me, the lettering was just as important, not only as far as *what* the characters were saying, but how it looked on the page. And this is actually an art that I think people don't pay attention to—once you actually dialogue a book, then the placement of those balloons, to me, is tremendously import-ant. Because sometimes I don't get to do that here on the *Spawn* comic book, and I always groan when I see the printed comic, "Oh, guys, that's not where you should have put that balloon." It's splitting hairs sometimes, but I just have four or five rules of how you do lettering, and where you put copy, and when you have it. And even things like when you go to all caps or when you go to lower case letters, when you go to block lettering, or when you do some-thing bold. I mean, they're just my own internal rules, but if I follow them, then my book looks consistent and it gets into a bit of a rhythm. And people then ultimately go, "I like the book. I can't really explain why."

DF: The lettering is a design element that, if you're doing it right, people don't notice.

TM: Right. And some of the best panels are the ones that are just, like, a closeup of a guy's lips on a profile. That's the only thing you see; it's only in the corner to the left, and then you've got 80 percent dead space. Don't draw anything there. Don't do crosshatching there. Don't try to do anything. And then you put a balloon off to the side, and it's very small, and it's floating, it's got a small tail, and the dialogue in lower case is the word, "No."

And let it just sit there like thunder on that page. And, again, it's about storytelling at that point. And this is that stuff where, when I've worked on full script, that I don't get a sense of the writer just letting the writing/balloon/artwork sort of do a dance together.

DF: So it sounds like, when you write and draw something, that you're doing the drawing and the dialogue simultaneously as you go along?

TM: To some extent, right. I mean, again, when I say we're going to pick up Spawn in the alley and pull back and see him melancholy holding a skull in his hand a la Macbeth, I just want that imagery—but I'm also aware of how close I want the camera when I start, and I'm going, okay, it's going to take me five panels to get to that shot, and then we're going to come into it. Or I might start with a close-up on a bug and then pull back to see that the bug is in one of the eye sockets of this skull, and eventually we pull back and there's Spawn holding the skull.

DF: Now, would you finish all the basic thumbnail sketches and then go back and do the dialogue, or would you do them both at the same time, or is there no hard and fast rule?

TM: Usually I would actually thumbnail it out, because if something didn't quite work in the pacing, I didn't want again to be a slave to "I needed six balloons on this page." If all of a sudden I came up with a different idea and I went, "Oh, cool, now you can get eight balloons in here," or I can expand the story, or add a visual element that means somebody's going to have to say something, or I'm going to have to add a caption, I needed to find that out after I looked at the thumbnails.

DF: So it sounds like you almost split yourself into two guys. First you do the drawing, or at least the panel-by-panel thumbnail pacing, then you go back and do the words.

TM: Right.

DF: That's very interesting. Now, you started writing *Spider-Man* in 1990. Has your approach to writing changed and evolved from that first Spidey story to where you are today?

TM: Yeah. You know, that was an interesting moment in my career, and I get reminded from time to time that people didn't see me as two people at that point. They saw Todd the polished artist, who was now entitled to draw his own book and had won some awards, and then there was Todd the novice writer. I never said then that I was a writer in the truest sense, and that somehow, magically, my writing was going to be up to par to my artwork at the very git-go, if ever. But by the time *Spider-Man* #1 came out, I'd been in the business, five years, six years, I'd done hundreds if not thousands of pages of art at that point. I've been able to get the kinks out of my drawing. While *Spider-Man* #1 is the *beginning* of me starting to put kinks on the page writing, which you have to then eventually, like all writers do, get through. I was in that weird situation on that first issue where, arguably, the worst story I ever write is going to be the one that most people bought. But I never said I was going to come wholly formed here. But I believe that, as time went by, two, three, four years later, that the writing became adequate at that point, and was better than the writing in *Spider-Man* #1. Ultimately, if an average person looked at *Spider-Man* #1 and then read something I wrote four years later, they'd go, "Yeah, there's an improvement." Not unlike if they saw the first artwork I did and looked at my artwork four years later, they'd see improvement.

DF: When you look back at that stuff, do you think it holds up?

TM: No, it's choppy. It's like anything else, you wish you could rewrite it, that you could go do it again and change stuff. But, you know, we do the same thing with our artwork.

So would I like to take it and rewrite it? Yeah, sure. But that train has left the station. And so you look at it and you learn. You, in hindsight, read it, and you go, "What would I do differently?" And you hope that you can apply that or take the criticism of it and move on and find your groove down the line as you write more and more stories.

DF: Now, once you started to have other people write or draw *Spawn*, you basically became the editor. Once you were in the editor's chair, did your perception of the editor's role change, and, if so, how?

TM: Not entirely, and I'll tell you why. I had the good fortune to have a couple years under my belt with Roy Thomas, who was, I thought, a good editor, and then later on with Jim Salicrup, who was a good editor for me. And I was able to take some of his editorial teachings, if you will, whether he knew I was going to be an editor someday or not. He was always questioning *why* I was doing stuff. And it wasn't because he wanted to redo it. He just wanted to make sure that I had a *reason* for doing what I did. There were times when he disagreed with me and he would say, "You know what, Todd?

We need to fix that." Or he would say, "Why did you do that?" And I'd give him a twenty-minute dissertation about why I'd written or drawn something a certain way. Then he would either go, "Fine, Todd, okay. I just wanted to make sure there was a reason." Or he'd go, "I understand your reason. I think there's a better way to skin this cat. Let me give you my perspective. We're not going to change it now. Just make sure, moving forward, that you sort of pay attention to this in the future."

And I thought that was a more courteous way, a more effective way, of getting an artist to change than saying, "Redo that page, rewrite that." Because, you know, we're all under deadlines, and nobody wants to redo anything. So he let me put a couple of raw dogs out, as long as he was able to say, "Next time, make sure there's a little bit of polish on that," and gave you a little bit of reasoning behind what he was saying. And I thought that was very fair-minded, and said to myself, "If I ever become an editor, then that's how I want to do it. I want to sit with my writers, artists, whoever else, and go. 'Here's what I see wrong with this issue. We're going to let it go to the printers. But I want to go through it with you so that, because we've got another issue coming out next month, let's not repeat this. But for now, let's just let this one go, and let's just chase our elusive holy grails on the next issue, and the next one after that, and the next one after that.'" So my editorial point-of-view was sort of taken from bits from the various editors I had. Roy Thomas, too. He was very kind and gave you a long leash but reminded you when you sort of went too far, or did something "wrong." Those guys were always there with constructive criticism, instead of just "redo it."

DF: Do you enjoy editing enough that if, say, hypothetically, Marvel said, "Come be our chief," would you go do that?

TM: [*Laughs*] You know what? I wouldn't mind it, and I think with the experience I've had being an artist, writer, and now with Image, running my own comic company, dealing with printers and staff, and having to deal with freelancers, and then expanding that into companies outside of the comic book world, you know what? I think I'd actually make a pretty decent editor-in-chief at Marvel Comics. It's just, I don't need the job right now, you know. So I'm busy. Maybe another day, but right now I'm busy.

DF: That leads me to another question. There are only twenty-four hours in the day and you're running a big company that's been expanding, as opposed to spending all your time at hands-on writing and drawing. What led you to make what seems, at least from my perspective, the decision to be more involved in business matters than you are in creative?

TM: I think that perception is out of whack. I think people see the business side of what I do, but I don't do nearly as much business as people think. The problem is that, when I was doing comic books, when you hunch over the board, what you do over that board or over that typewriter, the public sees. I'm now in a position where a lot of what I do artistically is preproduction work that the public will *never see*. And so what they see is the end product. But somehow, "magically," these toys come out of my company, but they don't just appear without there being drawings in advance of their production. And there are also drawings that go in advance of doing animation, and there's the music [video] directing that I've done, and the film work I've done, and designing characters for video games. There's still a decent amount of artwork that I do, it's just people don't' get to see it with their eyeballs, so they assume that I'm not drawing that I must be out with bankers or something like that.

Now what led me to some of the business tasks I've taken on is that I'm not a guy that likes to sit by water coolers and complain about things. I believe that we all sort of, for the most part, are in control of our lives. And it's like, if you don't like your job and don't like your boss, then *quit*. But people like to stand by a water cooler and bitch, but not do anything about it. I just think that, if I'm going to be the artist, or the musician, or the singer or the actor who's going to complain about their agent or manager, or about an executive, I've got two choices. I either figure out how to *be* that guy or I just shut my mouth. And so I took the path of, I'm going to figure out whether I can get smart enough to find how to produce and deliver my own artwork.

At some point the business part of it is like learning a second language. I am now fluent in "business." So can I walk into a meeting with a banker and a bunch of executives in Hollywood and say the things that are important to those people on that day, or to a guy that I'm dealing with at Walmart? *Absolutely.* Because I understand the words that matter to them and what's important to them. And a lot of times it's not about art. But I take that business hat off as soon as I can when I get out of those meetings, so I can breathe again and go back to just being the artist who wears a business hat every now and then. And this is a point that people don't understand, and they say, "Oh, Todd, you're a sellout." Okay. If your definition of a sellout is to figure out a way to get your artwork out to the marketplace in a successful enough way—and it has to be successful—nobody will give you an opportunity if you keep screwing up. This I know for a fact. So you must be *successful* enough in your business so that they will give you more opportunities to put out more *art*. So the only way I'm going to be able to keep putting out more art is I have to be successful in the *business* side of it. It's that simple. I don't want to run a big business and be successful in business so I can be a rich businessman. I want to be successful in business so that I can continue to do art when I want to. It's as simple as that. If I walk into a business meeting and tell the people I'm meeting with that the last ten lines of toys I've done have been successful, or the last two music videos I did won awards, or the last TV show I did, the ratings were up, I get a better chance of getting my next creative idea made than if I walk in there and say it was a failure.

DF: When you say you're "doing the art" on a lot of projects, does that include the storyline also?

TM: Yeah. Like the animation we're working on right now, I came up with the idea and wrote the script to it, and then I think pass it on to . . . Brian Holguin, maybe, he might have done a little polish on it, and then I came back and did some more work on it, and so on.

DF: This is a new *Spawn* animated project?

TM: Yeah. Like the new *Spawn* animation we're working on. And I'm eventually going to direct the new *Spawn* movie, or we're never going to see it. But I'm going to write and direct and produce it. Why? Because it's in my head, and I haven't had much luck translating what's in my head to other people. Every time I do that, it doesn't work out. I'm not saying that I'm better than them. I'm actually dealing with some skilled people. It's just that there are nuances and things that are in your head that just can't be explained to other people. Or people are so loyal to what it is that they think you want that they're missing the idea that I want them to reinvent some things. It's sort of the trouble I've had with Spawn as a whole. Everybody that comes on board is, in my mind, being *too* loyal to what's gone on in the past, you know? A little bit of ignorance, I think, will actually go a long way, for instance a writer going, "I've never really read *Spawn*, but you know what? Give me a couple of big, broad strokes to explain it," and then he would come out with some crazy stuff, not worrying about the continuity of the last 150 issues. I mean, it's a little bit like what happened with the "British Invasion" of comics in the 1980s and '90s. When the British writers came over here they were so ignorant of the history of, say, Superman, but "Here's a cool Superman story I've been thinking about," and you go, "Wow! That's trippy." I don't know that we want a steady diet of that, but it was refreshing enough that it was new.

DF: What's coming up? Is the *Spawn* animation going to be a series, or a one-shot?

TM: Right now it's planned for an eighty- or eighty-five-minute movie/pilot that I'm hoping that, when I've got enough of it together and I go back to LA, I've got cable stations that I've dealt with and other people that'll go,

"Yeah, cool, Todd, bring it in, we'll take a look at it," and they might go, "We'll take that eighty-minute as a pilot, and then give us episodes afterwards," like on HBO. Or they might go, "Hey, take that eighty minutes and cut it into three and we've already got our first three shows."

DF: And the second *Spawn* movie is still in development?

TM: Oh, yeah. And, like I said, I've been living with that one in my head, Danny, and there's no way I'm going to be able to get anybody else to do it the way I see it. I'm going to get the right cinematographer, because there's a couple of them that I know can hit the look that I'm going for, and I'll give all the money to the cinematographer because he'll make me look good. I'm very strong in what it is that I want visually, and how I want the camera to move, and what I want it to come across as being. I see bits and pieces of it. When I watch certain movies I go, "There it was. I just saw another scene in my movie. It looks like that, it feels like that." It's the same way I developed my own art style. You see bits and pieces of thousands of comic books, and you just cobble little pieces, put it all together, and it becomes a unique style called "yours."

DF: Would you think about doing that as a comic first just to show it to people and say, "Here's what I'm thinking of?"

TM: We're actually sort of doing that in the last couple issues of *Spawn* right now. You know, it's not about alien invasions at that point, and things from the pit of hell, which, bizarre as that is, is what Spawn is. It's just, how do we "ground-level" a story and still make it a cool, odd, creepy, singular story? When I was a kid, there were things like *The Omen* and *The Exorcist* where there was only one thing in those movies that was odd, and it was the kid. And earlier, when I was watching black-and-white movies, it was *Frankenstein*, and that was the same thing. Everything was normal in that world except for Frankenstein. So I don't want Frankenstein's bride, I don't want the villain, I just want, in this movie, in this story that I have, I just want Spawn to be the odd thing, and the rest of the world will be as realistic, art, dramatic looking, as anything you'll ever see.

DF: Have you ever thought about doing a sports comic or a sports movie? I mean, that's such a big interest of yours.

TM: I've got a couple of ideas for a movie. But in terms of sports comic books, I'm not a guy that's smart enough to invent wheels. I've had a little bit of skill, again, in trying to figure out how to *polish* wheels. So it's like, oh, okay, there's comic books, how do we make them slicker? There's toys, how we make them cooler? There's animation, how do we make that more sort of adult? I've just taken what's there and gone, "What's lacking?" and then added to it. But sports comic books, as I look at them historically, I go, "Nah." Because the history tells me that sports comic books don't work. So I'll debate anybody on it, because, somebody, please, give me an example. We've had over seventy years of comics now. Give me an example of a sports comic that lasted more than nine issues. Why would a kid want to read about Ken Griffey Jr. when they can watch him, or they can play him on their video game? "Well, what if we made Ken Griffey Jr. a superhero?" "Well, why?" As a kid who collected sports stuff when I was a kid, Danny, I just go, "Why do I want an unrealistic version of what I know to be true? I don't want Ken Griffey Jr. flying. I want to see Ken Griffey Jr. hit a three-run home run and win the ballgame!" So I never was able to make that leap and figure what would make a successful sports comic book.

DF: DC used to do "Strange Sports Stories."

TM: You know what? If someone had a good idea more in the vein of *Eerie* and *Creepy*, I'd go, "Yeah, cool!" Because now you're doing a true twist on something. I mean, you're doing *Tales from the Crypt* stuff. That makes sense to me. I go, "Yeah, yeah, that's cool." But doing some kind of superheroic sports comic because we think the five-year-old kids are going to read it? I'll let somebody else spend their money on that idea.

DF: But you are interested in sports, and I've always found that an interesting contrast to your comics and other work. On the one hand, you have your love of baseball and hockey and those sort of bright, shiny sports, and then your fascination with horror stuff. What's the relation between those, for you?

TM: I don't think there is one. For me, actually, it's not there there's a relationship, it's that there actually *isn't* a relationship. For me, at the end of a twelve-hour day of writing, or a twelve-hour day of drawing—or in some cases twenty-hour days like I used to put in—I, unlike some of my peers—and, again, I'm not saying it's good or bad, everybody has to do what they do to survive—I couldn't at the end of those long hours, sit down and watch *Star Wars*. I couldn't do it. I would go, "I need to get away from fantasy. I need to just get myself away from all this big, fantastic stuff, I need to just get out of that world." So, for me, stepping into the sports world is an escape. Movies, too, which is why I like the idea I just mentioned about the new *Spawn* movie being urban, because I like movies that are realistic except for one element. I've always liked the movies that—if I gave you my favorite movies, they'd all be art dramas that are very *realistic* movies, if not actually based on real events.

DF: What *are* your favorite movies?

TM: Number one, I'd put *Godfather*. Number two, I'd put *The Insider*, that one on the tobacco industry. Number three, *Crash*, I just thought that was a tremendous movie.

DF: The Cronenberg *Crash* or the more recent one?

TM: The new one. And then the remake of [British miniseries] *Traffic*. It's dark, it's gritty. To me it's all dark stuff. If you look at it, I mean, even in *The Insider*, you see the protagonist get deconstructed, and the world is trying to take something from all these people and they have to figure out how to get through it, you know?

DF: When you say "deconstructed," what do you mean?

TM: Well, you know, when the hero faces a situation of "If you don't toe the company line, you'll lose your job. We'll blacklist you." And the hero goes, "Hold on a sec, I've got a mortgage, I've got a wife." I mean, these are the true heroes our world, people who eventually stand up, to the point of putting, arguably, their own families at risk, to say, "No, I need to do the right thing." Because it's a tough one when, do you do the right thing if it puts your family in jeopardy, or do you just turn a blind eye and protect your family? And I don't think any of us can make that decision until we're there.

At some levels, when I'm dealing with Spawn, although I picked big ideas for him—there's heaven and there's hell, that's as big as it's going to get—to me it's all metaphors for the government and corporate America trying to control one man's life, and him going "I want to just live my life the way I see git. Just leave me alone." Arguably, I could go one more step and just go, you know what? It's basically just *me*. It's *my* life. The easiest way to write is to actually go from your own personal experience and just go, "No." You know, I've fought against forces my whole life. People said I couldn't do stuff, people tried to block me, people try to put you out of business, all of it. People are trying to sue you, bring you down and say, "No, you can't." Even from the early point of people saying, "You'll never break into comic books. It's too tough. You'll never get there." And, again, what kept me going is that stubbornness, and you have to keep that thickness of skin on you throughout the whole game, because there's always going to be somebody there that's going to say, "Can't be done." And you either just accept that or you can go, "No."

So those movies I listed take people, put them in these fantastic places that are still real, then go, "How are you going to get out of it? And at what cost?" To be Malcolm X comes at the cost of losing your family, but is it good for the community? Yes. Did it cost you your own personal life? Yes. And I'm not talking here about getting shot, I'm saying the home life goes out the window. So you protect the community, but you can't protect your own family, because to protect your family you have to *ignore* the community. At what point do you become a Good Samaritan, and at what point do you cover your own family? These are personal debates that we all may have to sometime make a choice on. And they're not easy choices by any stretch.

DF: Well, that's the appeal of Spider-Man, right? He's one guy, and how does he balance the heroic role he's taken on with his personal life, with his family life?

TM: Let's talk about that. I know that's Stan Lee's personal take on it, and I get it, and it's not a bad sort of mantra. I don't subscribe to it, though. Because there's also a character that is equally interesting and equally branded called Batman, and Batman is a millionaire, philanthropic, good-looking playboy. And he doesn't really have too many problems, so he can go date supermodels every day. The core of it is that what makes Spider-Man cooler than anyone else, is that he just *crawls up damn walls*. He *swings* on *webs*! I've got a seven-year-old boy who would love to do that tomorrow. And Superman can fly, but Batman can put on a costume and scare the crap out of people, and he's got a Batmobile! So one guy happens to be a college student, the other guy happens to be a playboy? Yeah, it adds some interest to them, but if Peter Parker were a playboy millionaire, he still would be cool because it's still Spider-Man crawling up the walls and spinning webs.

DF: I agree that, especially for kids, the costumes and gimmicks and powers are the appeal of superheroes. But what makes them appeal, I think, to older people, as well, is this business of having to make choices. Even Batman does have that choice between living that playboy life and going out and fighting crime. He's giving up different stuff than Peter Parker is, but I think it does come down to personal choices.

TM: Right, right. They're both making sacrifices to try and get someplace. So the sacrifices can come in a lot of different forms. It doesn't have to be a poor kid. It can be a rich guy who's giving up his comfortable, insulated existence to try and do something, too.

DF: Exactly. So, how did you like the way the Venom character came out in *Spider-Man 3*?

TM: I would have done certain things a little bit differently. Just tweaks on it. When I created Venom, I always wanted that character to be bigger and bulkier than Spider-Man, sort of a scaled-down Hulk, if you will. If Spider-Man is one finger thick, I always thought of Venom sort of as being two fingers thick. Why? Because I wanted this creature, which is what he was, he was a monster to me—and going back to the origin of it, they didn't tell me there was a human underneath it until after I came up with the creature part of it. So I was like, "Oops! Sorry." I didn't know a man was supposed to be in there, which is why I didn't give him true human proportions. I gave him sort of quasi-Hulk proportions. I gave him a bulky build that you wouldn't even find on a bodybuilder. I wanted something that was very formidable when it stood in front of the little, skinny Spider-Man. So what I saw on the screen was, Spider-Man and Venom, body-build-wise, weren't that dramatically different. And the body language of the way that I used to draw Venom was hunched over and sort of had a little bit of Quasimodo in it. And the head I designed was a little less human-shaped, and the jaw dropped down a little bit more. It was a true, true monster to me.

DF: What were your guidelines from editorial when you came up with Venom?

TM: I don't know if that came from editorial. I think it came from David Michelinie, and I think the phone conversation—there was nothing written down—was as simple as, "Hey, we've got to come up with a new design and a new character, and there's this black costume in continuity." And I'm going, "Cool." That was all I got. And then for me it was, the costume is alien, so, okay, I'm going to make a quasialien monster out of it. And then later on they went, "Uh, we're going to give it a human host, a human has to be able to wear it." I'm like, "Oh, okay." If you see the drawings I did, [Venom's host] Eddie Brock is a lot bulkier than the actor in the movie, Topher Grace. But even still, in the comic, once the costume comes on, it enhances Eddie, it makes him bigger. I'm a big monster fan, so to me Venom is about a creature, a monster that's big and strong, fighting the little skinny bug called Spider-Man, whereas in the movie it was two boys fighting each other.

DF: Any thoughts on the state of the comics industry these days and about breaking in, for anybody who's looking to?

TM: I don't think that the act of breaking in has changed that much over the decades. You still have to go and look at your trade, try and figure out how to put it together, sort of sit in a quiet corner and teach yourself whatever it is, I don't care whether it's coloring, lettering, inking, writing, whatever it is, and eventually get to the point where you're confident or delusional enough to take those samples out to the public, which means either putting them in the mail and/or going to conventions and/or knocking on people's doors. I mean, is there a more streamlined way of breaking in than the way you and I did? I don't think so. I think it's still the old-fashioned way. "Just go and make your own breaks, son."

DF: It seems to help to be a best-selling novelist or a Hollywood director these days.

TM: Well, yeah, but I'm talking about the kid in Ohio. Can that kid still break in? Yeah. Do I think that there's more chances on the art side? Yeah, just because pure math says that most guys can only draw one monthly book, whereas a lot of writers can do multiple books, so there's less opportunity for writers because there's less of a need to have one on every book. But most comics need, for the most part, one artist for every book.

DF: Makes sense. Well, this has been great, Todd. Thanks for your time.

TM: Thank *you*, Danny. This was fun.

INDEX

ABOUT THE EDITOR

Jake Zawlacki is a writer, translator, and scholar. His critical interests include popular American comics of the early 1990s, as well as Kazakh animation and film, with essays appearing in *ImageText, Inks,* the *Comics Journal,* and *Folklorica*. His translations of Akhmet Baitursynuly's poetry have appeared in *Guernica* and *Asymptote*. He holds degrees from Louisiana State University, University of San Diego, and Stanford University, and his creative work has been published in the *Saturday Evening Post, The Journal, Two Hawks Quarterly,* and the *Citron Review.*